UNSUPERVISED
and loving it

Sharon Row

Cover and Author photography by Michelle Steadman

Copyright © 2015 Sharon Row

ISBN-13; 978-1514748749
ISBN-10: 151-4748746

DEDICATION

Love is the only word to describe how I feel about my family. This book is dedicated to my daughter Michelle, her husband Kevin and my Grandson Logan. Thank you for all the years of encouragement, inspiration and support. To my son Brian, whose life was affected by the decisions I made for him as a child. I'm so proud of the man you have become. My Granddaughter Alana who will always be my pink princess.

This story would never have come to fruition had it not been for the tears shed, and laughter by my close friends Stephanie Baxter, Gordon Tareta, Joe Baldino, and Philomena Ojeda as I told them my story. My daughter Michelle who believes in me and lived this life with me since the day of her birth; and my grade school best friend that I refer to only as my sister Emma Knight. Thank you for being with me side by side as I had to relive each and every chapter throughout this journey.

The original story needed some major editing with help coming from Francine Robertshaw who did the grammar. Making it at least readable by Judy Walter who completely polished, tightened and turned it into a journey I can be proud of taking. Thank you.

AUTHOR'S NOTES

While writing my life's journey, I researched facts when I could. Otherwise I relied on my own memory of events and changed the names of most individuals in this book. I also changed as many identifying details to help preserve anonymity.

CONTENTS

UNSUPERVISED

and loving it

I knew I was about to be killed. My heart was pounding as I hid in the bushes outside the Palm Springs Police Station. I knew too much. Ricardo had been involved his entire life in the largest drug cartel business. He would want to make sure I paid the price for going to the police. He already had two strikes against him from being in prison twice, having served twelve years. I watched a man slowly get out of his car and remove what looked like a rifle bag in the darkness of the night. As he walked toward my direction, I quickly tried to call my daughter from my cell phone for what I thought would be my last call. How did I get to this place in my life, when all I ever tried to do was be a kind and loving person? Now, not knowing if I would ever see my family again, it was so important to me to have this one last chance to say goodbye.

Everything I had worked so hard for was right at my fingertips and in the blink of an eye it was now soon to be gone. My adult life had never been easy for me, but as long as I was able to make sure my family was well taken care of, I was happy. Now my life and my family's life were in danger.

I never made the right choices when it came to love. What I dreamed of was the one man I fell in love with as a young woman of twenty-three. He was my knight in shining armor. He would love me passionately, protect me from harm. But I lost him, and as many times as I searched to find someone with just one of his qualities, none came close. Instead I fell into the trap of trusting someone who soon became verbally abusive, a trap most women find easy to slip into with their hearts open, but before we know it, someone has taken over our life without our even realizing it, damaging our spirits, making us feel little self-worth in order to make the man feel empowered.

My life for the most part has always seemed to be in chapters. Each chapter has taught me great lessons, and many more than most women would know in a lifetime if they were lucky. I hope sharing my chapters of life will help at least one person and inspire others to make choices that aren't as destructive as mine have been.

Flashback Years Earlier

CHAPTER 1
The Bookie

The chief of police and the city's finest politicians and businessmen placed bets in the musty, smoke filled back room of the local barbershop, tables with cigarette burns, money on the table, talks of the odds on each race being spoken, dirty ashtrays, beer bottles, *Playboy* magazines and the daily green sheets always on hand for reading. The sounds of horse races played on the radio, the bathroom collaged with wall-to-wall cut-out-taped-on nude pictures of women and men's cartoon jokes, all to amuse while being detained for a moment. This was in contrast to the business out front where men were getting their haircuts and barbershop shaves. The scent of talcum powder filled the air as it was being brushed around their collars, the crisp white starched draping wrapped around each man's shoulders, and Harold outside the front door, polishing and buffing shoes on the large black shoeshine stand. All the while the red, white and blue barber shop pole ran at full speed.

My Mother was in labor and being rushed to the hospital but my father was nowhere to be found. He told the other barbers he was not to be disturbed. Mom sent a friend to the barbershop, where he rushed in and interrupted the bet making and the police had to help make a speedy trip to get my dad to the hospital in time to see the arrival of his first and only child, a little girl, Daddy's little girl. My dad was forty when I was born and the sun rose and set in my every breath, as he would tell me constantly from that day forward.

Having a bookmaker for a father was always an adventure. From the time I was old enough to walk, I was down on the ground being taught how to shoot dice and count numbers, while my dad would write down the odds of what appeared, as he was always thinking of ways to create a system, the perfect way to beat the odds of playing craps at the casinos in Reno, Tahoe and Vegas. I didn't understand gaming addictions until much later in my adult life. For a child it was just fun playing games. It was quality time with my dad. I remember him saying to always bet against the house on the "Don't Come" line and never play at a happy table, and he would bring self-addressed, stamped envelopes along to mail home the winnings so he wouldn't spend the money. Dad went gambling with a certain amount of money and always hoped when he arrived back home the money in the envelopes was more than he left with. Most times it was. My dad was better known as "Cal the Barber" around town, Monterey Peninsula's best bookie. Being the daughter of a bookie had its perks. When it was time for him to go off to gamble he would hang a sign on his barber chair saying "Gone Fishing." I would look forward to his journeys because when he came home he would bring me beautiful gifts fit for a princess, take me shopping for clothes and always made sure I knew he did it all for me. When I was in sixth grade, he returned once and took me shopping at the finest (at the time) jewelry store on Alvarado Street in Monterey and bought me a one-quarter karat flawless diamond solitaire ring. He said he always wanted me in diamonds and furs. My dad was the last of the big-time spenders, or so they were known in those days, living life large, and always being tipped well from his players who made money from their winnings. A nice newly-built home would be ready soon after my arrival. I would never want for anything.

As I grew older, at about age four, my dad would take me with him on the Del Monte train in Monterey as he traveled to Reno for gambling. All the conductors and ticket collectors knew me and made sure I was having a great time during my special trips with my dad. When we arrived, I would be dropped off at a day care facility called Jack and Jill, where I counted the minutes until Dad came to pick me up. Sometimes it took a couple of days, but it was all an adventure for me, and I was with my hero, my dad.

Every so often when we traveled we would take the train to San Francisco so my dad could go to the Veterans Hospital for his checkups. He had served in World War II and had what is now called PTSD, or post-traumatic stress disorder, but was then known as "shell-shock." He was always given uppers and downers, beanies, red devils and whites. But I never had a clue what the drugs were or did. Dad was protected me from anything that would make me worry that something wasn't right. I only knew that in my entire lifetime I never heard him speak in anything other than a kind, gentle, calming voice. Whenever I was ill, it was his healing hands on my forehead, checking to see if I had a fever.

My Dad always taught me to be an "Old Man's Darling, rather than be a Young Man's Slave." It's just as easy to marry a rich one as it is to marry a poor one." These were the mottos instilled in me. It was all about getting by on beauty and what appeals to men. The way you walk into a room, knowing you own the attention of all the men just from the way you carry yourself. There was no talk of, "Grow up, live the American dream of work hard, go to college, get a good career." A college education wasn't the ticket to it all. No, in my world it was all about the outside appearance of a woman, and how I was to be hanging onto some older man's arm, one who had money to take care of me for the rest of my life. I was never allowed to do my own school homework, but would come home from school, tell my dad what I needed to turn in the next day, and he would make sure he did it. Before I left for school the following morning he would sit me down at breakfast and explain to me all he had done and I would re-copy word-for-word whatever he had written. My grades suffered from that but I always passed with Cs and Ds. He was never concerned.

My mother, Rosemary, a fiery red head, was something to look at - natural red hair, white skin, a beautiful smile, and green eyes with a perfect thin model's figure. She had been married twice and divorced with an eleven-year-old daughter by the time she was in her mid-twenties. She lived in Pacific Grove and worked at the local drug store to support them both. My mother's mother lived nearby and was always the rock for my mother and her daughter. My grandmother was a nurse and caregiver for a retired school principal, and when he died he left his home to my Grandmother since she had devoted all her later years to him. The home was completely paid for.

My grandmother lived on a fixed income and wrote down every cent spent daily. My mom worked at the drugstore across the street from my father's barbershop. She helped the customers and stocked shelves. One day my father came in while my mom was on a ladder, her arms filled with cartons of cigarettes. The moment she made eye contact with my dad she accidentally dropped all the cartons and my dad helped her pick them up. When their eyes met, both were instantly smitten. They began dating and soon married in a very private, intimate ceremony, with the spectacular scenic background of Pacific Grove's Lovers Point overlooking the Pacific Ocean. Her daughter Carol stood by her side. My mom would describe my Dad as a matinee idol because of his tall, handsome, debonair style, always well dressed in his handmade suits. They made a stunning couple, my dad, John Calvin "Cal", with his silvery white hair, a touch of brown running through it; my mother so stately, with her tiny 18-inch waist, looking fabulous in everything she wore. I can still visualize her wearing those tall stilettos, making her legs look even that much longer.

There isn't a doubt in my mind that this moment of time in my mother's life must have been amazing. Always smiling, laughing, being social, she had the control of every room she entered. The way my father must have adored her, making her feel like she was the most beautiful woman in the world! She was in awe of my father, the high-roller, always seeming to be on a winning streak. She finally met the man she could depend on and would never have to worry. The first two husbands didn't work out, but this time it was going to be different!

He had a home being built for his new bride and her daughter. My father's mother and her husband also lived nearby, so there were many family gatherings and Carol (my half-sister) must have indeed felt blessed she had this loving family. The news soon broke that my mother was pregnant and since my father had never had a child or been married before, he was over the moon with happiness. Everyone at the drug store, the friends and family, my dad's barber customers and bookie clients all knew of my pending arrival, and they all shared the anticipation and excitement during the next nine months until that man burst into the backroom of the barber shop with the announcement that the baby was coming

A baby girl has arrived; six pounds – seven ounces, brown hair, brown eyes. Ahhhh! Just being blessed with taking my first breath of air in Monterey and having this magnificent place on earth be where my first footprints touched the ground, it is no wonder the soul of me resides in this part of paradise. I am often reminded to give gratitude for having this be my origination of life. The Monterey Peninsula was made famous by the novelist John Steinbeck. My parents worked a lot, so my paternal grandmother spent time with me and showered me with love and kindness. Her name was Pearl and she loved me tremendously. I know I must have been loved from all the pictures taken of me with her.

Soon after I was born we I moved into our new home on Cedar Avenue in Pacific Grove, across the street from the golf course and a few short blocks to the beach. Carol was forced to take me for stroller rides daily and in later years she confided how there were many times she wished she could push me out in front of a car since my walks and babysitting me were the cause of her not being allowed to play with any of her school friends. Her animosity toward me only lasted a year or so because she moved out of our home and was sent to live with my maternal grandmother. And it was there that Carol would remain.

By the time Carol was thirteen, she wasn't allowed to be with her friends. Stuck being caregiver for me, it is no wonder during the rest of her life there was always a hidden resentment. I was the one who took center stage. Her stepfather now had his own child and her mother seemingly didn't have time for her, sending her off to live with her grandmother like that. It was only a few blocks away on Alder Street, but she must have felt disposable by the family she had craved so desperately to love her. Carol was the center of my grandmother's world and there wasn't anything my grandmother wouldn't have done for her. She must have understood what Carol felt, being abandoned by her mother who had already tossed away Carol's real father and the following next two stepfathers.

I have no memory of this but it was around that time that Grandmother Pearl's husband died and she came to live with us. I'm sure it must have been helpful since Carol was no longer there to babysit and they now would have a built-in caregiver for me with my Grandmother Pearl. I must have been about five years by then, since I vividly remember her reading me stories, helping me to cut out clothes for my paper dolls, and always in the kitchen cooking to prepare my healthy, made-with-love meals. I lived close enough to walk to Lighthouse Elementary School each day. The school was adjacent to The Monarch Sanctuary and watching caterpillars growing into cocoons, soon to release a beautiful butterfly, is a vivid memory that has me drawn towards butterflies to this day. One day while walking home from school a car driven by a man driving pulled up next to me asking me to get in with him and he would give me a ride. Why I stood there listening I will never know. He told me how pretty I was and how he would make sure I was safe and get me home faster. As he got out of his car and came around and opened the door for me to get in, I knew it was time to run as fast as I could. He began calling for me, but thank goodness I hadn't let him get close enough to grab me and only had a few blocks left to run. He never followed me to see where I lived and as I ran to the house, there was my beautiful Grandmother Pearl waiting with open arms to comfort me and let me know that I was never to get in a stranger's car, that they might want to kidnap me and never return me to my family. Up until that point I never had anything to worry about, as life in this beautiful little ocean town, where doors were left unlocked, was all I ever knew, and the world was a beautiful place, with no danger, just love.

I awakened one night with my Mother hollering at my dad. I didn't hear my father's voice, just the loud sounds of my mother screaming, "How could you do this to me? How could you gamble, and drink, and risk losing your family?" I could hear my dad saying how sorry he was, but mom wanted a divorce.

Within minutes, my clothes were packed, along with my mother's. Mom went to stay in a hotel while she dropped me off at my maternal grandmother's house, where Carol, my half-sister, resided. This is where I remained for the next several years. My mother would come by daily after work and drop off some groceries and check on me. I wasn't allowed to see my father or my paternal grandmother, to whom I had grown so close. Instead, I was now sharing a full-sized bed with Carol, who resented me enough already, and now I was a burden placed upon my maternal grandmother. It didn't take long before I was moved to the living room sofa for my bed.

My grandmother, being a nurse, had a home that was always immaculate. I can remember her pouring bleach in the sink to wash the dishes and boiling water on the stove to rinse them. She made the best cakes with butter cream frosting. What wasn't used on the cakes was put into a small jar, and in the middle of the night I would get a spoon and sneak a little scoop. Whenever I was sick I received excellent care, not in a warm loving way, but in a professional caregiver way.

Soon Carol turned eighteen and graduated from high school, fell in love, and eloped with a man a few years older than she, and moved to San Jose. Word came that my father's mother, my Grandmother Pearl had died in the middle of the night from a heart attack. It was the first time I was allowed to see my father since my mother left him. My mother must have forgiven him long enough to allow him to see me. He came to tell me about my grandmother dying. He said he woke up in the middle of the night and saw the light coming from under her door and when he asked if everything was alright, there was no answer. When he opened the door he found her dead. My father had a very close relationship with his mother and when she died, I'm sure he felt as if losing me wasn't bad enough, but he had lost her now, too. So he went on a bender, where he drank and gambled until he lost everything and hit rock bottom.

CHAPTER 2
Music Became My World

I had no idea where my mother lived or much about her life except that she now had a new job selling cosmetics behind a counter at Holman's Department Store, and would sometimes bring me to the store to buy me school clothes. It was the only large department store in Pacific Grove, and being in cosmetics was always glamorous. I always thought my mom was very beautiful and was proud to have her for my mother because so many people who worked with her liked and admired her. Over the next few years, other than the fact she would come by daily to check on me and bring whatever my grandmother requested, I never saw much of her.

Around the time I was in fourth grade, when I would come home from school, I was made to go in my room and take a nap. It was time, I'm sure, when my grandmother needed to watch her soap operas and didn't want to be disturbed by me. A nap! Are you kidding me? So I did what any fourth-grader would do. I jumped out my bedroom window each afternoon and sneaked to a girlfriend's house across the street, coming back before her soaps ended. She never figured out that I left the house each day.

Good news came for me when my dad picked me up in a taxi and brought me to a beautiful historic hotel on Lighthouse Avenue in Pacific Grove where he was living in a small room. This is where he taught me to play Chinese checkers. It was a moment in time I will always remember. Being with my father, and actually feeling like Daddy's Little Girl once again was ecstasy! He explained to me that when my mother left him and he wasn't allowed to see me, then losing his mother, made him feel he had no reason to live, and he didn't care what happened to him.

But now he had received the doctor's care he had needed, and had just bought a beautiful house, and my mom was buying furniture and getting it beautifully fixed for all of us to be a family once again. This was the best news I ever could hear. My parents were getting back together and I would once again have the life I had only dreamed of!

The day came when they took me to our new house on Welch Circle in Pacific Grove. It looked like a home fit for a princess. A beautiful bedroom was all decorated in pink for me, and a new bike, along with all kinds of other surprises. I had my mom and my wonderful daddy, whom I loved more than life itself. This home was even more beautiful than the first one. I was allowed to have girlfriends sleep over and we even had a large formal dining room table where we could sit and share meals together. One time I put on one of my mother's beautiful long tulle slips on my head and pretended I was getting married. I had my girlfriends be part of the wedding. I was going to marry a ma just like my father, a man who make me feel beautiful and loved, and we would live happily ever after.

My father took me each week to the local horse stables for riding lessons. My mother enrolled me in Girl Scouts. I took ballet and tap lessons in a building on Cannery Row and started noticing boys.

On Saturdays, I was dropped off at my grandmother's and allowed to walk to downtown Pacific Grove to go to the movies. It was twenty-five cents to get in, with another fifty-cents allowed for popcorn and candy. The theater was always packed with other kids from school. Lots of flirting went on between the boys and girls.

I remember going to the movies to see Elvis in *Love Me Tender*, and when my parents picked me up afterwards, they drove to Cannery Row where there was an enormous fire. To this day I remember the flames from the fire shooting straight into the air in the dark night's sky. My father would tell stories of when he first came to Monterey and used to spend time in the "cat houses" on Cannery Row. It was big business for the madam who ran everything. She operated a restaurant in the front of the cat house where the men hung out. He spoke of the days when the canneries where a thriving business due to all the sardines. Then the sardines left and businesses had to close. Guessing that meant the cat houses, too!

All through grade school, my parents gave me money that went into a special savings account to help show me the value of what saving money could do. Once Disneyland had opened in Anaheim, it was my father's goal for just the two of us to ride The Del Monte train to Anaheim and travel to spend a few days at this magical theme park. We had almost five-hundred dollars saved over the years in my account and we looked forward to this father and daughter time together.

My parents started fighting again. My mother was constantly screaming at him. It was at this point where music became my escape, a place I could go to turn on the one local radio station and listen to all the current hits. When I was lucky at night I could sometimes reach one other station from Los Angeles and listen to Wolfman Jack. Just the sound of Wolfman's voice was exciting! It was also the first chance to listen to more songs with soul.

My father left for a few days (gone fishing) and along with him went my Disneyland savings, which he lost playing the Craps table. My mother started drinking around this time. Both my father and mother were chain smokers, he with his unfiltered Camels and Mom with her Marlboros. She had now started drinking Hamm's beer or vodka martinis with green olives on a tooth pick, while Dad had his Budweiser. Dad was back to the doctor getting prescriptions for uppers and downers for his periods of depression, caused by the war. Once again my mother kicked him out and they lost the house. I ended up back at my grandmother's, and who-knows-where my mother went to live this time. Both my father and I were so easily disposable to her. I probably would have gone to the doctor for drugs myself if I always had to hear all that yelling! My world was crumbling around me; my school work was suffering, and I was isolating myself from my friends. Missing my father, and yet so sad and disappointed that he had spent the Disneyland money we had saved for our special father-daughter trip together. But I got past it, because in my eyes, Daddy could do no wrong.

It became easier and easier to tune out the rest of the world. My sister was never around, so I was basically an only child. All I had left was one grandmother who would take me in but never was thrilled with the situation. Nevertheless, she gave me a room to sleep in and food in my tummy. Was everything in life to be so disposable? Music was my only friend.

My dad returned faster this time after losing his family and what he cared most about in the world ... *Me*. We moved to a small one-bedroom house on Sinex Avenue in Pacific Grove where the rent was seventy-five dollars a month. My mother had her own bedroom, my dad slept on a Murphy pull-down bed in the wall of the living room, and I slept in the laundry room on the back porch, just big enough to furnish with a narrow twin bed. There wasn't a washer or dryer, just a utility sink. A board was placed across the sink and pink shower curtain material was tacked on to hide the sink. It felt like I was being stuffed into a shoebox. There was no heat. A door leading off the laundry room opened to the backyard.

The fights between the two of them continued. My dad was not driving now. I suppose his license was revoked for drinking and driving, or doctor's orders due to the drugs he was on. The house always smelled like cigarette smoke from them both. But, I was at least in a home with two parents. The good side was the backyard was big enough for a tether pole, a wall to bounce a red ball off while playing dodge ball, a cement area for hopscotch, jacks and all my baton twirling, cartwheeling, and dancing to the music routines. The empty lot next door was filled with rows and rows of gladiolas and I would go often and pick fresh arrangements for the living room and the top of my bedroom covered sink. They made me feel good. To this day I love the beauty of gladiolas and have kept them in my bedrooms throughout my life.

I was sent off to church on Sunday. The Sunday school bus would come by the house to pick me up and drop me off. My father didn't attend church, claiming he was an atheist. He said he never received words or signs from his mother after she died, so therefore, he was not a believer. My mother couldn't be bothered, saying she needed Sunday mornings to herself. I will never forget each and every single Sunday getting off the church bus and hearing the yelling before I ever walked in the door. I would just go straight to my bedroom and turn up the music to tune it all out. One time my father was so out of it that Mom hit him in the head with the heel of her shoe, sending blood rushing down his face.

I looked forward to Mondays. It was my favorite day of the week. As soon as I came home from school, Dad would teach me how to cook something, usually a pot of soup of some kind and my favorite chocolate cake. It was always my dad who made my breakfast and dinner. My mother rarely cooked a meal until my teenage years.

Dad was a talented artist who used many different types of medium for his drawings. He would always make me fun cartoon characters to start my day off with a smile as I sat down to breakfast. Sometimes when I would go cut the gladiolas in the empty lot next door, the nice man who was the neighbor on the other side of the fence would come out and stand on his kitchen stairs and visit with me. His wife was very nice also. They would often bake cookies and offer me one. I would show them my dad's cartoons drawn for the day. After a year of becoming familiar, one day the man came to the stairs and said he had made a special picture to show me. He asked me to come around to the other side of the fence so he could show me. When I did he said he had left it in his car and to follow him into the garage, which I did. As he got into the driver's seat he unzipped his pants and pulled out his penis and asked me to touch it. He went to grab hold of my arm but I was able to get away and run. I was afraid to run home and tell my father, so I ran to my girlfriend's house down the street and told her, not realizing her mom could overhear. I was too afraid to go home, so I stayed with them the rest of the afternoon. When I finally went home, my father sat me down in the living room and told me my girlfriend's mother had told him everything and he wanted to make sure I was okay. Shortly thereafter, I found myself sitting in the office of the police chief, the same one who used to make bets in the backroom of my dad's barbershop, with him asking me to describe all the happened and what the man's penis looked like. I remember being very scared and nervous and recall my father leaving the room so I could tell the police chief what I saw and experienced.

I never saw the man again and the house he and his wife lived in was emptied quickly and a For Sale sign was posted. I never noticed the moving van come. The entire process must have been stealthily done during the dark of night.

I was twelve years old in 1961and part of a generation that started changing the world. AM Radio was King and the popularity of which songs made it to the Top Forty depended on how many 45 rpms were sold. I bought every new 45 rpm I could afford.

CHAPTER 3
A Teenage Princess

Starting seventh grade at Pacific Grove Junior High School was world-changing for me in many ways. This was going to be the greatest year of my life! The first time I didn't have the same kids in the same classroom all day long, but instead, put my books into a locker, shuttling from one classroom subject to the next. I enjoyed sitting next to new people in each class, making new friends, and concentrating on friends more than academics, especially since no emphasis was put on the importance of education and Daddy was going to do all my homework anyway. All I had to do was hand it to him and he would do the rest. He'd read, make the book reports, and if there was a map to be studied and colored in, he was thrilled to show his artwork skills. I only had to study the following mornings as I copied word-for-word what was written and learn as I go. More importantly was decorating my school books, covering them with blank grocery sack paper so I could write on them. I was big into making hearts, names of boys that would catch my eye, and new slang words of the moment, such as "cool." Annette Funicello was my role model; her clothes, the way she spoke, and her sweet romance and constant flirting with Frankie Avalon were what really mattered. I dreamed of owning a two-piece bathing suit to wear to the Pacific Grove beach on a sunny Saturday to show off the new girly figure I was beginning to acquire.

Having been an only child, I loved to finally be around so many new girlfriends. I was able to make friends easily. As my mother worked in cosmetics, she was always giving me samples to share, which was a great way to acquire new friends. This is where I started to blossom, became more outgoing, smiling more. And in order to be popular you needed to make sure you wore the cutest clothes to school each day. Mom even signed me up for a charm school held at the store that would teach me how to walk, sit and most importantly, model. At the end of the once-a-week six-week course the store held a large fashion show and all the teen girls from the classes were to be the models. The prettiest clothes to model were chosen for me, and I got to wear the bridal dress a showstopper for the finale. It was here that I knew my true calling was to be a model (or at least so I imagined).

I gravitated toward friends who were trendy and from upscale neighborhoods, including the elite Pebble Beach. We'd spend hours on the phone talking about boys, makeup, and hairstyles. We were typical of girls growing up in the sixties in America. When everyone started having slumber parties, I could not invite them to my house. No way did I want my friends to know that I slept in the laundry room. Nor did I want them to know that my glamorous mother spent her evenings in a robe, smoking and drinking, and yelling at my father.

Our school had a sock hop each Friday during lunch. The kids would meet in the gymnasium, kick off our tennis shoes. Boys lined up on one side, the girls on the other. The music would start playing and the boys would have to walk across and ask the girls to dance. I loved this time most of all; music, my girlfriends, and now boys asking me to dance! Gary US Bonds would come on playing *Quarter To Three*, Chubby Checker doing the *Twist*, *Let's Twist Again*, and *The Fly*. There was *The Bristol Stomp* by The Dovells, *Runaround Sue* by Dion, *Mashed Potato Time* with Dee Dee

Sharp, and The Shirelles singing *Dedicated to the One I Love*. This is when I could say I danced like no one was watching. It was a special time when music and dance became my world. Girlfriends, boys, music and dancing... life was but a song and music was the key to my happiness.

After being seen in the local fashion show by friends at school, boys and girls started watching my trends and fashion became very important to me. Who needed to worry about grades? I was sure I would be on the cover of *Seventeen* one day! Being 5-feet, 7-inches, and one of the tallest, if not the tallest in my class, I dreamed of the day I'd be a fashion model, as I'm sure many girls my age dreamed about as well. *Seventeen* was my Bible and I would read it from cover-to-cover.

I started to get my first real modeling jobs doing fashion shows. I was even asked to model for an ad in the local newspaper, *The Monterey Herald*. There was a photographer named Steven Crouch who did the photo shoots for the paper and he was very well-known for the quality of his work. On the day of the photo shoot I went with Steven for a location picture at Nepenthe Restaurant in

Big Sur. I was asked to stand on a ledge overlooking the beautiful ocean in the background, but not to look down because there was a danger of falling. It descended down a steep hillside to the ocean's edge. It was surreal, me, a girl who had never even been to Big Sur (although only a half-hour drive from home), now being photographed for the newspaper! This was truly without question one of the best years of my life.

That same night, Dad came home very excited to tell Mom and me the news that he bought a new house for us, a three-bedroom, two-and-a-half bath, den, with sliding glass doors leading to the patio, all on a big lot. My dad said it would require him to haul dirt in to make sure the front lawn would grow well and he was planning to build an enclosed patio and a waterfall. Dad would give me my own special space to grow whatever flowers I would like. It was being built now and would be finished in the next six months. My mother was very excited to hear the news. She went with my dad to go see it and fell in love with her new soon to be built home. Mom immediately started collecting everything turquoise to match her planned new refrigerator and stove. The house was being built in a new city on the Monterey Peninsula named Marina. There were new developments going in at a price my family could afford. It was about a thirty minute drive from Pacific Grove.

My dad surprised me by telling me I would have the master bedroom complete with my own bathroom, just perfect for his soon-to-be teenage princess. My mom and dad would each have a room of their own, but I would have the biggest and best room of them all. However, I would have to wait a few months longer to actually see my beautiful brand new house on California Avenue. But I just knew it was going to be amazing. And to go from the laundry room to a princess room -I could only imagine! Since I was still in the seventh grade and Mom had to drive Dad to work each day, she would keep me in the same Pacific Grove Junior High and I'd continue through eighth grade with my same girlfriends as I turned thirteen. So, new home, new princess room and same friends!

Finally, the time arrived when I would get to see our new house. Although Marina was only eight miles north of Monterey, it seemed to take forever to get there since my mother drove like a snail. The area was connected to the property Fort Ord used for military housing and training. We traveled the old Del Monte Highway known as Highway 1 as it progressed towards Marina. I had never seen Army recruits before. For exercise, they ran along the railroad tracks where we could hear them singing. I never understood the World War very well or the magnitude of it, only that my father was in it and it made him sick and he had to take pills because of it. At last we arrived and Mom and Dad announced this was Marina, my new home town. I looked around waiting to see something, anything other than sand. Oh wait! There was a small gas station, a little building that was the fire department, and a small street we turned onto called Carmel Avenue. On the corner was a bar, where according to the signs you could play card games. I was sure there must be a city somewhere up ahead. All I saw were a small church, one small elementary school, no junior high and no high school. Everywhere I looked I saw sand. Road construction was underway in this new development. There were three more houses being built near ours. On the other side of our house were a series of run-down tiny old houses with broken down rusted cars and clothes hanging on lines in the front yards. I was hesitant to get out of the car, but wanted to see what my room would look like.

CHAPTER 4

Home Sweet Home

We walked through the front door and saw a beautiful furnished house. I could see my mother's face light up, a sight rarely seen other than at work. She was so happy to see the final results of her creative designs and color schemes in her perfect new home. We stepped down into the den, done in a tropical island style, where the large sliding glass door overlooked a large hill of sand, what Daddy explained would one day soon become our enclosed patio.

I asked where my room was and they pointed to the end of the hallway. I took off running, opened the door, and there it was, my Princess Room, with twin beds for a girlfriend sleep over, my own color TV, larger than the one in the living room, with attached stereo record player that had a panel in the front that would change colors as the music played. On my nightstand was my very own pink princess telephone that lit up when the receiver was lifted, not a rotary, but push buttons to dial the numbers. I opened my closet and saw that my mother had already moved my clothes. I had forty skirts lined up from light to dark with the matching color sweaters on the shelf above. Then I looked in my bathroom and I had an actual shower with a toilet in my very own room for privacy. How could this be true? How could someone like me who was living in a tiny little laundry room that was so cold during the night be brought into a home as beautiful as this? It was thrilling!

Marina is a pretty name and one of my favorites, but that is all. Carmel Avenue was a two-lane road, with a few girls my age who appeared to have no fashion sense. There was a little hole-in-the wall café with a juke box where all the bad boys stood around smoking, their dusty old cars parked to look like they owned the town. Peeling out and laying rubber as they left was meant to impress anyone who might be getting groceries next door. That was the one tiny grocery store on Reservation Road in a little strip mall, which included the only beauty salon. There was a small recreation center for teens to hang out on Friday nights, complete with juke box, dance floor and pool table. Only two main streets connected all the streets, Reservation Road leading to Salinas, and Carmel Avenue. The population was 6,000. The town had a two-man paid fire department in an unincorporated sandy open field. But for me, once I was in my very own Princess Room, the rest of the world didn't exist as I escaped, listening to my music, polishing my toes pink, reading *Seventeen*, and talking on the phone to girlfriends, often all at the same time.

I could hardly wait to get back to school and invite a girlfriend to spend the night at my new house in my very own Princess Bedroom. It seemed a long drive away from my school and my girlfriends, but as promised, I was still able to attend the same Pacific Grove Junior High for eighth grade, walk downtown with my friends after school, have a coke, and go check in with Mom before I had to go catch a bus to go to New Monterey to stay with my father at his barber shop named Cal's. It was located next door to the Monterey Beauty College, where all these beautiful girls with white uniforms and bleached blonde hair, sometimes pink hair, would walk past the shop. I wanted to be old enough to get my hair done there someday. But my dad always cut my hair since I was born. He would even put a bucket outside to collect rain water for rinsing my naturally curly locks. I loved the way he would put that brush with talc powder that smelled so good all around my shoulders, always finishing with a touch on the tip of my nose.

The barber shop was very small compared to most. It still had the nudes plastered all over the bathroom walls, *Playboy* magazines, but no backroom for bets, and my father had stopped drinking and I never again saw him take the uppers and downers. This shop had only two chairs for his cuts and no Harold doing shoe shines outside. I hoped Harold and his family were okay. I liked them so much. Harold always pretended to shine my shoes when I would climb up into one of those big chairs to read my comic books. I enjoyed each day there with Daddy. I think my father must have closed his other two barber shops before this, one on Forest Avenue in Pacific Grove and one on Bonifacio, off Alvarado in Monterey, all named after horses Dad must have made big money on, Citation and Salamander. I'm surprised he didn't name one after Willie Shoemaker who was a household word! Each day I spent at the barber shop was fun. All the men getting their hair cut often would give me twenty-five or fifty cents to go shopping on the block. I was always allowed to take quarters from my dad's wooden tip box. Cuts were two dollars and always included a fifty-cent tip that went straight into the box. These men were regulars each and every week and they all knew me from the time I was a little girl coming to sit in the back room where the action was happening.

First stop with the tip money was next door at the Farmers Insurance store. A blind man owned a book store in the back room. The books made the room smell old and musty. I would go spend time helping to keep everything dusted and clean and put away. He was such a nice man to visit with and I know he enjoyed hearing my voice when I would say hello to him after school each day. I loved picking out comic books for my dad to read. He loved the ones with naked girls and dirty jokes. I was so used to being raised around nudes it didn't mean a thing to me. I, on the other hand, loved reading *Richie Rich*, *Archie and Veronica*, *Superman* and *Casper*. Often I'd go to the five-and-dime store across the street or the pet store at the end of the block. I'd also get an after school snack at Monte Mart or I would go to the local tavern called The

Halfway House where they made the best hamburgers. Of course I had to wait outside for my order. The owners of all the stores knew me and always had a special sandwich made for me in what I assume was in exchange for weekly haircuts. It was like family for me to go visit each day.

For the next year this was my daily routine and my dad would leave work early, while still daylight, and drive over to my grandmother's house, park across the street in an empty lot, and for an hour shovel loads of rich dark dirt into the trunk of the Chevy. He shoveled enough dirt to completely cover the sand at the new Marina house. He built a wooden fence around it, planted a beautiful lawn, two palm trees (which weren't seen much in the area), and added a cement walkway. In the back patio area Dad placed redwood two-by-fours in big squares and then filled it all in with concrete. He built a massive cement waterfall out of beautiful rocks. He left a big space open and filled it with dirt for my flower garden, which I filled with gladiolas, gardenias, and my number one favorite of all time, sweet peas, grown on trellises covering two walls, giving the sweetest smell to my bedroom and bath.

Once all his hard work was completed, Dad sold the Chevy and bought a brand new white Ford Galaxy 500 straight off the showroom floor. It was just beautiful and had that wonderful new car smell. Since Marina was so small and you never saw any highway patrol, sheriff, or police, Dad would always let me sit next to him and practice with the steering wheel. I felt so grown up. Now we had this new car and I knew in a little more than a year, at age fifteen-and-a-half, I would be allowed to drive as soon as I got my permit.

It was during this summer that my father had a heart attack at his shop and was taken to the hospital in Carmel, then transferred to the Veterans Hospital in Palo Alto. Mom came home from work to pick me up and drive us to Palo Alto. I had never been to a hospital before to visit and the smells, plus the intravenous needle stuck in my father's arm, were a little overwhelming for me, I suppose, because I started to feel ill and asked to use the restroom and the very moment I walked inside and closed the door I fainted and had to be revived by a nurse with smelling salts, then was seated in a chair with my head hanging between my legs. But once

I was better I was allowed to go lie next to my dad and all seemed to be better in the world again.

It was another few weeks before my father came home, and when he did, everything as we knew it seemed to change. My father was not permitted to work any longer and the barber shop had to close. My mother had to quit her job at Holman's to stay home to care for him. I was now not allowed to continue my schooling in Pacific Grove due to transportation issues and since there wasn't a junior high in Marina I was sent by school bus to Fitch Junior High School on the base in Fort Ord, which taught grades seven through nine. I was going into ninth grade and didn't know a single student. I was going to miss all my girlfriends from all my school years in Pacific Grove. What were these new students going to wear? How should I dress? Those were the things important to me. Did they read *Seventeen* magazines? My dad was always so comforting, with his soothing voice, promising me all would be fine, that he would be waiting for me the second I got home from school, that we could play Chinese checkers or card games together, and how much fun that would be.

Fitch was a totally different school. Many of the kids who went there were transients since it was located on a military base. Kids came and went and I quickly learned not to get too attached because they were used to moving from state to state, keeping contact through letters. Calling was not practical because of the cost of long distance. I did learn many things from these kids I'm sure my parents would disapprove of. My parents would have been very upset had they seen how I looked when I left the house in the morning to go catch the bus and how I transformed my appearance by the time I arrived at school. My tight skirts always had to be at my knees, but while standing waiting for the bus they were always rolled up to become a mini skirt. I wasn't allowed to wear anything but mascara, but on the bus I outlined my eyes in a black Maybelline eyeliner pencil. My brown hair was teased very full, and I always added a touch of Tabu cologne on my neck. Pacific Grove was very Noxema clean and *Seventeen*. Fort Ord was all about being noticed by the bad boys. It was just like out of the movie *Grease*. I was the new girl, sweet innocent "Sandy" who had to learn quickly how to defend myself in case of fights. At this school there were fights every day, usually the blacks against the whites or this gang of guys versus that gang of guys. It was also a time where I was taught by my new best friend, another Sandy-type from *Grease*, but that was actually her name, how to kiss by holding a mirror and practice kissing it, lips never too tight but with barely just a pucker. Eyes closed and head tilted slightly to the side. She also taught me how to smoke a cigarette in the girls' lavatory so I would look cool. I had watched my parents long enough, so I had a pretty good idea of how to do it, and at the time cigarettes cost only twenty-five cents a pack in the vending machine in the movie theaters. Our choice to look cool was filtered Winston's.

On the weekends when my parents would allow me to spend the night at Sandy's house, her brother would take us downtown to Alvarado Street in Monterey and drop us off at the movies. All the bad boys that Sandy knew, thanks to her brother, went to shoot pool at Louie's Pool Hall a couple of blocks away. Then the guys would go stand around the Rio Theater across from the State Theater and check out all the girls across the street. It really was just like a scene from *Grease*! The way the guys combed their hair to look just like that! I never did meet any boy I really liked, except for one, Tommy, who had that James Dean look. I never made it as far as getting the kiss I had practiced for. Thank goodness for Sandy helping me to master my flirting style. I'm sure I must have flirted with a hundred different guys during my high school years. I went so far as to change my name from Sharon to the flirtier "Shari." It became popular to dot an "i" with a small circle or a heart above it. Yes, I was very cool, or so I thought!

Still, music was the main thing that held my attention. I danced to songs like *It's My Party* by Leslie Gore, and *Louie Louie* by The Kingsmen, and came home quickly from school to watch *Where the Action Is* and *American Bandstand*. There were still drive-in movies. There was James Bond as 007. It was also the beginning of the war in Vietnam, when one hundred troops were killed. Over two-hundred thousand took part in the Civil Rights March on Washington to hear the Rev. Dr. Martin Luther King give his *I Have a Dream* speech. President Kennedy was assassinated in Dallas. It was the beginning of change in our times. It was still a very innocent, fun, flirty time for me with very little time given to any school work. No need, my dad would still do it all.

By the time 1964 came around I had new friends and didn't have much contact from the ones in Pacific Grove any longer since I didn't live there and their high-end life styles and fashions were really not "the look" at my new school, Seaside High School. I was more concerned with learning the new slang lingo. Boss, crash, dig, far out, out of sight, tough, freak out, hang loose, right on, stoned, flipping the bird, threads, pig out, make out, square, stacked – I mastered the new language! A new transistor radio allowed me to listen to music anywhere, anytime. Chuck Berry and "Beatlemania" were sweeping the nation. The Ford Mustang instantly became the "It" car. I learned who Audrey Hepburn was in *My Fair Lady* and *Charade*. The *Pink Panther* was on the scene, and I learned how to twitch my nose like Elizabeth Montgomery on *Bewitched*. The Surgeon General linked smoking with lung cancer.

Seaside High School was a brand new school, big and beautiful. In the last year it opened with the first tenth graders now moving up to be juniors, while my class made up the new sophomore class.

I was able to hang out not only with own my class, but with some of the students in the two upper grades. At lunchtime music played over the loud speakers. I remember being impressed that a very high percentage of the students were black, and I couldn't help but notice that, man, could they dance! And I loved every chance I got to be able to attend school dances. But my most favorite nights were when the Fort Ord bus would come to Marina and pick up kids to take them to the Fort Ord Youth Center. This was actually one of my favorite places growing up. The cool guys would shoot pool and check out the girls coming in to dance. When the songs played, the guys would pass along the pool stick to someone else while they tried to get a girl to dance with them. If you could get Raymond or Ronnie to dance with you, you had the best dancers, the ones that all the girls wanted to dance with. My favorite song was *The Stroll,* and I loved when Raymond would ask me to dance. Raymond was my "Fonzie." He could just walk into a room and the guys would want to be just like him. He had a swagger when he walked, and would always drink a little rum and coke he stashed away. Like all the guys that were in his group, he was COOL. Even at this point I still had never had a real boyfriend, but lots and lots of boys that were my friends. With me they could all look but not touch.

This was the year I got my driver's license and just like everyone else in the small town of Marina, now it was my turn to practice laying rubber. Hanging out with friends at the small drive-through hamburger place on Carmel Avenue, the same one I used to make fun of was where I wanted to be and be seen. With my cut off short jeans and short tops with my bare midriff showing, I wanted to stand out. Driving skills became important and I would go out on back roads with the guys where they would teach me how to drive fast and what to do if I lost control of the car. There was no such thing as seat belts and the maximum speed limit was raised to 55 mph on the freeways.

Every Sunday afternoon my parents let me take a girlfriend and drive to Salinas to go drag Main Street. Round and round in circles we drove, making a loop, the same as all the other cars with the guys and girls flirting as they passed each other. We would pull into Mel's Drive-in where a carhop would come out to the car and take our order, mine usually being a Coke, with French fries and gravy poured on top. When the server brought the order, she would attach a tray to the window. When finished, I would be able to get out of the car and saunter off to the rest room to show off what I was wearing, with maybe a little subtle hip movement as I walked. These were the days when guys did actually whistle when girls passed by, especially construction workers. Nothing could make a girl feel more like a girl than being whistled at. Oh, yes, the times have changed!

I always had to have the car back home by five o'clock, and on this one afternoon, as I was driving my girlfriend and me home, I was running late so I sped up to 100mph, but it was raining very hard. I was on a two-lane road and attempted to pass the car in front of me but when I did, there was a car coming head-on. I couldn't slow down fast enough to avoid hitting the car in front of me in my lane, so I tried to pass it on the right-hand shoulder. But due to wet road, the car spun around in the mud a few times and careened down into a ditch, landing on its side. We were very lucky that the mud slowed us down. Passersby stopped to help and were able to unlock the driver's door and helped both of us climb out to safety. When the highway patrol showed up I told them I put on my brakes in the rain and they locked up and all I could do was try to pull the car off the road into the mud. There were no skid marks due to the pouring rain and my story was bought and no ticket given. The bad part was my mom and dad came in another highway patrol car to the scene to pick us up and make sure we were okay. No word was ever mentioned about the car. It was towed and fixed right away and all that mattered was we were safe.

The hard part was that the following day my father had another serious heart attack. By this time, I had grown even closer to him since spending so much time at home with him each day after school.

Luckily, when my dad bought the new car and all the furniture for the new house, it was put on a monthly payment plan that carried an insurance policy to cover certain health conditions so the loans would be completely paid up. When he had this heart attack, he qualified, and everything was now paid for.

CHAPTER 5
Daddy's Little Girl

The Veterans Administration now granted him total disability since he had been under doctors' care since the war. Now he was able to get many extra benefits. Shopping on the Fort Ord base was one helpful perk, plus he was entitled to paid art lessons at home. The teacher would come over and two other disabled military men would come in their wheel chairs. The teacher was a free-spirited hippie woman, who traveled all the way from Big Sur once a week to teach this class. The VA even paid for the nude models. Can you believe it? So I got used to coming home and walking around nudes lying around in poses as the men sketched. They really did a fabulous job and they enjoyed a particular beautiful blonde model and always made sure she and the teacher enjoyed a glass of wine during the sessions. It never bothered my mother at all. She was rarely at home anyway when I returned from school.

Mom, not quite fifty years old, still loved going out to lunch with her friends, or to the movies, and my father never denied her anything. It did get to the point where he thought it would be a good idea if they married one more time because he wanted to make sure if something happened to him she would receive his VA benefits for the rest of her life. So they did marry again for the third time. My father had me drive him to a clothing store where he wanted to surprise me with a new full-length mink coat, but I had to turn it down. I didn't want to hurt his feelings because I knew he dreamed of me in diamonds and furs, but I didn't want to wear the poor animals that had to give their lives. We left the store and he took me out for a nice lunch in Carmel. He wasn't sad; he just wanted to make sure he knew how proud he was of me and how much he loved me. My father always told me he loved me, but never once do I remember hearing that from my mother, not that she didn't love me, she just didn't know how to express it. But I still loved being Daddy's Little Girl no matter how big I was getting. We would laugh at how I used to dress up like a bride so I could marry him. I told him I wanted to marry someone just like him one day. He would always talk about men and how I had to trust him, and to make sure I married someone older who could afford to take care of me like he had.

My dad tried to explain what his doctors were telling him, that he wasn't able to have surgery and from now on he would have to be homebound except when he went for his doctors' appointments, and that a wheelchair would be arriving along with a hospital bed. He didn't want me to worry; the VA hospital was providing everything for him, including a nurse coming in once a week to check on him, bathe him, and take his vital signs.

As the coming months progressed, the summer between my junior and senior year, my parents sat me down in the living room and told me they had decided to take me out of school. My grades were not that good and my father had decided that he wanted me to go to beauty college and learn a trade; if anything ever happened to him he wanted to make sure that no matter how old I got I could always use that trade. Dad said the VA had a program to help the dependents of veterans get vocational educations and they would pay all expenses for tuition. He said once I graduated and got my license, which would take nine months, I could always return to high school to get my diploma, but that he needed me to do this for him.

I went to take some special tests at the VA office to qualify. There were hours of psychological tests, ink blots and many more. When the results came back we were all shocked, especially my father and me, to learn the results which said I was gifted and had a very high IQ. Hilarious! Me with a high IQ and Dad doing my homework all those years! I always wondered - what if? If only I could have worked in the field that all through my school years, tests told me I would do well in! They determined then that I should become a social worker. Now that I am older and look back, they were 100% correct. I would have loved devoting my life to helping others. Little did I know in my very distant future I would spend my happiest hours volunteering, doing for others.

I did always dream of being in the world of beauty and fashion so now was my chance. Since it was summer, I didn't have the chance to tell many friends at school that I was leaving. Many friends were hanging out at Del Monte Beach learning to body surf. But I would always have more summers and was still just a teenager. The fantasy of looking like those girls I so admired next door to Cal's Barber Shop was soon going to be me; bleached blonde hair, a white uniform and nurse's shoes. I felt so grown up and yet, was really just a child. But I knew how to drive and smoke cigarettes, so I looked very grown-up. The boys would just have to wait one year for me to return to high school, when I would look foxy with my gorgeous blonde hair!

This was the summer of 1965. I was Sweet Sixteen and had just barely been kissed. The war in Vietnam escalated with over one-hundred thousand American troops and an intensive bombing campaign. Campus protests began against the war. I witnessed two months' worth of nationally watched civil rights demonstrations in Selma, Alabama. President Johnson won Congressional approval for the historic Voting Rights Act which allowed for a mass enfranchisement of racial minorities throughout the country, especially in the South. Get Smart was the show to watch on TV. Doctor Zhivago was my favorite movie and The Rolling Stones' *I Can 't Get No Satisfaction*, was #1 on the billboard charts.

Beginning beauty college at age sixteen was completely different than high school. This time I really did have to study. There was so much to learn from Marinello School of Beauty. I found I was a natural at it. The bad part was the State of California would not permit me to get licensed until I turned eighteen. It would be much longer than the nine months I had anticipated and I wouldn't be able to go back to high school, but would have to go to adult education classes to get my high school diploma.

I was learning to cut women's hair, to curl it with the proper sized rollers, and how to make pin curls with just the right twist. There was no such thing as a blow dryer or an electric curling iron at the time. It was a shampoo and set, put them under the big domed dryer, put their feet up, and bring them a cup of coffee and a magazine. When they were finished drying, it was comb out the hair, backcomb it and style it smooth to conceal all the teased cushioning packed underneath, then spray it like crazy with pure lacquer. It was reminiscent of making an art sculpture, especially if it was an up-do, which required the need to make curls that were inter-woven inside each other. I learned how to wrap a head-full of permanent wave rods. I was very well-trained in hair color and it became a specialty for me when I learned to do a few colors at once on one client. I knew I was becoming an expert when regular weekly clients came back asking just for me!

In order to learn how to practice facials I had to practice on dummy wig heads. I held them in my lap, the head balanced between my knees, as I practiced massage strokes.

The owner of the beauty college liked to use me as her model to win hair-styling contests. She would get me a hotel room, a new evening gown, new heels, all to look fabulous for her hairstyles. Models were spoiled and she took especially good care of me, since we always took first place. I helped her win money and status for her school. I can remember going to Los Angeles and staying at the Ambassador Hotel where The Grateful Dead was playing that night in the Coconut Grove nightclub. I tried to get in but, darn, I was too young!

Soon it was 1966 and the military draft calls for the war in Vietnam continued. Protests expanded, monthly draft calls rose to ten times what they had been in 1965. For the second time in two years there was violent rioting in the Watts section of Los Angeles. Miniskirts were the rage in England and the US, and boots on women became popular, with Nancy Sinatra recording *These Boots are Made for Walking*. "Mod" clothes and Nehru shirts and jackets for men with no collars were the latest fashions, along with shaggy long hair-styles and color shades in round and square shapes and sizes. *Batman* and *Mission Impossible* were on TV, Dusty Springfield on the radio, the movie *Hawaii* in the theaters, and The Lovin' Spoonful recorded *Summer in the City*. Yes, they were hot times.

By now my dad was enjoying watching his "princess" come home from school brimming with excitement. He was now qualified by the VA to be a teacher for the art students. The same two men came by our house twice a week for life drawing classes. I often smiled to think that here were three men in wheel chairs, at least able to look at pretty girls, often two modeling at a time. I found the oil paintings and charcoal drawings of the nudes to be beautiful. I always thought the sight of a naked woman's body was beautiful no matter what the shape or size. Often times I would grab a pencil and paper and draw, too, but know I would have been very uncomfortable to draw a nude male because I had never seen a naked man. Luckily, their models were always female!

I really loved beauty college. One of my best friends from Seaside High School, Emma, who had just graduated, enrolled in beauty college with me. It was great fun for the two of us to reconnect and knew I would be happier having her along during my extended stay. She shared all the stories with me of how many of the boys in our school were now drafted into the war. She said I was lucky I left school when I did; so many of our friends were smoking pot and girls were getting pregnant. It was then I knew I was blessed that I was taken from the school during that time. I had matured tremendously being around all the older students. Emma was still in love with her high school sweetheart, who was the star of the school's wrestling team. She talked about their love for each other every day. Oh, how I wished I could find someone like Emma had! But in beauty school, all I met were women all day long.

One day Emma and I were walking down the block to get some lunch when two guys pulled up at the stop sign in a 1963 Corvette Stingray. They revved the engine to get our attention and I couldn't help but smile. They proceeded to pull in where we were having lunch and asked to join our table. Emma wasn't at all interested but I found the driver to be very handsome. It turned out he was much older than me by seven years and worked at the Defense Language Institute. His name was Jim and he asked if he could have my number and call me sometime, and I complied. I told my father all about him and he said both he and my mother would look forward to meeting him. Jim invited me to go to the movies, but I wasn't allowed to go until they met him first. So I invited Jim to come over to meet my family.

My dad got along very well with Jim. They seemed to have some male bonding going on. It wasn't that long before I received another invitation from Jim to go dancing, but he must have thought I was older than seventeen. Going to where alcohol was served was out of the question, but going to the movies was a great idea. I suppose after the long talks with my dad, Jim never tried to take advantage of me in any way and was always a perfect gentleman and my parents grew very fond of him. My dad encouraged me to see him more often and said he liked the fact I was with an older man who would take good care of me in case my dad's health got worse. Jim was also a great artist and would come over while I was in school and join my father's classes sketching the nude models and having a cocktail along with the group. Jim and the other men all smoked and it was just normal for me to arrive home to a smoke-filled room. Mom never minded and would say, "More power to them."

Jim seemed to be good for my father, mother and me. Jim was kind and gentle and never spoke a harsh word. I do not remember ever having a disagreement. He was happy to do anything to make me happy. His birthday was the day after mine. You would think we were brothers and sisters. Our personalities were very similar.

The year was 1967 and in Monterey everyone was looking forward to the Monterey Pop Festival. I was now wearing flowers in my hair as a flower child for the big event, along with flowery bell bottom hip-hugger pants in oranges and pinks with a cropped top showing my bare midriff, completing the look with a beaded choker necklace. It was June and I was able to see, in person on stage, Janice Joplin, Big Brother and The Holding Company, Jimi

Hendrix, The Mamas and Papas, The Who, The Byrds and many more. It was a time to be a Love Child, smoke a little shared pot with friends and live in peace. It was the time of Haight-Ashbury in San Francisco, Love-ins at Big Sur, and listening to Joan Baez and Bob Dylan talk about peace. I lived in an area where hippies now roamed the streets, hitchhiking their way down to Big Sur. While the rest of the country was still suffering racial violence, and over five-hundred thousand troops were in Vietnam. The big movies were *Bonnie and Clyde, The Graduate* and my favorite, *Guess Who's Coming to Dinner.*

This was the year I became engaged to Jim after he got down on one knee and proposed to me using the solitaire diamond ring my father had bought me; I didn't want to wear any other diamond but that one. I was just turning eighteen and even though I was still a teenager, in my mind I was fully ready to do as my family wished and marry Jim and live happily ever after.

On August 3rd 1967, I received my cosmetologist license and three days later I was given the most lavish wedding in my beautiful white wedding dress and had my father in his handsome new black suit walk me down the aisle. My parents' wedding gift to me was their house in Marina. My father wanted to make sure I always had a roof over my head, a loving husband, and a job to fall back on. Being intimate with a man, wasn't at all what I had dreamed it to be, not passionate, very mechanical, and almost like two people doing something expected but not enjoyable. At least for me. Even if it wasn't a romantic love story, I couldn't have been happier. I felt safe and secure.

As long as my dad was okay, I was okay. I knew if I needed anything, my dad would take care of it.

As the war in Vietnam raged, violence continued to rage in the streets of America. The Reverend Dr. Martin Luther King Jr. was assassinated in Memphis, triggering even more racial violence in hundreds of cities and towns. Two months later Senator Robert F. Kennedy was fatally shot in Los Angeles after the Democratic Presidential Primary. I felt blessed to be able to say I shook hands with him at the Monterey Peninsula Airport. What a tragic world this was turning into! What happened to the days of rock and roll oldies but goodies, my sock hops, *Seventeen* magazines and shopping for 45 rpms? The brightness and laughter came from the TV show *Laugh In,* with the Fickle Finger of Fate and Goldie Hawn. I enjoyed Barbara Streisand in *Funny Girl* and the Beatles singing *Hey Jude.*

Our first Christmas Jim bought me a silver toy poodle. It was my time to practice the responsibility of taking care of something so helpless. It was also the year I became pregnant. I wanted to make sure I gave my father a beautiful grandchild, not knowing in those years whether it was going to be a girl or a boy. But I was ready to be a mommy and I was going to love this child with every ounce of my being. My father had a long talk with Jim and they decided Jim and I would sell the house on California Street and move in with my parents during my pregnancy so they could be closer to me. We would jointly purchase a much bigger house with an extra-large back yard for the expected child. We found the perfect one, still in Marina, where the costs were still affordable and both families shared expenses.

Dad and Jim also went in together and bought a new navy blue Lincoln Continental. Jim sold our 1963 Corvette, which I was sad to see go, especially since Jim was the president of the local Corvette club and we had enjoyed going to all the rallies. Then my 1967 Super Sport Camaro was sold as it was decided I would need a station wagon to keep my new precious cargo safe. Our beautiful new house was on Young Circle in Marina. It was at the end of a dead end street next to a large field filled with magnificent eucalyptus trees where horses were kept. What beauty I was able to wake up to view each day! My new home was extra-large and spacious compared to the California Street place. It had an oversized living room and a step-down more, intimate den with sliding glass doors that lead out to the massive back yard with huge trees, totally landscaped. I could visualize an Olympic pool here one day. But for now I was going to plant rows and rows of gladiolas and trellises of fresh smelling sweet peas. My father's favorite were red and white carnations which he bought for me each time he went to the commissary grocery shopping, but now I would plant them and surprise him with fresh cut bouquets made with love.

Dad and Jim decided to purchase a pool table for the living

room. Everything in the room was as if you stepped into Louie's Pool Hall on Alvarado in Monterey; pool sticks of varying lengths all lined up on the wall, blue chalk for the cue tips and the rack to rack them up. My dad was great at shooting pool and playing "call shot." Jim and Dad had running scores against each other daily. I learned how to play, too, and did very well at playing against them. I would study Minnesota Fats' books and practice my combination shots. Dad bought me my own personalized pool stick in a case. All three of us had them.

CHAPTER 6
Michelle

I had quit smoking when I wanted to try to get pregnant. The doctor advised it was better for the baby. But Mom, Dad, and Jim still smoked and left unfortunate burn marks on the edges of the pool table from laying their burning cigarettes down as they made the calls. My dad's charcoal pictures of nudes hung on the walls of the new house and became the place where all the gentlemen in the neighborhood came to hang out, enjoying shooting pool.

I had never tasted alcohol due to my age and because I didn't like the smell. I also remember once when my Mom was so drunk I had to help get her to the bathroom to throw up her vodka martinis with two olives. I could never eat green olives or stand the smell of them after that. Even to this day I have never tasted a beer due to the smell. In any case, besides giving up tobacco, the doctor needn't have worried about me drinking alcohol during my pregnancy, but I suppose that, unknowingly, I was inhaling "second-hand" smoke, something that was never mentioned in those days.

In the new house, Jim and I were given the master bedroom with bath. Mom had her room and Dad his, and the baby's new room was mine to decorate as I pleased. These were the days of long shag carpets, using a garden rake between vacuuming to make them look fresh all the time. Not knowing if the baby would be a boy or girl, I decorated the nursery with an animal theme. Somehow, I just knew I was going to have a beautiful baby girl and every time I petted my growing tummy, I referred to the baby as "she" or "her." The bassinet, crib, and rocking chair in the room were all white. Large stuffed animals were given as gifts from friends at my shower, along with lots of clothes in white, yellow, and green. But hidden under my bed were bags and bags of my little girl's clothes that no one knew I bought. I had everything picked out to bring the baby home from the hospital and my suitcase was packed and ready to go at a moment's notice. The last month of my pregnancy became very difficult. I developed preeclampsia, a condition that caused high blood pressure and water-retention, that required my being bed ridden. I had to go to the doctor's office each day to have my blood pressure checked. One day the doctor said my blood pressure was at stroke level and I needed to be induced to have labor start right away. He couldn't take the chance of something happening to either of us.

Jim drove me straight to the Carmel Community Hospital where I had been a Candy Striper volunteer during my teen years one summer, when I would wheel around carts of books to the rooms and be kind to the patients, offering a pleasant smile and warm hello. This hospital looked more like an elegant hotel with water fountains in the lobby and a dining room that was first-class for doctors and visitors to enjoy. Now it was my turn to lie in a bed while waiting for my baby to come into the world.

The IVs were started and hours were going by I could feel the contractions but nothing really hurt. My Mom and Dad came to check on me during the evening visiting hour but only one person was allowed in at a time. Soon everyone left except Jim, in the waiting room with all the other expectant fathers. The fathers never knew when the wives were taken into delivery so were always on high alert each time the doors swung open with the announcements. Close to twenty-four hours later I was given a spinal injection that numbed me from my waist down, then wheeled into the delivery room where I was able to fully enjoy the birth, pain-free. I will never forget my doctor telling me I had a beautiful baby girl. I just knew it! I started crying, filled with so much joy to think I had given birth, let alone a beautiful baby girl! The word got out to Jim and he went to the window where our baby was held up for him to see. Mom and Jim were in the hallway to see me as I was wheeled back to my room, a room filled to the brim with pink flowers. Dad wasn't there. He wasn't feeling very well but would come by the following morning during visiting hours. It was Dad who I really needed to see and watch him smile as he saw his beautiful granddaughter for the first time.

That evening, after getting some rest, I was in my room alone when the nurse asked if would like to see my baby girl and feed her. "Yes!" I said, as she brought her in all wrapped up in a pink blanket and handed her to me. She didn't have a name yet. I was alone, just the baby and I, and I was almost afraid to touch her, afraid she might break. I started to undo her pink blanket; I wanted to examine her to make sure she was just perfect. I counted her toes and fingers to make sure there were ten of each and then I saw her crooked little pinky fingers that matched mine perfectly and I smiled knowing she was really my baby. This sweet angel that lay in my arms, so perfect, weighting 5-pounds, 9-ounces, and 19-inches long, looked just like me when I was a baby, as I could tell from the photos I had. Jim and I looked like brother and sister and we created a real beauty. We talked about the name and I said I loved the song *Michelle* by Paul McCartney and I would like to name her Michelle, and Jim agreed. What about the middle name? I said I would like her middle name to be the same as mine; Kathleen. Jim also agreed Michelle Kathleen would be a beautiful name. As so it was made official. The following morning my dad came to the hospital. He went to see Michelle in the viewing window and then came to see me with tears of joy in his eyes. I had never seen my dad with tears before, and all he could say was how proud he was of me and how perfect Michelle was. I buzzed the nurse and asked if someone could bring Michelle in to meet her grandfather. It was against the policy but they made an exception. My dad was allowed to hold her and he fell completely in love with her and she stole his heart from that moment on. My mother took my father home. She wasn't allowed to hold Michelle yet and still only one person at a time allowed in the room that day. Mom came back later that night and finally had her turn at holding her granddaughter. My Mom said from the moment she held her that she was holding the apple of her eye.

On the third day, we went home. Mom and Dad had found a new home of their own within a mile. I would miss my family but now I had a full-time job of being a new mommy.

In 1969, Apollo 11 astronaut Neil Armstrong was the first human to set foot on the moon. Woodstock was three days long with four-hundred thousand participants, making it *the* landmark event in music history. Charles Manson and his cult killed Sharon Tate and six others. Midnight Cowboy was my favorite movie. The Fifth Dimension sang *The Age of Aquarius*.

My days as a teenager were coming to an end. I was almost twenty and had the beautiful role of Mother, caring for my daughter, and Wife, caring for my husband. Jim loved Michelle very much and they spent a lot of quality time together. Jim was still more like a brother to me so there really wasn't the passion I had dreamed I would feel, the passion I had read about in my magazines. But we got along well with laughter and dancing and he was a great cook. For the first four years of marriage it was great. But by the fifth year, the older man I had looked up to was no longer the man I wanted to spend my life with. I felt I had little in common with him but my daughter, and when I went back to work doing hair six weeks after giving birth, I began finding new interests and new friends. I found a new job at a beauty salon. One of my weekly clients, Cissy, owned the drive-in restaurant where I used to hang out in as a teen. Michelle and I would go to the movies with her, and sometimes to dinner, and it became the perfect escape. Slowly I was looking less and less forward to driving home after work. I even took a second job selling cosmetics at Del Monte Center in Monterey.

I found the perfect caregiver for Michelle; Helen, a Filipino lady who was a widow with five daughters living at home, the youngest aged five, the eldest, fifteen. She was amazing and I felt blessed. We were made to feel like family, and since Michelle was only six-weeks old, I felt it was important that she be surrounded with nothing but love.

It was two years later when I asked Jim for a divorce. We never had any bitter words between us and he completely understood since I'm sure he felt the same way. This marriage was something created by my parents more than us. When I talked to my dad and explained I wanted a divorce, he was concerned but wanted me to be happy above all else and felt Jim would always be there for Michelle and take care of us. So we sold the house. Jim found his own apartment in Monterey. Michelle and I stayed in Marina about a five-minute drive from my parents' place.

It was a beautiful life. Michelle and I were never apart from the moment I got home from work till I had to leave again. We spent lots of time with my parents. They had a fenced front yard with a nice lawn. Michelle would play outside while Dad would sit on a pillow right next to me and we would do our gardening side-by-side. Mom would be in the kitchen cooking up some yummy meals. Even she seemed happy. It was as if when Michelle came into the world Mom came alive again, always smiling and happy. Dad wrote love notes to Mom each morning. One night in the middle of the night my mom called and said Dad wasn't feeling well and wanted me to come drive him to the hospital, half an hour away. On that night my car happened to be running on empty, and since there were no gas stations open that time of the night, Mom had to come pick me up in her car. She had to leave my dad for a few minutes to come pick up Michelle and me. When we got back to their house, the fire department was just arriving. I rushed into the house. Dad said he had called them to assist him into the car and have me drive him to the hospital, which they did. He asked my mom to stay with Michelle and to call a taxi in the morning so she could drop Michelle off at the sitter and then come to the hospital.

During the drive to the hospital my father was very talkative, saying that if he needed to spend a few days there, for me to please take good care of Michelle and my mother. He told stories of me growing up, that he really loved me, and what a loving child I had been, and how Michelle would grow up to be just like me. He was so proud of me. When we arrived at the hospital they were waiting for him and took him directly to ICU and asked me to wait in a private waiting area. About an hour later the nurse came and told me my father wanted to see me. It was so hard to see him hooked up to those machines and IV drip. My Dad didn't look very good and was very pale, but he held my hand and told me everything was going to be fine. That I was going to be okay. That Mom would be here in a little while with me. He kept telling me how much he loved me, how proud he was of me. He made me promise to take good care of Mom while he was gone. He told me how much he loved Michelle and how Michelle looked just like me when I was little, and what a wonderful mother I was. The nurse then asked me to leave so he could get some rest. I kissed him goodbye and went back to the waiting room. I laid my head down on the arm of the sofa and fell asleep.

I was awakened by my mom early in the morning, asking how my dad was, and I told her he was fine, and getting some rest. She went to go check at the desk and they said the doctor was in with him now and would come see her when he was finished. It wasn't much longer when the doctor opened the door and looked at us both and said he wished he could have done more. I had no idea what that meant at first and I don t think my mom did either. But he continued to say they had done all they could, but just couldn't keep him alive. He said he was brought back to life a few times but he just couldn't stay with them. We were both still in shock; it was numbing. The doctor asked if we would like to see him. Mom said no, but I said yes, and the doctor advised against it, saying I would not recognize him from the trauma his body had been through. He asked my mom to start making decisions on where she would like his body to be taken. It was August twenty-first, 1972 and he was only sixty-four years old.

Mom and I left the hospital and she asked me to drive home. Neither of us spoke a word that I can remember. Later that afternoon, Mom called and asked me to meet her at the mortuary to make arrangements. She said my father had all his requests clearly written out. So Michelle went back with Helen, and I met Mom at the Mortuary. Mother said this was something she could not deal with and dropped off Dad's suit and gave me the instructions prepared by him, and asked me to do all the talking and arrangements. I was then led alone into a room filled with caskets and picked out the least expensive wooden coffin, which my father had requested. Dad knew the VA would cover the cost of it, saying on the paper, "Once you're gone you're gone." I made arrangements for the VA to fold and hand the American flag draped over the coffin to my mother, and requested the gun salute and taps to be played. He only wanted my mom, my grandmother, Jim, and me to be at his gravesite, not Michelle, and specifically requested he "didn't want any lousy preacher." My Dad left us handwritten letters of his love for us. The mortuary told us my father would be ready for viewing at four o'clock. So Mom and I left and returned later in the day, she in her car, and me in mine.

When we entered the mortuary the greeter showed us to the room my father was. The lighting was very soft and I remember slowly walking up to the coffin. I had never seen a dead person before. But there he was, lying there in that wooden box that looked so nice with the grey fabric lining it. He looked so handsome. I hadn't seen him look so wonderful for years. He was wearing the suit he wore the day he walked me down the aisle. Mom also thought he looked handsome. Mom didn't want to stay long. The mortuary was going to close at five o'clock and I asked if they would mind if I stayed a little longer. The man told me they were going to be celebrating a birthday party that night in another room and they didn't mind my staying longer if it didn't bother me to hear music and celebratory sounds. I said no, that it would be fine. I continued to sit and stare at my father for the next three hours while the music played and the mortuary was filled with the sounds of laughter. I couldn't help but smile and knew in my heart that this was exactly what my father would have wanted. I had brought a picture of Michelle and me that I knew my father liked and once I was brave enough to touch his hands, I slipped the picture under them. My dad's hands did not feel cold as I expected them to, but had the same soft, soothing, comforting feeling I loved feeling all my life. I also brought my father's favorite cologne, Chanel for men, and I lightly dotted some around on his suit. I memorized every wrinkle and recollected my entire life spent with him. For twenty-two years he was my life and I was his. Now he was gone but he would never really ever leave me. The following morning we all met at the mortuary and a limousine drove the few of us across the street over the bridge, past Dennis the Menace Park, where my took me often as a child, where he helped me climb up on the large old train. I can remember him buying me candy at the snack bar and taking me to watch baseball games. Then we rode past where he would take me to feed the ducks and ride the paddle boats. What a perfect place to be buried; next to his mother. The prayers were said silently by each of us. The flag folded, the gun salute, the taps played. I laid a handful of red carnations on his casket and we walked back to the limousine, then each leaving and going our separate ways. I went to Del Monte beach and sat in my car for hours, never crying, almost without emotion, just contemplating what to do now without him. What would my life be like now? He had been my world and now that reality was gone.

CHAPTER 7
Life Goes On

It was 1972 and music was the key for my survival with the help of Al Green singing *Let's Stay Together*, Roberta Flack's *The First Time Ever I Saw Your Face*, Johnny Nash's *I Can See Clearly Now*, and another soon-to-be favorite of mine, Billy Paul's *Me and Mrs. Jones*. We had the Watergate Scandal, and the end of the war in Vietnam. The Equal Rights Amendment passed creating equality of the sexes. World leaders banned biological warfare. Governor George Wallace was shot. Popular movies were *The Godfather, Dirty Harry, Diamonds are Forever* and *Cabaret*.

Life might not have been exactly as I had dreamed in my fairytale existence, but the reality had to be dealt with. I was a single mother with the most beautiful little girl that I felt was ever born. Michelle was my whole world now. I was working full-time doing hair and I would pick up some occasional jobs with Laguna Seca Raceway working for L&M cigarettes during the Formula One Grand Prix races, wearing hot pants, cropped tops, and boots, handing out free gifts of cigarettes and autographed pictures as a way of promoting Jackie Stewart, whom they sponsored. Money was good and this led to fun parties and events with the top drivers, Stewart, Sterling Moss, Brian Redmond, and Peter Revson, who was the son of Charles Revson, creator of Revlon cosmetics. I made some great friends and had some really wonderful times.

Cissy, my weekly customer at the beauty salon, went through my divorce with me and I went through hers with her. Sometimes when Michelle was with her dad, I would go spend the night at Cissy's and we would go out to listen to music and dance at local clubs. Neither one of us drank but we both loved to dance. When we would come back home we would stop off at her drive-thru restaurant called "Drive-n-Eat", and open it up to grill some sandwiches. It never failed that the local police would come by to check on us. Those cops were like family and there was never a charge for their food and they were included in the midnight snacks. Since Cissy lived nearby, the cops were very protective of her and came by her house checking on our safety often throughout the night when I was there. It was fun to do "ride-a long," where we got permission to spend the evening riding in the police cars on calls. I enjoyed the adrenaline rush when a good call would come in that included some kind of high speed. I had always viewed the police as fun and a protective lot to be around, since my father had taught me that. I suppose I was drawn to it since my father was now dead and I needed to feel protected. I had been known to leave a bottle of Boone's Farm Apple Wine in a selected place in the cemetery for them to enjoy after work as a thank-you gift after a ride-along.

The time came a few months later when I realized I needed to make more money, and move from Marina to give Michelle a better childhood. My mother took up drinking full time as her escape from loneliness. If she would have gone back to work she might have gotten the support she needed from her co-workers, but instead, she sold her house, paid ten thousand dollars in cash for a single-wide mobile home in a park. It was actually a very nice place with a small yard. I'm sure it gave her peace-of-mind not to have many bills, and she had my father's Veteran's widow's benefits to help her survive without working. Just like every week since I was sixteen, I would go and do her hair, shampoo, set and comb out. Since I was working, I really only had that one day a week to give for our quality time together. The hardest thing for me was when she went on her daily drinking binge that started around noon with lunch, then it was nap time, or pass-out time, followed by an evening of the same. Night time seemed to be the worst for her since not a single night would go by without her calling me, drunk, and saying mean things that she would never remember the next day. That was the problem; she would say so many terrible things and then never remember. But I had to remember everything. When Mom was sober she was wonderful, loving and very giving, especially to Michelle. But when she was drunk on cheap red wine by the gallon, it was awful. I had to search really hard to find the good. Getting the phone calls in the middle of the night was like water torture giving me drips of how I would never be any good at anything and using horrible language to express how she felt about me, yet never remembering it the next day. The one thing that seemed to help her was when I would bring Michelle over to visit. I would make sure it was early in the day and they would always have fun. Mom would cook her special treats and spoil her. Michelle knew she was the apple of her grandmother's eye.

Some people, when they drink, are really funny; my Mom, on the other hand, became mean. She would say that my Dad loved me more than her, how he chose me to take him to the hospital, how she never got to say goodbye. Now that I'm older, I'm more understanding of the grief she was suffering then, and I feel really bad about what she must have gone through, still being a young woman. I had suppressed all grief myself, mostly by escaping through music which was always where I turned to help me feel emotions. I couldn't afford to be weak at this particular time in my life. I had to be strong. I was a loving parent at twenty-two, with a mother who was dealing with her own survival and an aging grandmother my only relatives. My half-sister and I were not close but she did reconnect with Mom once my father died.

I needed to set priorities and worked three jobs in order to provide the best I could for Michelle. My first full-time job brought in good money. I worked during the day at a beauty salon in Pebble Beach. It was across from what was then called Del

Monte Lodge. Pebble Beach was familiar to me while growing up. I never missed a Bing Crosby Golf Tournament from the time I was five. My mom always took me to watch and had me bring a small book to collect autographs. I was used like a cute puppy to get attention for her. But I didn't mind a bit. I was always spoiled and gifts were always given to us. Free complimentary meals, drinks for mom, and lots of autographs in the Tap Room at The Lodge as the golfers finished the eighteenth hole and came inside. Being around celebrities was a very common thing. The first time I ever saw snow was on the golf course in Pebble Beach, white everywhere, and a deer running across. I tried to chase after the deer and an announcement was made over the loud speaker: "Would the little girl in the red jacket please get back on the sidelines." My mother wanted to die from embarrassment, I'm sure. I loved deer then, and still do.

Working in a beauty salon, especially in Pebble Beach with all the rich and famous, was fun because you heard all the dirt and rumors. I wasn't into dating - since my divorce I had only one thing on my mind; my daughter. But I did have one occasion to go on a date with the tennis pro at Pebble Beach Tennis Club. He needed a date for the Clint Eastwood Celebrity Tennis Tournament cocktail party to be held at Del Monte Lodge that evening. I wore a floor-length white halter backless dress, cut low in the front and slit up the front, revealing lots of leg. A real showstopper that was done in very good taste, even if showing some leg, back and cleavage! My hair was up and I felt like a princess. My little Fiat pulled up outside for valet service. As I walked into the lobby of The Del Monte Lodge, I walked straight ahead to the stairs leading down to the ballroom. I paused at the top looking across the room to find my date, when at the bottom of the steps, Merv Griffin walked to the center of the first step and started singing to me, "… somewhere across a crowded room, you will meet a stranger…" All eyes were on us as he ascended the stairs singing, took my hand and walked me down to the ballroom, where my date came at once to claim me. Later that evening, as the party wound down, my date and ten more celebrity golfers and their dates were invited to be Mr. Griffin's guests for dinner in the private wine cellar of The Sardine Factory restaurant on Cannery Row. What a beautiful evening! The following morning my picture, along with the others, was posted in the *San Francisco Examiner* and I was listed as a guest.

I loved the job in Pebble Beach, but I especially loved a new thing that had just come out; instead of a full strip of eyelashes like I had worn since beauty college, they now had individual ones. I started booking appointments to put them on our clients and it didn't take long for me to be totally sold out applying individual eyelashes that cost fifteen dollars and took fifteen minutes to attach. Once I learned that, I started doing the clients' makeovers and found my favorite calling was in the world of beauty and cosmetics. But for now I had to stick with hair and lashes to keep my income up high.

My second job was two nights a week at the Del Monte Hyatt Hotel as a dining room hostess. My third job was serving cocktails at the Holiday Inn on the beach in Monterey, overlooking Monterey Bay. I had enough money finally to cover all expenses and was able to afford a beautiful newly built apartment right on the beach. Michelle and I were among the first tenants to rent there. This will forever be my favorite place to live in my lifetime.

We could look out our bedroom windows to the beach and across the Bay to Cannery Row where the red lights of the radio station would blink in the dark. Cannery Row was always one of my favorite places to go as a child with my parents, and as a teen. I once took a job working for a man who was an entertainer on Cannery Row at the Outrigger, who also owned a florist business. He asked me to work selling roses on Friday, Saturday and Sunday nights to guests having dinner at each of the restaurants on the Row. He paid me twenty dollars a night, plus tips. I did very well going from table to table with a basket of roses. It gave me some extra money as a teen.

Since I was busy working five days a week now, holding down three jobs, while Michelle was at her babysitter's or at my mother's, I was able to spend two or more complete days devoting myself to her. We would go feed the ducks at Lake El Estero, or play on the trains at Dennis the Menace Park. We spent time on the beach outside our front door at home and were always together with no interruptions during our special time. Michelle loved dressing her dolls, playing card games and coloring. No matter what it was, we did it together. I made sure Michelle went to a private pre-school, Santa Catalina in Monterey. She was getting a good education and it was worth the extra jobs in order to pay the tuition. Plus, Helen and the girls who watched her for me were always teaching her.

Working three jobs and raising a small child can be daunting, so every once in a while I tried to do something fun for myself. I was invited to go dancing with co-workers from The Hyatt. They wanted me to come to a new place that everyone was talking about on Cannery Row. They said they heard the music was great. The band consisted of "Joe" on drums and "Rock" on the keyboard. What a voice Rock had! Once after a set I had the chance to meet Rock face to face, eye to eye. The sound of his warm, soothing, comforting voice, and the way he walked into a room, how tall this amazing man was took my breath away; he would sing and my heart would melt. It was as if I was the only one in the room. Rock's singing made me forget any sadness I had from the loss of my father as I completely escaped into believing he would be mine forever, which I'm sure happened to musicians all the time. He looked at me with kindness; spoke to me so sweetly. Rock knew what to say with sincere honest words. And all I knew was this was the man I wanted to spend the rest of my life with. For the first time in my life I could say I was madly in love, not because someone else suggested it but because he was The One; the one who stole my heart. He became the center of my universe without even trying. A few months went by with flirting and trying to catch his eye. For me it was a feeling I had never known. I went dancing only one night a week, but one night was enough. There is no way I wanted to go anyplace but where Rock was performing.

Since Michelle and I lived across the Monterey Bay on Del Monte Beach, I would sit in my bedroom window watching the red light blinking from the radio tower, high in the air, knowing exactly where he was singing. Dreaming and lost in a world of love, I couldn't wait to hear him sing each week. When his sets were finished, he would always come to sit at my table of friends. I'm sure I acted stupid with those goofy looks of love, but it couldn't be helped. If Rock could only see into my heart he would understand what had happened inside there. As he would sing *The*

First Time Ever I Saw Your Face, it was as if he only sang to me. I had screamed during the Beatles and dreamed of Mark Lindsay of Paul Revere and The Raiders, but this was different. I was still so young at twenty-two and this feeling was so new to me. Rock must have been into me also, because he stopped playing once and came out from behind his keyboard and actually had a brief moment of slow dancing with me with only the drums being played. As time went on Rock eventually asked for my phone number and if he could give me a call.

When he did call, we set up a night for him to come to my place and spend an evening getting to know each other, since we were always surrounded by friends at the club, with no time alone. So on this special night I made sure I was home alone. I took my bubble bath, put on my favorite body cream and perfume, lit a fire in the fireplace, and placed lit candles and fresh flowers arrangements about. I dressed carefully, trying to look as cute as possible as my plan was to knock his socks off when I opened the door. From a man's viewpoint, he must have known from the moment that door opened he was in trouble! This girl was in love.

I watched him walk up the few steps to my door as my heart was beating fast. He wore a black hat with a tan leather jacket. I invited Rock in and poured our drinks. Since I didn't drink much, I needed to find a drink where I couldn't taste the alcohol. Usually at clubs I would always order Perrier water. But tonight was special so I had hot buttered rum. Rock had brought me the most romantic gift I have ever received or ever would receive. It was a trilogy album of music by Anita Kerr and The San Sebastian Strings with the poetry of Rod McKuen. *The Sea, The Sky, and The Earth*, was romance spoken in every song. He asked if he could put on his favorite "The Sea." While there are many songs that had special meanings I could relate to over the years to come, it was *While Drifting* was playing that stole my heart and made me his forever. Rock said this was the one he wanted me to hear; beautiful strings gently playing music with ocean waves in the background and poetry being spoken gently as if it was kissing my ears. *While Drifting* was the one song that imprinted on my heart for the rest of my life. I would play it hundreds of times throughout my life as I needed to escape through music when times became more difficult than I was able to deal with. It is powerful what music can do.

Rock held me tightly, letting me know I was safe in his arms and feeling that no harm could come to me, I remember walking with Rock down the hall to my bedroom, windows wide open looking out onto a crystal clear night across the bay, with lights glowing, sparkling with reflections of the boats in the bay and businesses along Cannery Row. He slowly undressed me and put me onto the bed. What a beautiful sight to see my skin lying next to his. Rock took complete control and for the first time in my life I understood what it felt like to be made love to. Now I knew what had been missing. When he said he loved me, I knew his heart had also been touched as had mine. I felt the passion and total pleasure, and knew this was a love never to be forgotten. The next day, I couldn't wait to call to tell my mother I was in love. Finally, I had found what I had only dreamed of. When I told her Rock was a musician, she was very upset. She said a musician had a different girl every night and that I was nothing to him, that he had thousands like me, some much prettier and smarter, and what could he offer me - a life of running off without me to play different gigs? I told her she couldn't control me or stop me from loving who my heart had chosen and hung up on her.

Later that night I got a call from Rock saying my mother had called him at work and told him to stay away from me or she would kill him, that she would not allow him to ruin my life. I immediately called my mother and found she was completely drunk. I had to hang up. I couldn't take the verbal abuse any longer.

Days and weeks would go by without me picking up the phone when she called. I spoke to people at work about moving, wanting someplace new that had sunshine most of the year where Michelle could swim. I didn't want her stuck inside like I was as a child due to all the foggy weather. More than one person suggested I go to Palm Springs. They said it was small and filled with tourists just like Monterey, and it was where all the celebrities like to go, so I would be able to find work doing hair and be able to serve cocktails or do hostess work when I needed to find a job. I mentioned my plan to Rock so we might escape together and live happily ever after. Rock suggested I go on before him and get settled, find a job, and then he would follow. He didn't want to be without me either.

When speaking to my mother again, I told her I was moving to Palm Springs where Michelle and I could get more sun. She asked about Rock and I told her he no longer wanted to see me. I knew she was going to miss Michelle, but I promised to let her come visit. Michelle's father, Jim, had remarried right after our divorce, and he didn't have any problem with me taking Michelle. I knew I would still need his $100 a month child support, especially until I got settled with a job.

I sold my Fiat for a newer used car, a Mercury Cougar that my florist-entertainer boss Jerry wanted me to buy, telling me what great condition it was in. I felt that Michelle and I would be a lot safer driving a larger car that had a back seat. I gave all three jobs my months' notice, along with my apartment manager, and I sold as many unnecessary possessions as possible. I was still seeing Rock romantically, mostly at his apartment in Seaside. I never felt so loved and I couldn't wait to have us start a life far away from my mother in a place no one would know us. A new life. Palm Springs, the home to the celebrities where I knew Rock would be one.

I was given a going away party with music, food, drinks, gifts, and cards of love from friends. Rock, on the other hand, gave me the best gift of all; a tape cassette player with a custom-made cassette he had made of all the special songs he would often sing to me. But the part I liked the most was when he paused and spoke messages to me in between the songs, confirming his love for me, telling me how much he loved me and how he would be with me soon.

CHAPTER 8
Palm Springs Here We Come

It was time to move, no longer had my jobs, or a place to live. Michelle and I were on our way to start a new life in Palm Springs, to a place I had never even been before, let alone in the middle of summer! But I was sure with my cosmetology license I wouldn't have a problem getting a job. I had great letters of reference from all three of my jobs. But I was in for an experience! I never knew of anything bad in the world. I came from an area that was practically crime free. I had my new used car and I was towing a U-Haul trailer with what few things I wanted to keep. It held our clothes and important things like our matching bean bag chairs. We went to say goodbye to my grandmother, who told me how much she loved the heat in Palm Springs, and that sometime when we were settled, she, would take the Greyhound bus to come visit us. Then we went to say goodbye to my mother; we found she had already started her drinking for the day, so we didn't stay long, and started off on the road to Palm Springs.

We had only driven two-and-a-half hours when our car overheated and we were broken down on the side of the road. We were close to the off ramp leading to Paso Robles. The tow truck towed us to a Ford dealer. They said the engine had cracked and it would cost five-hundred dollars and two weeks to fix. They had their tow truck take our U-Haul and park it outside a small motel where Michelle and I were to spend the night. I didn't know what to do. I couldn't turn around and go home. I was only two-and-a-half hours away, but I had no place for Michelle and me to live. I would have had to call my mother to come get us and live with her until I could get a job and a place to live. Everyone had given us a going away party; I couldn't go back! I noticed a pool hall across the street from the motel. I took Michelle across the street and went inside and asked if anyone could tow my U-Haul trailer and give my daughter and I a ride down to Palm Springs in the morning for a one-hundred dollars. Two old farmers said they would, so it was Palm Springs or bust! Well, not quite that fast. During the evening Michelle came down with fever of 103° and I had to call a cab to take us to the ER. They told me it was her tonsils, that they would need to come out before long, and gave her antibiotics to help the infection and aspirin to help lower her fever. By morning, the fever was gone and Michelle was fine.

The two farmers showed up in a beat-up old white truck, attached the trailer and off we went, Michelle sitting on my lap, all four of us in the front seat; there wasn't a back seat. It was a long, somewhat scary drive, especially over the treacherous Grapevine (Highway 5) in the rain, but Michelle slept in my arms most of the way. Finally we arrived in Palm Springs on Highway 111, right before the main part of town. The farmer said, "Here you are, this is Palm Springs." He pulled over to the right side of the road where there was a Ramada Inn, and unhooked the trailer. I paid the hundred dollars and they left. It was over one-hundred degrees in middle of July. I had never even traveled in the state of California other than by train to San Francisco with my Dad. This feeling of brutally hot air was new to me. I had two apples left over from lunch so Michelle and I sat in the grass under the shade of a palm tree and ate our apples. While we sat there I kept wondering what to do next. I couldn't just let this U-Haul sit on the side of the road.

Then I remembered when I used to work doing promotions at Laguna Seca, that one of the top mechanics said he lived in Palm Springs, so Michelle and I went into the lobby of the Ramada and I found his name and number listed in the phone book and gave him a call. Jerry said he had to leave to go out of the country the following day, but he would come get the U-Haul and bring it to his house where Michelle and I could spend the night, and it would give us a chance to make plans for tomorrow.

Jerry's house was huge compared to what I was used to on the Peninsula. He gave Michelle and me a beautiful room with a view of the swimming pool. He took us to dinner that evening right in the center of town on Palm Canyon Drive. I learned there were two main streets in town; Palm Canyon Drive was one-way going south, and Indian Avenue was one-way going north. These two streets were famous for being the top location for teens to go cruising over Spring Break. While we were at dinner, Jerry mentioned he knew a girl in town that had a little boy the same age as Michelle and that her roommate had moved out and she was looking for another. It wouldn't be very expensive and at least a temporary roof over our heads. He said I wouldn't like the girl much, but since he had to leave to go out of the country the following day, this was the best idea he could think of to help. I was grateful to have at least one opportunity to find a room for us to stay, especially since we didn't have a car to go out searching.

Early the following morning the girl showed up alone. Her name was Lulu and she was, without a doubt, the most beautiful California girl I had ever seen, with gorgeous long, straight blonde hair, a perfect figure, and... she seemed very sweet. She said it was a two-bedroom, one- bath; she had one bedroom, and her son had the other, but in the son's room there were twin beds and if I didn't mind, Michelle and I could share the other twin bed. Lulu wanted me to split her month's rent. She paid five-hundred a month so my half would be two-hundred-fifty. I agreed and gave her the money, sight unseen, and Jerry towed the trailer to her place where it was a very quick unload; then Jerry returned the trailer for me.

So here we were in our first home in the desert! It was very small and not even close to how clean I would need it to be in order to stay there, but I was going to make the best of it. I always made sure Michelle saw the best of everything from my eyes. Lulu's little boy was well-behaved and they were both very nice to be around. Since I didn't have a car, we were pretty limited in what we could do, so for the next week, while Lulu went off to work and her son to day-care, I made sure the place was sparkling clean, did the built-up laundry, and made sure there was a nice meal when they got home each day.

Michelle and I never had a problem amusing ourselves. Between our coloring, reading stories and playing games, we also had a TV and could watch cartoons together. It was nice having a phone so I could call my mom and Rock to let them know we were okay. Rock would call me each night to see how we were. I made sure he knew I listened all day long to the cassette he had sent with us. Just hearing his voice and knowing once I was settled he would come be with us was all I needed. At night it was a little hard because we only that one twin bed, so I made sure Michelle and her doll had the bed and I slept in a sleeping bag on the floor next to her.

Lulu was really very nice to me especially since I did all the work around the house. I had told her my story and about the love of my life, and how once I got a job, I was going to find a home for all of us to live in and how much I missed Rock. I would let her listen to his amazing voice from my cassette, and told her how music had always been my escape when times were difficult. Lulu knew I needed to find a job. I had told her I did hair, modeling and hostess-cocktail work. She came home one afternoon and said one of her customers was looking for someone to do a modeling job for an album cover. He was a recording star who had had a top hit, and would I be interested to interview for it. I said I would love to. Lulu called Charles and he asked if he could come by and pick me up that evening and take me to dinner. Lulu said she would stay home with the kids while I went, so I accepted his invitation.

When Charles arrived he was driving a black Rolls Royce. Things like that never impressed me since I was raised around them when I was in Pebble Beach. But I guessed it was the car to be seen in in the desert, having noticed a few of them my first night on Palm Canyon Drive. Charles was very polite. He was tall and looked like a used-up surfer from back in the sixties. He wore

Buddy Holly-type glasses. The restaurant was really beautiful with tiki torches blazing outside the front door. Everyone working inside dressed in Hawaiian attire that reminded me of The Outrigger on Cannery Row. The wait staff called him by name and he seemed to be well-liked. Sitting at dinner, all I could talk about was Rock, about him being a musician, and that he was the true love of my life. I told him how I had moved just so we could start a new life together. Lulu had told him how I was a model and that I was starting to look for work until Rock could join us. Charles was very nice and said he looked forward to meeting Rock, and there were lots of places in the desert that needed good musicians who could sing. Charles said the album cover was to be shot in the middle of the desert on location. It paid five-hundred dollars for an afternoon of work. He said his company was paying me more since it needed to be shot in the desert in the summer heat. His company would be providing the clothes, makeup artist, and hair stylist, so I didn't need to bring anything except my own high-heeled shoes. I explained I wouldn't have my car for another week and he said not to worry, he would send someone to pick me up. Charles said he would show me the location after dinner, and that it was right on the way home. We didn't stay very long. Valet service had his car parked right in front. I was so excited I had gotten the modeling job and it would be starting in the next few days. Plus, making great money, which was just what I needed to get Michelle and me our Greyhound bus ride to Paso Robles to pick up the car. No more money worries and I could soon start job hunting. On the way back to the house Charles insisted he show me the location since it was only five minutes away and he promised to make it fast.

Charles drove not far from town and he was right, it was only about five minutes away. He pulled onto a small paved road in the middle of the dark desert with nothing around. He wanted me to see the lights from the cars on the freeway down the road that would be used in the background. He asked if I would mind taking my top off so he could see how I would look in a bikini for the shoot. Of course I refused and that is when Charles started acting in a more aggressive way, saying he couldn't guarantee me the job without seeing my body, and trying to convince me it was okay since no one knew we were there and no one could see us. I told him no and to take me home, and when he tried to start to force himself closer to me I slapped him, and when he tried to hold my arm down I pulled it loose and scratched his face very badly. He got very angry. He took me home and never said another word as I slammed the door to the car.

When I got inside, Lulu asked what was wrong and I told her what had happened and she seemed upset that Charles was mad. Lulu told me Rock had called and she had told him I was out for the evening. When I got hold of Rock, he didn't sound the same. He never said why, but he thought it was best he didn't come to the desert. He wished me the best, but he wouldn't be able to come. That was the last time I spoke to him.

My world had shattered that night. If it hadn't been for going into my bedroom that night to lie on the floor next to my little girl, I don't know what I might have done. I just prayed to God to help us and spent the rest of the night crying silently. I could never tell anyone what happened that night. I felt so ashamed and scared. I knew God would always forgive me and protect me and this was a way to help me to become a stronger and more determined person, to survive and let my beautiful little girl have the best life I could possibly give her.

The very next morning, after Lulu and her son left the house, I was busy doing some cleaning when a knock came at the door. It was a very pretty girl who introduced herself as Josette. She said she didn't expect that anyone would be there and so was happy when I answered and she found out Lulu wasn't there. She asked if she might come in and talk. Josette said she and her son, Daniel, were roommates there for one month, and that Lulu had stolen some of her clothes and jewelry, and she had come to get them back. Josette said that she found out Lulu was a prostitute and worked in a massage parlor in Palm Springs. She told me she also paid half of the month's rent, as I was, then she found out the entire rent was two-hundred fifty, not five-hundred, and that Lulu hadn't paid it yet. Josette said she didn't mention a word to Lulu but she found another place to live in nearby City of Rancho Mirage, and one day when Lulu went to work, she and Daniel moved out. It wasn't until later she realized some of her most valuable jewelry had been stolen and that was why she waited until Lulu had gone to work to try to find a way to get in the house to get her things.

It all started to make sense to me now, why Lulu had wanted me to meet Charles. He was probably one of her customers and she had told all about me being her new roommate. Now I understood why he had come up with the pretense to offer a modeling job. She probably told him how nice and sweet I was, and I suppose it made him want to take on the challenge. Little did he know he would meet a tiger ready to scratch his eyes out! I might be nice, but after going to high school, I had learned how to fight off guys trying to get into my pants!

Josette said she and her son had rented two rooms from a single man in his sixties who wasn't in the best of health. He needed a little help in cleaning and cooking, and charged her two-hundred fifty a month for the two rooms. Josette said she would call James and see if he would be interested in renting to Michelle and me also. She explained our situation living at the same place where she had been, and James said sure, he would rent to us too, that there was plenty of room. So right then and there Josette found her stolen things and we loaded her car and in two trips within the next few hours, and Michelle and I had a new place to live.

The new house was huge; it had four or more bedrooms, three bathrooms, an Olympic swimming pool, and was located in a fast-growing area of the desert. Michelle and I would share a room with twin beds. I was so grateful not to have to sleep on the floor! It was only at night, after Michelle fell sound asleep, that I would be able to finally have a chance to listen to my cassette with the music and words Rock created just for me. I had suffered the loss of my father who was my protector and provider, and now the loss of my heart and the very soul of me. I would cry myself to sleep, sobbing in silence, never to share these private feelings.

James could not have been nicer. He was on oxygen and had to have it with him where ever he would go. Josette thought of him like as a father-figure, and James had taken a real liking to Daniel. He would often send Josette out to buy some special gifts for them both. A cleaning lady came in two days a week. Josette was great at cooking her French specialties and Michelle and I had a new family to love and make us feel loved. We were no longer alone. God, overnight, felt my heart, gathered my tears and heard my prayers, and we were so loved and blessed, and many more miracles were to happen for Michelle and me.

Michelle and Daniel were both four years-old and got along as if they had known each other since the day they were born. They were instant brother and sister. Josette and I taught Michelle and Daniel how to swim and they were like fish. For the first time, I felt assured I had a chance to give Michelle a beautiful life, one that was in the sunshine and not in the cold fog. Yes, I would always miss my hometown of Monterey, but the man I loved no longer needed me and I had to learn to make a new life the best I could, living one day at a time.

My car was finally ready, but after having to pay both rents and the farmer's towing service, along with groceries, I didn't have enough money left to pick up my car. What I did have was enough money to buy two tickets on the Greyhound for Michelle and me to get to Monterey. I called my mom and she said she would pick us up at the station and she would loan me the money for the car to be fixed and she would even pay for our bus tickets from Monterey back to Paso Robles. I never told my mom about what happened when we first arrived in the desert, but Michelle and I gave her great stories about where we were living with the pool and swimming each day in the sunshine. My mom was so happy to see Michelle, the apple of her eye, and for the next two days we had a wonderful stay at my mom's. I guess that short time away made us appreciate each other more. She was my only connection to my father and my childhood memories. Mom barely had any drinks while we were there, except one before her dinner. She was kinder and very giving. She loved spoiling us while we spent the next two days with her. She bought Michelle and me Doodle Art and we would color for hours, side by side, creating our masterpieces. Then it would be mom's turn with Michelle, and they would play Old Maid card games for hours. Michelle was good at learning how to mark a corner of the Old Maid card so she wouldn't pick it. It didn't matter. They would just laugh if Mom caught on to Michelle trying to cheat. Mom would just go buy a new set of cards and hope for the best. I loved to hear them laugh. We also went to Pacific Grove to visit my grandmother. She also was delighted to see us. My grandmother used to live in Palm Springs behind the El Mirador Hotel and loved the dry desert heat. She said she had always wanted to move back. I still wasn't very familiar with the location but promised when I returned I would take some pictures to send to her.

It was time to leave and because of my mother' attitude and kindness, being right there to help me when we needed her, it was time to forget the past and try to be more understanding from what she also must have suffered through the loss of her husband. Those two days of us with her, helped to fill that sad, lonely void, helping to ease the grief in my life, and changed how I looked at her. Once I returned to my new home in the desert I started sending her weekly letters, as well as the promised photographs to my grandmother.

Michelle and I did make it to Paso Robles to pick up the car and drove it back to the desert. God always has a plan never to be questioned. The car stopped running the second I pulled up in front of the Rancho Mirage house, never to run again. A week later I had it towed away, never to be seen again, and I was without a car. But ahhhh! It sure felt good to be home in Rancho Mirage. I happened to be very lucky because my new landlord had an extra car he wasn't using and offered it to me. This gave me all kinds of new freedom. One was getting a full-time job doing hair at the Rivera Hotel. It was great, always busy and never saw the same people twice. At the hotel salon I did individual eyelashes, makeovers and hair on the hotel guests. It was easy daytime hours so I was able to spend every single night with Michelle. I had tried taking on a weekend job serving cocktails in the evening at The Howard Manor in Palm Springs, but it only lasted two days when a man put his hand on my butt under the short skirt they made me wear, and I dropped a tray of drinks on him and quit.

Josette worked as a dining room hostess in the evenings at a new local restaurant, Las Casuelas Nuevas in Rancho Mirage. We put both Daniel and Michelle into a private pre-school. A bus picked them up every morning and returned them early afternoon. I was able to make breakfast and get the kids off to school, and Josette was always home waiting for them when they arrived. One thing nice about Josette, she was dependable, and the more time I spent with her the more I learned what a wonderful person she was. When I got home, Josette left for work, and it was such a nice smooth flow, with us looking out for each other. I enjoyed my evenings with both kids. They got along really well and were great company for each other.

James thought it would be really fun for him, Josette, Danny, Michelle and me to take a weekend vacation down to Tijuana, Mexico. It was about a two hour drive and James arranged for top accommodations in a really nice hotel right down town. James had errands to go run for the day and Josette and I, spent the days with the kids going shopping and tasting all the new flavors. I think this is where Michelle first started loving the taste of a spicy hot sauce. She loved the street carts with fresh-cut fruits in a cup, squeezed lime juice with sprinkles of chili powder. All the bright colors of the clothes and hats along the street were my desires, but my favorite was finding a store with nothing but perfumes and cosmetics. At our hotel we enjoyed the pool and felt like millionaires, since everything was so inexpensive. Going through customs at the gate was an interesting adventure also. You could tell we were tourists with our fresh sunburned cheeks and all our souvenirs. It was surprising we had room for passengers. I had felt like I was in Disneyland and a new world of adventure and I couldn't wait to return with everyone and try it again.

About a week after we were home James gave Josette and me each five-hundred dollars in cash as his way of thanking us for going to Mexico with him. He went on to explain that while he was out running errands, he had met up with a man he had made contact with in the desert and that man helped him to load marijuana into his huge oxygen container in the trunk of his car, and we unknowingly helped him bring it back across the border without having the car checked! I was grateful for the money, but I couldn't believe how used we all were. James said pot was the only medicine that made him feel better and seeing how sick he was I could understand his desperation for coming up with a scheme to get it. He asked if we would like to do it again sometime, but Josette and I both turned him down.

Michelle started to get sick often with high fevers and problems with her throat and tonsils, with her temperature spiking to 105° I learned to put her in a cold tub of water to cool her off. To this day I'm sure she won't forgive me for my cooling skills but they did work. I found an ear- nose-throat doctor who said the tonsils had to go. So hospital arrangements were made and my mom felt she also needed to be there for the surgery and drove down to the desert. It was so nice to have my mom with me and I know Michelle loved knowing her grandmother would be there, too. Surgery went well, but Michelle was expected to spend the next twenty-four hours in the hospital in recovery. I never left her side for a minute, even during the night. The hospital chair wasn't very comfortable for sleeping and since they allowed me to spend the night with her in her room, I got a pillow and blanket and like old times, slept on the floor all night right by her side.

My mom spent the following week helping me care for Michelle. Josette, Danny and James seemed to like having her there. She stayed busy and enjoyed spoiling all of us with her home cooking. I even had fun swimming with her in the pool. Michelle and I knew we would miss her very much when it was time for her to leave and return to Monterey. We seemed to have learned the hard way we needed each other.

Things were back to running smoothly again when I got a call at work from Josette, saying she was at home with James when he had a heart attack and died. The kids were in school, thank goodness, and didn't witness the commotion of the ambulance coming and taking him away. I had protected myself from getting too attached to James since I knew he was not well, and at that point, I knew I couldn't handle another loss very easily. However, since I was the one with the most experience in picking out coffins, when his two children arrived they asked me go with them to the mortuary to help them. It was another moment of grief and loss.

It would also become another loss of a place to live. But I needed to remain strong and act as if everything was okay for Michelle, Josette and Danny, and I knew and believed God would help us. And sure enough, God helped Josette find us a new affordable house. It was beautiful, and only two blocks away on Sahara Road in Rancho Mirage. The property was huge. It was a ranch-style house with a large veranda we could enjoy on warm nights. It had three bedrooms and two baths. At the back of the property was a one-bedroom guest house where the owners stayed when they came to the desert. For the first time since Michelle and

I lived on Del Monte Beach in Monterey, we each had our own bedrooms. It had a large kitchen, cathedral ceilings, and a huge fireplace in the center of the living room with built in circular seating. I had to buy beds for us so I bought Michelle a twin bed, and a queen size water bed for me. I loved that bed, especially when the water heater was turned on and it felt so toasty to crawl into at the end of the day. Michelle loved sleeping in my bed; I think she loved being close to me but the bed was so soft and soothing for her. She rarely slept in her own bed. I would tuck her in and tell her stories in her own bed, but by middle of the night she always brought her doll and came in with me. I loved every second of that closeness with her.

Michelle always had long hair until one afternoon when I came home from work and she came running out of her bedroom to show me how proud she was that she had given her doll a short haircut with her paper doll scissors. Then she turned her head to show me how she made hers to match. One side cut completely short and one side long. I should have been upset but she was so happy with her new do, I suggested we make the other side match.

I sat her up on a bar stool in the bathroom as she watched the transformation take place. She loved her new short hair and the way her doll looked. She could always grow it back, but scissors were forever placed on a high shelf unless there was adult supervision!

Our landlady was very nice; she didn't come down to stay often in the guest house, but one weekend she didn't seem be her friendly self. I decided I would bake her some homemade chocolate chip cookies and surprise her. When I went to knock on her door the door had been left open. I called her name and no answer, but her little puppy was barking. I had a feeling something wasn't right as I started calling her name even louder. I set the cookies on the kitchen counter and as I was about to leave I heard a noise coming from the bathroom. The door was open and as I got closer I could hear water running and noticed water coming out onto the hallway floor. Slowly I peeked around the corner and there was my landlady sitting naked in a tub of bloody water. I quickly turned off the water and noticed the knife and the large slits on her wrists. I quickly let out the water of the tub and grabbed two bathroom towels to wrap around her wrists to help stop the bleeding. I ran back to the house and called 911. When the ambulance arrived they quickly took her away. I was left with a bloody mess to clean up and a little dog to take care for. I contacted her husband and let him know what happened. The following day he stopped by to pick-up the dog and when I asked how his wife was, he only said she would be ok. He never offered more than that. He was the only one we ever heard from after that.

CHAPTER 9
The Crusher

It was 1974, and almost a year had passed since we moved to the desert. A gallon of gas was fifty-five cents. Nixon resigned after the Watergate scandal, and President Ford granted him an unconditional pardon. Patty Hearst's kidnappers demanded seventy-thousand dollars in food be given to every needy Californian. Pocket calculators started selling like crazy. The top songs of the day were Barbara Streisand's The Way We Were, and Time In A Bottle by Jim Croce.

I started creating fantasies in my mind about Rock. No one could take his place and I had no desire to date since I arrived in the desert. All I had time for was work and Michelle. Nothing else mattered, but in order for me not to lose the memory of Rock, I started escaping to dreams of him. I realized he was no longer in my life, yet I didn't want to let go. Visions of love making with Rock danced through my mind. This was part of my fantasy world. It was my escape, and I was not willing to let go.

I know it will be very hard for anyone else to come into my life and replace Rock. I always felt blessed that I understood what it felt like to love, to really be in love. I was so sad not to have him in my life any longer. I never let him know where I had moved once I got settled. I doubt it would have made any difference.

Work was going well at the Riviera Hotel beauty salon. Palm Springs was at its best with celebrities on every corner and everyone knew when the annual desert season would start. Opening day of the Palm Springs Racquet Club in mid-October. A big percentage of businesses closed in the summer but made sure they reopened in October in order to be ready for the season. It was the people from the entertainment world, old money and new. Anyone who was anyone came to the opening. Since I worked at the Hotel across the street from the Racquet Club, I was invited to the opening as a guest of one of the members. I had heard a lot about it. It was created by Charlie Farrell and Ralph Bellamy on Christmas Day 1934, and celebrity members could play tennis all day for one dollar. Everyone wanted to become a member in this Palm Springs hot spot to see and be seen, private club, with the famous Bamboo Lounge, whose bartender at the time was well-known for his Bloody Mary recipe. There were the tennis courts, a swimming pool and cabanas tucked away for discretion, celebrities seen coming and going after tennis matches, a few cocktails at the Bamboo Lounge followed by lunch and dinner in the restaurant.

I hadn't been to any special events since I arrived in Palm Springs, and finally I was able to dress in a long classic black evening gown, which Josette loaned me for the evening. I accessorized it with black stilettos and a long black feather boa thrown over one shoulder. I parked a block down the street and walked, since I felt my car wouldn't exactly fit in. The entrance was graced with a red carpet and spot lights shooting into the sky. At twenty-five, I felt like a celebrity as the cameras flashed as I walked in. The opening was grand on every scale. All the celebrities, millionaires and wannabes showed up with all their chauffeur-driven Bentleys, Rolls Royce's, and limousines. Women dressed in furs and diamonds looked like they were arriving for a Hollywood premier. I was in awe of all these beautiful women; the way they carried themselves as they held a glass of champagne, hoping to get everyone's attention.

It was fun listening to the live music and I couldn't help but wish Rock was with me to enjoy. As the night wore on, and since I didn't want any alcohol this evening, I started to notice that the women I admired earlier for their beauty, after a night of cocktails, looked so sad in my eyes. It was from that night that knew I never wanted to be caught in public drinking in excess. They had all the money and success, hanging onto some old man's arm as a trophy, but I felt happier and prouder of the life I had, and could hardly wait to get home and look at that sweet little girl's face that I had given up an evening to be with the in crowd.

It was only a few months later when I found another salon, with a higher-end clientele, where I could work closer to home, not in Rancho Mirage, but an adjacent city, Palm Desert. Rancho Mirage, where we were living, was growing like wild fire, developing a Restaurant Row with six high-end establishments on Highway 111, the route that linked all the major cities together going west to east; Palm Springs, Cathedral City, Rancho Mirage, Palm Desert, Indian Wells, La Quinta and Indio. Palm Springs was the happening spot;

however, growth started heading east to continue the desert building boom and more jobs were created. Cathedral City (known locally as Cat City) was known for its gay bars and great night clubs. The desert seemed to have a large gay population and being in the beauty business, all the top stylists seemed to be the most fun outgoing gay men. They made working in this field the best job! We always served cocktails to the clients, had lunch delivered when they were getting longer processes, like color or perms. Music played and often dancing and singing created a lively social atmosphere, making the client feel like family.

One afternoon when both Josette and I were home at the same, she said she had heard about a guy who played saxophone in a band that everyone was talking about because he used to play with a major rock band. She suggested we should go out for the evening together since we had never done that without the kids. She knew a lady who was a nanny that worked for an agency that catered to the rich. We could hire a nanny for that night through the agency. It was fourteen dollars an hour and we could split the cost and be gone for just a few hours. It worked out great. Danny and Michelle had a professional nanny and we had a night out!

I could listen to music for hours and just slip away into my own world that I had reserved for Rock. But tonight would be different. Josette and I walked into the Trinidad Hotel in Palm Springs and headed to the Purple Room. Back in the sixties it was the sweet spot of the swinging supper club scene. Frank and Dino and the Rat Pack hung out to eat, drink and play. We felt like VIPs as we were seated in the front row. The music was phenomenal, Pat was amazing. I had never been where blues and jazz was being played before. The entire atmosphere of the room, which was large, but very intimate, seemed a great place to go for celebrities who might not want to be seen by fans, but just hang out with friends.

There were six or more men at the adjoining table. They talked to us in between sets, and flirted, but not enough to be annoying; more gentlemanly, harmless pickup-type flirting. They asked to buy us a drink and had champagne sent over. They were friends of the musician and had come to listen and support him. They asked us to join them and had our table connected to theirs. The men I sat between were a photographer named Vince and a man named Jilly

Rizzo. We had a great time laughing, listening to music and when it was time to leave, Jilly asked for my number to perhaps go out to dinner one evening, and I gave it to him.

I hadn't had a date or even given thought to having a date in over a year since I arrived in the desert. Somehow I knew I needed to force myself to go. Jilly was a much older gentleman. He seemed to be the man in charge of the table when we sat with his group, picking up the tab for all expenses incurred with his friends. He was a relative to sax player Pat and seemed very well-liked. It was fun hearing all the laughter of the men bantering with each other. I learned new slang that night; "Oh, marone!" "Forget about it!" and, "In the bush" (referring to a woman s pubic area). I felt safe and protected around these men. Of course being young didn't hurt, while I'm pretty sure most of them were in their late forties and early fifties. Jilly asked a lot of questions and seemed interested to know how I came to the desert. I was completely honest and told him I came because I wanted to start a new life with my musician boyfriend who decided not to follow me, how I hadn't been out anywhere since I arrived in the desert, and this was such a fun night getting to hear music.

I didn't hear a word from Jilly for over a week but when he finally called and asked me to join him for dinner, he said he would send a driver to pick me up, and we would be joining another couple. I chose a black cocktail dress with black nylons and heels. Jilly was taller than I, and I figured I couldn't go wrong in basic black. There was a knock at the door and when I answered, a short, heavy set Italian man asked for me, introducing himself as "Crusher," announcing he was there to drive me over to Jilly's. He was very pleasant to me. When we reached Jilly's house, he said he also lived there, and was Jilly's right-hand man. Jilly's place was a large, single-story, like most of the desert houses, with the entire living and dining room glassed looking out onto the pool, with mirrors on the walls making everything look that much larger. All the sofas, chairs and carpets were white. It felt classically elegant, and yet, had warmth to it. When Jilly came out he gave me lots of compliments and said we'd be off right away to pick up another other couple.

The ride to pick up the couple was only three minutes away on

a street named Frank Sinatra Drive. I remember pulling up to the front entry of large, green electric gates that slowly opened. We parked and started to go inside when the couple walked out to greet us. I was introduced to Barbara Marx, a stunningly gorgeous woman who was model-thin with shoulder length blonde hair. Her date was introduced as Frank Sinatra. Francis, as he was referred to from then on, said he would drive. He drove an olive green jaguar, while Jilly and I sat in the back seat. I knew of course that Frank Sinatra was a popular singer with the older crowd, and I was excited on the inside and knew I would tell my mom first thing in the morning about the evening and who drove the car. He and Jilly told stories to each other all the way to the restaurant, and the laughter was infectious.

We pulled up to valet parking in front of a small restaurant named Ruby Dunes. Immediately upon entering, it felt like family, with warm friendly hugs all around. I realized right away that I was amongst "royalty" by all the attention. My major concern became what to order and to make sure I picked up the right fork!

Barbara had been married to one of the Marx Brothers. Her son

came by to join us for a cocktail, but couldn't stay for dinner. He seemed like a very nice young man and Francis seemed to get along really well with him. The evening went smoothly; dinner was grand, and Francis tipped everyone from valet to busboy to waiter to hostess, with a one-hundred dollar bill. When it was time to leave we went to the home of a professional golfer. He and his wife were good friends with Jilly, Frank and Barbara. I got the impression that the golfer's wife was one of Barbara's closest friends. I felt a little out of place with Barbara talking to her about who they have come to their homes to do their manicures and pedicures. I was still so young, and felt nothing in common with them. I could barely keep Michelle in a private school, let alone afford the obviously expensive designers clothes these two women wore. But they were very kind to me and did their best to make me feel a part of the group. Jilly, being the gentleman, included me in every conversation. After-dinner drinks were served from the step-down bar in the living room, and I continued to stick with Perrier. Ruby, owner of the restaurant where we had dined, also came over after he closed, and that's when the fun and laughter really started! We were sitting around in the large living room, laughing and

talking about things they had seen and done, when Frank and Jilly decided to "pants" Ruby, who must have been in his late sixties or early seventies. The term to "pants" someone is when you pull down a guy's pants leaving him with nothing other than his boxers. They laughed so hard they were rolling on the floor. When the evening was over and we got in the car to leave, Frank told Jilly we should drive by Bob Hope s house, and as we did they pulled up along the fence to the back yard and both started throwing cherry bombs over the fence, and then jumped back in the car as we quickly drove away. There was lots of hilarious laughter.

When the evening was over and Jilly and I returned to his house, he thanked me for being a perfect date, remained a perfect gentleman, saying he hoped to see me again soon. He had The Crusher drive me home.

As I lay in bed that night and thought about the experience I had just been a part of, I couldn't help think that no matter how much money one might have, it wasn't necessarily the material things that mattered; it was all about good friends, doing for others, not losing the child-like humor we all should have, and to just enjoy

laughing and being silly sometimes.

Jilly had The Crusher drop off a gift for Michelle the following day a beautiful Mickey Mouse necklace, definitely a collector's piece. It was very thoughtful and a beautiful gesture. He also sent word with The Crusher that if I needed anything at all, to just let him know. Groceries, anything…

For the next six months, I had many occasions to double-date with Barbara and Frank. One thing I can say about Barbara she arrived a lady and left a lady, and was one classy broad, meant in the nicest possible way. We always went to local restaurants where Frank made sure those hundred-dollar bills went to anyone who helped him in any way during the evening. I was fortunate enough to be invited to Frank's house for a home-cooked meal he prepared using his special gravy, a wonderful marinara sauce he cooked for hours. Jilly often tried to impress me with his late night cooking skills when we returned to his home after our evenings on the town. His specialty was a cauliflower dish with olive oil and garlic - out of this world yummy!

I was always made to feel very comfortable. One day while I was visiting and was left at Jilly's home alone, the next door neighbor, a Vegas entertainer, came over to ask Jilly a question, and since no one was there he spent some time talking to me. He invited me to come next door to see his house and give him my opinion on some decorating he had done. He gave me the tour of his lovely home, showing me all his art work, walking along a hallway, showing me the bedrooms. When we reached the master bedroom, he got a big coffee table book of art, sat on his bed, and asked my opinions on a couple of pictures, nudes, and he started talking about nudes. I was really interested in the artwork since I had loved nude drawings from my childhood, but no, this wasn't his real intention. He was really trying to "show me his etchings" and get me into his bedroom. I guess he thought seeing the pictures would turn me on. I laughed so hard when I figured it out; this was a man trying to seduce me! I wasn't insulted at all. It was just so funny to hear someone giving me a new line, one I hadn't already heard. I got up and left, telling him I couldn't help him, as I laughed all the way out the door. I did tell The Crusher (whose actual name I eventually learned was Jerry), and we both laughed about it. I don t know if it ever reached Jilly's ears or not, but he never mentioned it.

On the weekends I usually stayed away because Jilly's place became what seemed like a house full of Italian men who came to play cards, and where some imported escorts would often come for a round of fun. Large sums of cash changed hands. Josette and I were present at one of the card games (sans hookers) and I happened to be in the line of fire when a wad of rolled up hundred-dollar bills came flying across the table and accidentally hit me in the side of my face. For some reason it felt so normal for me to be among this group of men who were placing bets and gambling. It was like living the life of the high rollers. And although it was fun to be on the inside hearing all the stories and sharing in the laughter, it just wasn't a comfortable place where I wanted to be. I couldn't wait to get back home to my sweet precious daughter. We were always so happy to spend quality time together and she was more important to me than anything in the world.

My Mom came to visit for a week. Jilly went out of town with Frank, which he frequently did, he made sure Jerry came to check on us each day. My mom and Jerry, aka The Crusher, hit it off very well. Jerry would come in the house and would say, "Hi, Mom!" Then he took right over like he was the man of the house to help her if she needed anything. Jerry became like family to us. He'd come by with big bags of groceries, and loved to help in the kitchen cooking when he had time.

I had the chance to spend a lot of time with Jerry at Jilly's, where I would occasionally go to do some topless sunbathing poolside, and Jerry always treated me with respect. Jerry and I would talk for hours and I asked how he got the nickname, The Crusher, and he told me that people think it's because it has the connotation of being a tough guy, but it was because he used to have a business that crushed cars and metal, I think in New Jersey. He had a heart attack followed by open-heart surgery, and it was Jilly who paid all his medical expenses and took care of him while he recovered. There wasn't anything he wouldn't do for Jilly or Frank. He was willing to literally take bullet for either one. Jilly brought him to California and had him move in and get healthy. Every morning Jerry would drive to a liquor store on Palm Canyon Drive in Palm

Springs and pick up copies of the Green Sheet and deliver them to Frank and Jilly for the horse races. I never did mention my familiarity with the Green Sheet or that my father was a bookie.

Jilly had a fundraising golf tournament called, of all things, "In the Bush," which most people assumed meant the golf ball getting lost in the shrubbery, but that was the funniest part, seeing all the ads and television commercials advertising the "In the Bush" tournament and watching Jilly laughing so hard about the name. Frank did a concert at The Rivera Hotel, and both events raised money for Frank's mother Dolly's favorite charity. I got to sit in the front row to watch the show and it really was the first time I had paid attention to the music of Frank Sinatra. He put on a great show, and I did enjoy his style of music from then on. I knew I had to move on with my life because this was not what I really wanted for myself or for Michelle. I wanted a life that was all about family and giving her a real life, not one of glamour and material things. I was just "a small town girl living in an uptown world," as Billy Joel would sing.

Josette took me to meet a lady she called "Mama" who lived in

Palm Springs. Mama lived in a small, one-bedroom second-floor apartment. She was a very petite woman from Romania. Josette had been going to see her for a few years for Romanian coffee grounds readings. She wanted me to have my fortune read after hers and she was going to pay the twenty-dollar fee for me. I could ask "Mama" whatever I wanted. It was interesting to watch. Josette would bring her cassette player with blank tapes to record what was said. Mama would make the cup of coffee and you would take a sip (my first time to ever sip what coffee would taste like), then she would pour out the coffee and turn the cup over, tap it, then spin it a few times saying some special words, then when she turned the cup back over, the cup looked like lace and it was the pictures Mama saw inside the lace that would tell her something, and then you could ask a couple of questions. On this day, she told Josette she would be going to Australia for a vacation, and that she was going to fall in love and marry a man from there. As for me, she said that there would be a man in my future who was going to come to my door under false pretenses and will look like a regular person, but underneath, he would be a man of the law.

139

Life for both Josette and me was really great. Michelle and Josette's son Danny were about to graduate from kindergarten at the private school. Summertime was fast-approaching and soon Jilly would be leaving and not returning until next season. I wasn't his girlfriend and although we did end up several times under the covers, it wasn't about romance as much as it was to feel good, really good. I enjoyed our times together and he was always so much fun to be around. I was Jilly's date, a companion, to take along when he had very special occasions to go to. There were some great times and fun memories.

CHAPTER 10

Should I or Shouldn't I

It was 1975 and the Vietnam War ended. The United States carried out Operation Baby Lift, bringing Vietnamese orphans to America. For me it was all about disco and dancing. This was a wonderful time of life for me. My job at the salon was going well. All my regular clientele had returned for the season. It wasn't but a few months later when Josette heard from her mother, saying she was moving from Paris to Australia, and could Josette come spend a month helping her move and get settled. So Josette and her son Danny left and Michelle and I had the big house all to ourselves. It was pleasant just being the two of us.

There was no leaving Michelle unless it was a Saturday night. Then it was off to the number one gay bar in the desert called Oil Can Harry's (later to be called Aunt Hattie's, then Daddy Warbuck's). If you were gay you spent most of your time socializing in Cathedral City, often referred to as "Cat City." This was where all my co-workers at the salon went to dance on the weekends. It was the most fun I had had since dancing on Cannery Row to the sounds of my one true love, Rock. Most of the world didn't recognize gays as being normal. But neither was I, and living life with Rock's songs in my heart gave me reason and motive to escape through music. Some of my favorite songs playing at the time were, *Never Can Say Goodbye* (Gloria Gaynor), *Can't Get Enough Of Your Love* (Barry White), *Rock The Boat* (Hues Corporation), *Where Do We Go From Here* (Trammps) *The Hustle* (Van McCoy) *Get Down Tonight* (K.C and The Sunshine Band), and *Love To Love You Baby* (Donna Summer). Finally I found a place I could arrive alone and leave alone and not have men interested in me whatsoever, which was exactly what I needed; work hard, play a little and bestow love on my daughter every free second.

The one thing I knew, I didn't need was the material world of the rich and famous. I wanted to give my daughter a loving life with a new father who would treat her well, put a roof over our heads, and have another child so Michelle wouldn't be raised alone as I was.

Josette returned from Australia and told me she had fallen madly in love while away and he had asked her to marry him and move to Australia. (A prediction "Mama" had made to her through reading her Romanian coffee grounds). So a month later Josette wanted to move. Michelle and I needed a roof over our heads once again.

One of my clients at the salon owned three townhouses in Palm Desert, just a quarter-mile drive from work. One was available to move into immediately at three-hundred dollars a month if I managed the other two and collected the rent. Since the owners had been leasing it as a vacation rental, the condo was turn-key, and was decorated with very expensive Danish Modern wooden furnishings. It had a community swimming pool directly across the street. This was surely a God-given blessing for Michelle and me. We would have a new home and I could still afford her private school, if I took on an extra job.

A very popular restaurant, The Iron Gate, was nearby, known for its prime rib and king crab legs. On Saturday nights I valet parked cars, and two nights a week I was the dining room hostess.

The tips were great and the extra money came in handy for all the fun activities Michelle and I would enjoy such as going to Disneyland, or going to Laguna Beach, just being California beach girls. We spent many afternoons swimming and playing in the pool. Then off we would go, beach blankets, tanning oil, and our portable battery-operated radio to listen to music while sunning. Michelle's babysitter had a daughter the same age as Michelle who went to the same school and they had lots of fun together each day after school until I came home from work. It was comforting knowing I was only five minutes from home in case I was needed.

My car was starting to require a few repairs and the mileage was climbing so I put a sign in the back window and hoped someone would see it while parked in the carport at home. There came a knock at the door and it was a very handsome tall man with black hair and blue eyes, wearing nice slacks and shirt. He had come to ask about the car. I went outside with him and he said he was interested and wondered if he could take it for a drive around the block. Michelle wasn't home, so I went with him. He was funny and very flirty. It was kind of nice to have the attention.

144

When we came back, I invited him in and we sat around and spent some time talking about the car, but also about life in general. His name was Mike; he lived in Palm Springs, and worked as a sheriff.

It felt really nice meeting a sheriff, since I have always had a great respect for law enforcement, especially back in the days of my dad's best friend being the police chief, the one who helped me with my predator, and my two friends in Seaside who were policemen, who had made me feel protected. Just for the moment, knowing that someone who could keep Michelle and me protected from harm seemed extremely sexy to me. It was the one thing lacking in my life, feeling helpless in case of emergency. I wasn't very street smart and was always too trusting of people. Perhaps because I was raised in a time and place where danger was pretty rare, where doors were left unlocked.

Mike asked if he might take me to dinner one evening. I didn't commit to that, but he did have my personal number from the car ad and asked if I would mind if he called me sometime. I agreed. All of a sudden I started to realize I was spotting him in his patrol car when I would go to the gas station, or he passed by where I worked. I didn't acknowledge him at the time, but didn't really mind being watched, and felt secure and protected. It was kind of flattering to me in a way. If this had been forty years later, I would find this behavior to be creepy and would have recognized he was a stalker. But I was still young and naïve ad thought like an adventurist teenager.

It took a week for Mike to actually invite me for dinner and I accepted. It turned out to be very enjoyable, and wherever he took me after that, everyone seemed to know him and like him. At restaurants we were always offered complimentary desserts. Mike said it was because he made sure he checked on these businesses and had helped with some problems they might have had. He never did bring up the idea of buying the car again. He mentioned where I go for gas, that he knew the owner of the station, and he asked the owner to tell him what conversations we had so he might find out if I was single and where I worked. Seems Mike had been following me long before he came to my house in pretense of buying my car. I soon learned he had watched me from a distance for several months and thought I was beautiful. At the time, I found this to be very romantic. Mike was so down to earth and yet took control of everything. I had learned to be so independent and it was nice being spoiled. It was really nice to be on a date with a man alone, and not on a double date, as it always was with Jilly.

Mike had never been married. He was four years older than I, and was a Vietnam veteran who flew planes in the war. He had a very close family in Riverside; an hour drive from the desert. His father was an elementary school principal and his mother worked as a sales associate in a local department store. Mike came from a very strict Catholic family, where values meant something. He said one day he hoped to marry and have children. I never told him of my childhood growing up, losing my father, or about Rock. None of that seemed to matter. What did matter was someone wanting me for just being me and liking me because of the kindness I have for the world. I was never the type to go hang out in a bar, and even up until this time, rarely drank alcohol. What was more important to me was giving Michelle a brother or sister and a real family. I wasn't Catholic but since I was sent off to any church that had a school bus, I didn't have that much preference, as long as

God was present and knew my heart.

Over the next several months Mike slowly worked his way into my life. If I was at Oil Can Harry's dancing with my friends, his sheriff's car would be parked close by to make sure I got to my car safely. He never followed me home, but made sure I was safe. I really liked that feeling. I liked knowing if there was an emergency or trouble happened, he would be right there. He also would make sure nothing would happen to Michelle since he had started to get close to her also. I don't remember him buying her gifts and that was usually the first things guys would do in order to get to me. Get to the daughter first and win her over. He was doing all the right things, and so far the only fault I could find in him at the time was that he couldn't dance. Not even a little bit! Since music and escaping to my private thoughts of Rock would exist forever, I would just have to give up dancing in exchange for a better life. It also was reassuring to know Mike had a great job with good benefits. I never felt concerned for his safety as a sheriff, since this area was filled with mostly part-time winter residents. You rarely heard of any crime. Anyway, I lived in such a fantasy world that I only saw the good.

When Jilly came back into town in time for the new season, I made sure Jerry the Crusher told him I had started dating someone else. There were never any bad feelings between us. We had become really good friends. Even with Jilly and Mike, I still went to sleep listening to *The Sea* and remembering that one night spent in the apartment on Del Monte Beach. I knew sooner or later I had to start moving on with my life.

A few months into seeing Mike on a regular basis, he started buying me some beautiful, thoughtful gifts. He frequently included Michelle when we would go out. Soon he started spending the night. Michelle was not aware, since he would be gone when she awoke in the morning. He knew I loved the perfume *L'air du Temps* by Nina Ricci and bought me the two-ounce size in a Lalique crystal flacon with two love birds on the stopper. It seemed so romantic, since I loved fragrances and collected perfume bottles. To most girls, this might not be a big deal, but to me, for a man to really give thought and take the time to romance me, that was sacred.

No one could ever be at the very center of my heart, since Rock would always hold that spot, but at least Mike was spending time romancing and showing a concern to protect Michelle and me, plus he wanted children and had great family values. I wasn't in love, the way I was with Rock, but on the other hand, I wasn't with someone who felt was like a brother to me, as Jim had. I didn't want to be alone forever either. I couldn't figure it out why no one could take Rock's place, especially since our relationship was brief. He never even knew my last name. Could it have been the memory of Rock's kisses, or my night with him on Del Monte Beach? Or was it because when I listened to music and closed my eyes I never really left him? That moment in time, that true feeling of my love for a man, pure passion, romance, love, music, Rock had it all.

Soon the day came when Mike took me to dinner and proposed to me. I accepted and felt so excited to know that my life was about to change. Everyone at all the jobs thought Mike was a great guy for me. We would take Michelle to go listen to music in Indian Wells and the minute we would walk in the door the singer would start singing *I Shot the Sheriff*. Michelle would be brought up on the stage and would sit on a stool while the singer sang her a love song. Being only five years-old (and adorable!), I know she loved all the attention. And now I would be able to give her a loving big family. Mike took me to his jeweler to arrange for a beautiful custom-made diamond ring with six large diamonds. He took me shopping to buy my wedding dress and Michelle's. My dress was a pastel coral floor-length gown with beautiful pleating. Michelle's was long and white and she would have her own flowers to carry down the aisle, because Mike said he was really marrying us both. Michelle helped me choose the invitations and flowers. Being a sheriff in a large department, Mike had many friends to invite, along with his big Irish family, and I had many friends and co-workers.

Mike invited Michelle and me to come meet his parents in Riverside. I was very excited, yet nervous. I wanted to make a good impression. We pulled up to their house, high on a hill overlooking the city of Riverside. It had a magnificent view of all the city lights. It was an older house with three bedrooms and two bathrooms. Clearly Mike's mother, Donna, was a wonderful homemaker and cook since the home was immaculate and the dinner smelled wonderful. Donna went out of her way, I was sure, to make one of Mike's favorite dishes. There was a small living room and a family room with sliding glass doors looking out onto an enclosed patio with a small kidney-shaped pool. Michelle and I were given a tour by Mike as his mother finished making dinner, while his father, Mike Senior, sat in the family room watching the news, not being very social, but I didn't give that much thought since his mom seemed to have such a kind heart. I offered to help in the kitchen but wasn't needed. All through dinner Donna wanted to find out more about Michelle and me. She was very gracious, but his dad would barely look at me.

After dinner, we sat in the family room for dessert. I remember asking Mike's father what he thought about private schools, especially since Michelle was in one that I was so proud of in Rancho Mirage. He told me he didn't think they were worth anything, that the teachers hired were untrained to the level of public schools, and if Michelle was finishing kindergarten, she needed to take kindergarten again at a regular school, and he went on and on about the difference. It wasn't, I suppose, the best ice-breaker question I might have asked. He was gruff and never once smiled, so I asked him why he seemed so unhappy. Did we come to visit on a night that he was tired from working so hard? Then I joked light-heartedly and said please smile for me. Then he let me have it!

He was not happy with the fact his son was marrying a woman who had already been married, who had a child, and wasn't Catholic, let alone the fact that I had never graduated from high school. His mother remained quiet, but eventually did try to soften his harsh words, saying they only want what's best for their son. "If Mike loves you and your daughter, there isn't much we can do about it. We would have just liked it to be different for him," she said. Mike spoke up and told them how much he loved us and they asked him to do them one favor and at least have me convert to Catholicism. I thought to myself, if this is what they need in order for this to become a real family in their eyes, then I didn't mind going to classes to become a baptized Catholic. But I left feeling defeated and somewhat worthless. I was very quiet during the hour's drive home. Mike didn't want me to give any thought to what was said. He was happy they met me and knew they would grow to love me as he did.

I acquiesced by going to catechism classes, but since I was already taking Michelle to Sunday services at the Presbyterian church that was within walking of where we were living, I made the decision that this is where we would get married. This was my wedding and I wanted it to be perfect for Michelle and me, and to feel comfortable on our special day. The church had a cathedral ceiling and a wall of stained glass window panes. Mike didn't object to my decision and said whatever I wanted was fine with him as long as I was happy. We could always have a Catholic ceremony at another time. I was feeling dejected since his parents judged me without knowing me. I was determined to win them over. Mike continued to be very supportive. We started talking about where we would move to once we were married. Mike suggested we first rent a house with a pool before jumping into making a purchase, which sounded fine to me. Finally, we'd have a home with a pool and a chance to become a real family for Michelle, a family with a mom, a dad, and hopefully one day, a new baby. It was fun for the three of us to go house hunting for our rental, getting ideas of price and location. Being a sheriff and driving in the neighborhoods all day long, Mike was able to pick out some great places.

We had set the date, my ring was ready, and I sent out invitations for the wedding. It was time for me to start a new life. Even if Mike's mother and father weren't thrilled with me, I was certain others in the family would be supportive and we would eventually have our own big family with events filled with love and kindness, at our new home. I would look forward to seeing the doctor and then to try to get pregnant before I was too much older, and Michelle would not be raised alone.

Two days before, my mother and grandmother drove down from Monterey to stay with Michelle and me and prepare for the wedding. The first time they met Mike, when he stopped by the condo while on duty, they thought he was handsome and loved him in his sheriff's uniform. My mom was on her best behavior and with my grandmother with us she never once asked if I had any wine, beer or alcohol, knowing I didn't drink. That night while trying to sleep, I kept tossing and turning, picturing Mike's Dad telling me how they didn't want their son to marry me. Then I thought about Rock and how this marriage was a Band-Aid to help fill a void. I would laugh to myself thinking how Mike didn't even like to dance and that he preferred country music. Although Mike and I were opposites in many ways, I had to concede that being with a musician like Rock probably would not have been the best life for me to give Michelle.

Would my Dad have liked Mike? I don t think so. I know my Dad would never have cared for Mike's father. My dad would only want me to be with someone who could offer Michelle and me the world. By the time morning arrived I had a talk with my Mom and grandmother and told them I just felt uncomfortable about the marriage and told them about Mike's parents not liking me and how I felt I couldn't go through with it. They both told me it was my life and I was the one who would have to live it. If this was not the right man for me, I should not marry him. With their support I called Mike and asked to meet him for lunch where l told him I had changed my mind and needed more time to be sure, and that I wanted to give it more time to see if his family would come around. Knowing all the time I was getting married, not because of a deep passionate love, but out of a need. Something just told me this should not happen. Mike was upset, but he understood. I called all the invited guests. I'm sure Mike was very concerned and worried at my sudden change, but said he would do whatever it took to make sure it was right.

CHAPTER 11
Life In The Real World

From that moment on, I felt like the weight of the world had been lifted from my shoulders. Instead of getting married, I had a wonderful vacation with my mom, grandmother and Michelle. I took them all on a tour of the desert, and drove my grandmother past the house in Palm Springs where she lived many years ago. My grandmother suffered from some arthritis in her hips and always had a heating pad on her lap in Pacific Grove, but the entire time they stayed with me, she never had the pains in her legs and felt one day she would like to move back to the desert. Soon it was time for them to return home and for life to return to normal for me.

It was about two weeks later when I read in the paper where a sheriff ran into a burning house to save a life before the fire department could arrive, and was in the hospital from smoke inhalation. It turned out it was Mike. I went straight to the hospital to make sure he was okay. He told me he didn't care if he lived or died. Being without Michelle and me was too disturbing to him, and he didn't want to spend his life without me. It was at that moment I told him that as soon as he got out of the hospital I would marry him.

Mike was really happy and I was ready to commit to a wonderful life of being a sheriff's wife, a loyal partner and mother one day, hopefully, to our new child or children to come. Our wedding would be just Mike, Michelle, and me. I went to the church and made arrangements for a few days later for an afternoon wedding. I stopped by the florist to reorder the flowers that had already been paid for. When I told my mother what happened with Mike in the hospital and the soon-to-be wedding approaching, she cautioned me, due to my hesitance from before, but I convinced her it must have just been from being too nervous and scared of the commitment. All the while knowing in my heart, this isn't going to fill the void I feel from the loss of my Dad and Rock, but it was a start in the right direction to heal from my sadness of both losses. Plus here I was, a single mom, wanting to give my beautiful daughter a home and family. I didn't want her to be bounced around like I was as a child. I wanted to give her a loving home with a brother or sister or both. I knew I'd be happy when the day would finally come and we could buy our new home. In the meantime, wedding bells were about to chime. We said our vows and there was no turning back now. We didn't take a honeymoon and the three of us spent the rest of the month living in my condo. Mike got his things packed from where he had been living in Palm Springs.

We found a perfect three-bedroom house with a beautiful enclosed backyard and swimming pool. Mike always looked so handsome walking into the house dressed in his uniform, his shiny badge, his holster. Plus he came home during lunch time since he worked the day shift. It was really a happy time for me, as Mike and I laughed often. He was home in the evenings when I got off work and I no longer needed to work extra jobs, just the hair salon. Life couldn't be better.

We started building up friendships and became more social. Mike's parents came around, and put together a wedding reception in the large party room at their Catholic church. I knew I could quiet my mind with my thoughts of Rock, and perhaps now he could lie dormant in the center of my heart. While I tried to move on with my life, I was sure Rock had never given any thought of me after all this time anyway.

It wasn't but a few months later when Mike and I decided the time was right for me to get pregnant, especially since he knew that was one of the main reasons I considered getting married in the first place. Michelle was already six years-old and seven years was going to be a lot of age difference as it was. Even before I had missed a period, I knew my body was changing. The following month we went back to the doctor for confirmation and YES, we were pregnant! This was the best news! I couldn't wait to tell Michelle and she was so excited to hear she was going to have a brother or sister.

Mike was doing great at his job and was given the responsibility of being on the detailed assignment of working with the Secret Service for President Ford during his up and coming visit to the desert. Mike got along well with the Secret Service and asked if I would mind having them over for a barbeque. I said sure, I'd love that. Of course all my clients and friends at work wanted to be invited, too. I had to be very discrete in my choosing of guests, and it had to be "top secret," that the Secret Service would be at our house. Of course, the President has many shifts of Secret Service agents, and this was only one of them. My guest list was checked, and all had to have quick background checks. There would only be about six agents coming, but nevertheless, the food I would be making would have to be tested before they were allowed to eat it. I kept the menu simple for that reason. Someone was brought over to watch me in the preparation of barbequed chicken, homemade potato salad, along with a few other side dishes, garlic bread, and my fresh-out-of-the-oven chocolate chip cookies. Hopefully no morning sickness would get in the way, since it was just the previous day that the doctor said I was pregnant. My friends arrived, and one was with the local press who got permission to write a small blurb in the newspaper a few days later after the President had left town.

Once everyone arrived and started eating, swimming, and socializing, the fun began and it wasn't my being the hostess that made the party special but, Michelle, who would made the Secret Service agents bring the dining chairs from inside the house to place around the pool and line them up like seats on a train. She made them sit in the chairs as she drove the train and had them each blow the whistle when it was their stop to get off. Between her taking charge, and showing off her swimming skills, she stole the show for the rest of the day. The afternoon went very well, and as they all left, each left agent left Michelle a special gift. One was a pen that President Ford had actually used. It went so well and I was thinking how I would look forward to entertaining friends again at our lovely home.

But it was not to be. I was three months pregnant and really happy. Michelle was about to start first grade. Mike came home from work one day pretty shaken and said he left his job working at the Sheriff's Department. He later admitted they had given him the choice to either quit or be fired. He said they had some crazy idea that was completely untrue of something he had been involved in regarding prostitutes who lived closed to the apartment where he had been living before we were married. Mike never went into any detail and I never asked. All I was concerned about was what were we going to do now with him out of a job. He said since he resigned it wouldn't or hurt his chances of working for another department. But we would have to move. He would have to give it all some thought and come up with the best answer for us.

As it turned out, Mike decided we would have to move in with his parents in Riverside. He said he had spoken to them and they would do anything he needed to help him and his family. He was going to go spend a few days with them and try to come up with a plan and start preparing his résumé. As Michelle and I waited for his return, all I could think was I finally had a beautiful life, a great job I loved, a baby on the way, Michelle was doing well in school, and now we will have to leave. And worse yet, another move, let alone to his parents' small house. I hoped Mike would return with some happy news on how we could make this work somehow where we could have our own place.

But as it turned out I had to leave my job, my friends, our new home, and Michelle would have to leave her school and friends. We had to move in with Mike's parents, who weren't thrilled he married me in the first place. And now, we'd all be under their roof, one happy family? *Oh please, Rock, come and take my away from all this.* Let me escape to music and thoughts of happier times.

Living with my in-laws wasn't really as bad as I envisioned it would be, but Michelle was forced to repeat first grade in a public school, so a another new school for her with new friends. I took catechism classes at the Catholic Church, was baptized, and received my first holy communion. I felt good going to church on Sundays with the family. This was not Monterey, this was not Palm Springs, this was Riverside, and I did not want to be here, but I didn't have anything to say about it. My life and Michelle's was now completely out of my control.

Was Mike ever involved in prostitution? I wondered if he even mentioned it to his parents. It was never a subject that came up again to this day. But the Sheriff's Department must have had some proof or there would not have been an issue. Perhaps it was nothing more than being caught at some point hiring one. I will likely never know. What had I done? I lost my identity, my voice to even speak up it seems. Mike became very controlling. Even his Mother started saying he was a different man when he came back from Vietnam. She could see a different side of him now that he was living back at home. I suppose this type of stress would get to any man.

I'm sure being pregnant wasn't helping with my emotions either. I was starting to gain weight and my pregnancy was not going well for me. I was getting a lot of swelling from preeclampsia, just like my first pregnancy. My blood pressure was rising. It was all so overwhelming to me. I worried about Mike finding a job before the baby came. But I had to put it in God's hands and wish for the best. I didn't speak to my Mom on the phone since none of my calls were private any longer. I started writing her letters to let her know what was going on.

Mike's family and the people at the church couldn't have been nicer. Mike enrolled in some college classes to qualify for a higher degree. I took a job doing hair in a small shop for as long as I could. Mike found a part-time job working in security for an amusement park. He found us an apartment close to his college in

Riverside, and now at least it was a place to call our own. Another move and school for Michelle. I can't imagine how she must have felt with all the changes and seeing me so different, not my usual happy self. But I made sure we still had our quality time.

Mike finally found a job as a police officer in a city only half an hour away. Mike worked the graveyard shift and continued working part-time in security at the amusement park. He could not have worked harder to try to provide for us. I admired him very much for that. Mike also never once made me feel unattractive or ashamed because I was gaining weight. He was very protective and I was under his complete control. I guess my dreaming of having a man protect me wasn't as nice as the fairy tale I had made it to be.

I was into my ninth month with my blood pressure going sky-high, yet still no signs of labor. The doctors decided I needed to be bedridden now and had to be checked daily. It was almost ten months when I started having slight labor pains. Mike took me to the hospital and my blood pressure was so high they said they would induce labor to make the baby come sooner. I would not be allowed any spinal injection. The baby was not in the right position and would need to be turned in order to get it out and I would have to help push. I was in labor for the next twelve hours when finally the time came. The doctors were very concerned and told Mike there was a chance that one of us, the baby or me, might die. Then the moment came when I could hear a baby crying and I was told I had a beautiful baby boy who weighed close to ten pounds. He was perfect! After they stitched me up, I would be like new again. I had Mike call my mother and he left for a while to go tell Michelle, who was staying with his parents, the great news.

Michelle was very excited about her new baby brother. You would think she was his mommy, the way she hovered over him every chance she got. We named him Aaron. No wonder I had a hard time when he would kick me while still inside my tummy. He had a lot of power behind those kicks! Life was better. I was still a little depressed, but figured it was mostly due to the trauma my body had just gone through. With Mike sleeping all day and Michelle in school, it was my special time to bond with my son. I loved this little boy so much! I knew as soon as I looked down at that sweet face that no matter what I had gone through I will love him with all my heart and make sure he knows it. What a perfect son and daughter I had brought into this world. I had so much love to give them both.

Life again was back on track, and I was now blessed with not one, but two beautiful children. This little son of mine was getting cuter by the moment, and Michelle wanted to help change diapers, feed him, sing to him, dress him, and help in any way possible. Aaron could feel the love from us, but the minute Mike got home, Aaron belonged to him. He was a devoted father.

My grandmother and Mom decided to move back to the desert. I was thrilled to know that they would be living only one hour away from me and would be able to be closer to Michelle and Aaron and enjoy watching them grow up.

This was a very exciting time for both of them. My Grandmother was happy to be able to live with her daughter in the warm weather where she already felt so good that even after only a few days in the desert, she didn't need a heating pad on her legs and was able to get around much better. From the time I can remember, she had never been sick a day in her life. The same with my mother; I don t think she ever missed a day of work, even when she had a hangover. But now all was new and these two ladies would be starting a wonderful new adventure.

I was so excited to bring the children down to visit them. Just to be back in the desert again and out of Riverside, it felt like home sweet home for me also. Michelle loved spending time with her grandma and always as a tradition they would play Old Maid. My grandmother was just crazy about Aaron. She loved it when I would set him on her lap and let her rock him in the rocking chair.

I kept trying to convince Mike to please find us home in the city where he worked so we could be close to him, so we could actually have a dad and husband in the home. I reminded him how I didn't feel much like a woman very often, since he was always either working or too tired to spend time with me, and I missed feeling sexy and beautiful like when we first met.

When I said the words "when we first met," it made me think back to what a wonderful life Michelle and I had before Mike came along, and how now it all changed. How I used to go dancing, Michelle and I having our fun time at the pool, the friends I had made at my jobs, all gone now. I wasn't the woman pretty enough to model any more. I still needed to lose weight; not bad, but not great. I just knew if Mike would find a place closer to his work, it would all change, a nice home where Mike could come home for dinner with his family, and always drive by to make sure we were safe. .

As a year passed I'm sure Mike must have been able to tell I wasn't happy because before Arron had turned two Mike had found our new rental home, and we were living in the same city he worked.

Aaron loved being able to play outside all day. Michelle was in her new school and even had new friends on the same block where we lived. She joined Brownies at school and started having lots of activities I could take her too and also participate in. I decided to work from home and since I loved kids I created a pre-school. We had a very large family room that lead outside that I transformed. I had business cards made, and went and bought all kinds of craft projects and ABC learning tools so it wouldn't just be all fun and games, but the children would get to make crafts and learn new pre-school skills. This was all kind of amusing to me, coming from someone who wasn't very well-schooled herself, but at least was a quick learner when given the chance.

This was really working out well. It really started feeling like we were a family again. Mike and his partner came for a home-cooked meal each evening and always made sure our house was patrolled often throughout the night. He had really tried to get me to change my mind about living close to his work. But I didn't give much thought to that, to what could possibly happen. If anything, I felt safer because he was close. The daycare business picked up quickly. I limited it to ten children per day. Even that seemed a lot, but the income really felt good. The kids, often screaming and crying when they got tired, would get on my nerves, but I could handle it. Life was better. I was a little depressed, but figured with all the moves I had made and the worry of being married to a policeman who was in harm's way wasn't helping. We weren't living on the Monterey Bay or Palm Desert where life seemed much safer. This was different and dangerous. Mike didn't even like the idea of my going to the grocery store alone.

CHAPTER 12
Badass Gangs

One day I realized that I had slipped into a state of total melancholy. I was going through the motions at home with the family and at the daycare, and things were still good, but I relished the quiet moments when I had a chance to listen to some music that helped me escape to Rock and much happier days. If I slept for a short time I wasn't so sad. At least when I slept, nothing seemed to bother me, as long as I went to sleep with *The Sea* music, remembering my one and only special night when this album was given to me. If only Rock could know how this album was helping me get through this feeling of overwhelming sadness.

A month went by when I got a call from my mother saying my grandmother was very ill and she had taken her to the doctor and was waiting for tests to come back. I let Mom know as soon as the weekend would come and I didn't have all these kids at my daycare, I would come down to see her. I will never forget the sight of my sweet grandmother lying in her bed in a room so bright and fresh-looking in all yellow and white bedding. My mother had hired a wonderful German woman, Clara, a registered nurse, to help each day in caring for my grandmother. I adored Clara. She had the heart of an angel and took really great care of my grandmother. It turns out that my grandmother, now aged eighty-five, had pancreatic cancer. Clara happened to live on the same street just three blocks away and would walk to our house anytime she was needed over the next month. I had to get back home and planned on coming each weekend, never realizing this would be my last time I'd see my grandmother again. Perhaps in my gut I knew that, but never wanted to acknowledge it.

Mike always made fun of me and my sensitivity when it came to death and dying. Once a baby bird fell out of our front yard tree and I wept for the loss of it. He would laugh and make fun of me and tell me how he had to see dead bodies every day that were brutally murdered, with brains splattered all over, and still go about his day and have a hamburger for lunch right afterwards. He was very insensitive, and somewhat sadistic. I guess that was his way to deal with and survive in his job. I was happy to be his sounding board and give him comfort at the end of a long day, but I had to start forming some of my own survival methods. I found I wanted to listen to music and sleep as much as I could. I also noticed I never stopped cleaning and rearranging furniture. I had always been a neat freak, keeping everything spotless, but this was more. This was moving furniture, changing things constantly. Mike used to joke when he came home about how he had to make sure he turned on the lights so he didn't fall over something placed in a new spot while he was gone.

My Grandmother died peacefully in her sleep with Clara and Mom by her side. My half-sister Carol, her husband and two daughters also came to express their sorrow. My sister always thought of my grandmother as her very own mother since it was she who had raised her more than her own mother. It was nice to see my sister giving loving support to our mother and having all of them staying at her house for a few days before heading back home to San Jose.

After my sister and family left, I could tell my mother went back to drinking to help ease the pain. How sad that Mom, still only in her fifties, wasn't able to find the happiness and a life she should have enjoyed. If only she had gone right back to work after my father's death, instead of turning to alcohol. But who was I to judge, since I turned to music and sleeping? I had never had alcohol in my home except for some beer for Mike's occasional indulgence. Mom needed me and I knew it. My mother was still a mean drunk, calling me and saying terrible things. It got so I had to keep the phone off the hook for periods of time, but it was hard to do this for too long, as I worried about how Mike wouldn't be able to reach me in case of a real emergency. I remember hollering at my mom once, telling her how much I hated her and what a horrible drunk she was. But by morning she called and when I answered, she acted like nothing had ever happened the night before. I realized she had probably finally passed out and didn't even remember what either of us had said. Mike, in the meantime, was getting upset because of the way my mother would upset me. But we agreed it wasn't his place to get involved. He understood that her behavior was a result of losing her mother, and we all have different ways to show or hide or emotions. I would still try to go visit her on the weekends. Having the kids around her really seemed to help. She behaved better and loved to spoil us with her home cooking, and I just loved being somewhat close to the desert again.

Meanwhile Mike was dealing with the first gang-related shooting that happened in front of the local church. I had never heard of gangs before until now. This stirred up an outpouring of concern and worry for the residents of the city. The pressure was on the police department throughout the city and the officers on patrol were out to arrest known new gang members responsible. They formed the first task force to end this type of crime and violence. Newspaper reporters and all forms of media started arriving in the city to have live coverage on the murder on the doorsteps of the church. This shooting occurred during Mike's shift and it was as if he was out to hunt for bear. He wasn't about to let these gangs start up in his city under his watch and once he found the area where they lived, he started harassing them daily.

This started a new phase in not only my marriage but in Mike's life. It became his goal to eliminate gangs. He learned as much as possible about how they lived, ate and breathed. The gangs took notice of him, as he made sure they did. Mike came home from work boasting of how proud he was while laughing and bragging how he had the chance to make a dirt bag Mexican gang member's life a nightmare. He felt a sadistic pleasure in handcuffing one of the gang members while beating the shit out of him. When I would comment that handcuffing was not right, he would tell me I didn't understand anything and that these were the worst elements in society and they had to be stopped, that these types of gangs would be happy to run over a child and get out of the car to laugh about it. This created a visual picture in my mind that did indeed help me to understand the type of criminals he and other law enforcement were working against.

It wasn't long before I became even more withdrawn and found it more difficult to deal with life. When I told Mike how I was feeling he was very supportive and asked me to go to the local Catholic Church for counseling, and I complied. I confessed to the priest how hard life seemed to be getting for me and all I wanted to do was sleep most of the time and was feeling very depressed. It was never suggested I go to a doctor, but rather I should turn to

God to help give me strength during this time. I was asked to come back and see him in a week, which I did, and each week it seemed to get worse instead of better.

On two occasions when Mike was patrolling in his police cruiser, it was hit with bullets. The gangs were trying to assassinate him! This was becoming very serious now. One night while Mike was working the graveyard shift and I was home alone with the kids, I heard the sounds of someone walking around the house and shooting a few gun shots in the air. I immediately got Michelle out of her bed and grabbed the phone on the way as we crawled into Aaron's room and took him out of the crib in the dark, staying on the floor, as I held them both closed to me. Shaking and so scared that my children and I were about to be killed, I called 911, and soon the home was swarming with police, and Mike and I knew they had found out where we lived.

The following day another attempt was made on Mike's life, and it was then that knew I could not go on living like this. I went to the church and told them what had happened and how I was getting much worse instead of better, and later that day, the priest came over to our house and suggested to Mike that I get admitted right away into a mental hospital where I could get the help I needed. Michelle and Aaron were outside playing and came in to say they were hungry, so I went to the refrigerator and quickly gave them each some yogurt to eat, to quiet them while we had company. Later that afternoon, Mike and I decided that the best thing, in order for me to get well, was to check myself into a Neuropsychiatric Hospital.

CHAPTER 13
Search and Rescue

The daycare customers were notified I would be taking a few days off, that I wasn't feeling well. Our children went to stay with Mike's parents. Michelle, I'm sure, was confused by the goings on, while Aaron was too young to understand. Under the circumstances, due to the shooting attempts, with the gang members knowing where we lived, it was best the kids and I were removed from the house anyway. I felt blessed Mike's parents were always there for us. So I packed a small suitcase and off we went to Brea.

The Neuropsychiatry Hospital was a single-story building surrounded by large forests. It immediately felt calming. As Mike and I walked in the Admitting waiting room, it looked very clean and we didn't have to wait long, since Mike had called ahead and they were expecting us. A mature woman greeted us and asked me to fill out a questionnaire, while Mike filled out my personal insurance information. The questions on my papers were similar to these: Did I feel sadness, depressed in my mood most of the day, or every day, all day long? Did I feel a loss of enjoyment in the things that once were pleasurable? Did I notice a change in my weight? Did I frequently experience insomnia or the need for excessive sleep? Did I feel fatigue or loss of energy? Did I have feelings of hopelessness or excessive guilt? Did I have recurring thoughts of suicide? Did I have feelings of low self-esteem? YES was checked in every box.

Then there were the health questions: Did I suffer from mental illness before? Was I on any meds? Did I have any health concerns? A heart condition? (Yes, but Rock wasn't here to help!) NO was checked for each of these.

And on it went, page after page. When I finished with the papers and the woman started asking me questions, tears began rolling down my cheeks. I told her I did not know why I was sad. I did not know why I cried often and I did not know why I wanted to sleep all the time. All I knew was that this was not normal and I wanted to get help. I explained that I tried getting counseling through my church. I also went to my doctor who gave me pills for the ulcer in my stomach and Valium to take if I felt depressed. Nothing seemed to work and I was just feeling worse and worse. I told her I did not like to take medicine, even aspirin, and did not drink alcohol, that I did not believe in taking drugs to cover up the symptoms. I wanted to find out what was wrong with me. The priest suggested I come to this hospital to spend a week and hopefully get the help I needed.

The woman was very lovely and calming and said that they specialize in acute, atypical depressions with one-on-one meetings five days a week with the psychiatrist assigned to my case, and with my group psychotherapy counselors, I should feel better really soon, that the feelings of sadness and helplessness would go away, and I'd be able to return to my normal life. That sounded great to me and Mike felt it was also the right thing to do since the priest had referred me to this hospital and his insurance would help cover the cost. So he filled out all the important paperwork and was told to say his goodbyes since he would not be allowed to go beyond Admitting, that the hospital itself is completely private for protection of the other patients.

Mike said goodbye and told me he would be back tomorrow and each day this week and hopefully this time next week I could come home. The woman said she would make sure I was safe and well-cared for, but told Mike it would probably be best if he stayed away for a few days to let me adjust and work on getting well. They would contact him if any problem arose. So Mike hugged me and said to get well fast and come home quickly, that he Michelle and Aaron would miss me very much, as well as all the kids in my daycare.

I was given a room with two beds but on my first night I had the room to myself. I was taken on a tour and shown the beautiful large social room with different sections of tables and chairs placed throughout, where family and friends were allowed to visit once a week on Sundays. Hopefully by next week this time, I wouldn't need this room because I'd be home already. The dining room was set up buffet-style. No portion controls, just help yourself, which I knew I would have to watch since I still hadn't lost all the weight from giving birth to Aaron. There was a building adjacent to this where we could do crafts and psychotherapy games that our counselors would choose for us. We walked down the hallway where different rooms were filled with patients having group therapy. There were offices where you would go to meet privately with a psychiatrist. All in all, the rooms looked very clean, floors mopped, with no bad smells like a regular hospital. I was told a nurse would take me to my room and unpack my bags so everything I brought could be gone through. No razors allowed, or many other things I had brought along, due to the harm they could cause me or another patient. I understood that and didn't mind.

Soon it was dinner time. I was nervous to be in this strange environment, but all that mattered to me was getting well. As I sat eating my dinner alone, I could hear screams coming from down the hall. A patient had gone off the deep end, I supposed, but other than that outburst, I didn't hear many other sounds, at least not that first night, but in time, those sounds became a regular occurrence. The other patients seemed drugged, almost in a catatonic state, many sitting in the hallways, some talking to themselves. They were like a bunch of zombies walking around the halls with no place to go but in circles, since their brains had no idea what was going on.

After dinner, it was time for my shower, and then I was told to go to the nurse's station for my meds, to help me with anxiety, I thought. The nurse's station was behind heavy glass windows with a little slot where the pills were handed out. The nurse behind the glass gave me the pills and another nurse on the outside made sure I took them. I went back to my room and crawled into my bed, missing my family already but getting excited for tomorrow to come so I could start on my intense therapy, get well and go home.

The following morning when I woke up, I was helped into the shower. I was so groggy and had never experienced this complete feeling of being drugged before. This was a feeling I did not like although I could understand why others would. If you had something bad happen in your life and you wanted to make your brain stop thinking about it, this was the place to come. I was told I had a guest waiting to see me. I took my shower and went to the visiting area where Ed was waiting to see me. It wasn't morning after all, but late in the afternoon, three days later from when I signed in. I had slept all that time and didn't even remember getting up with help to go to the bathroom. Whatever pills they kept giving me over those days were so potent they took away all my memory. The same thing would continue for a few more days where I was awake but didn't have a care in the world. I had no recollection of Mike's visits, although he would tell me he had been there and we spoke, but I just couldn't remember.

By week two I started to remember going to my counselor's office for meetings. He started me with blotch tests and asking me many questions, always giving me tests. The group therapy meetings were never really about me very much since the others in the room spoke up much more than I, and really had some serious problems. I didn't find myself getting better and the drugs were keeping whatever was buried deep inside of me from coming to the surface. Each day seemed like the day before. Being as social as I was, I enjoyed making new friends and found most to be hospitalized here due to drug abuse or having been involved in some very tragic situation in their life, where they perhaps witnessed a murder, or tried to commit suicide, and they were being treated with shock therapy. On several occasions, in the middle of the night, I heard an alarm go off, meaning someone tried to escape and run out into the surrounding woods. They would send out search and rescue teams of staff nurses and security. When the person was caught they were put into solitary confinement, given tranquilizers, and days of shock therapy and other treatments for the deeply disturbed. It wasn't surprising to me that these patients stayed locked up in here for months at a time, never getting better. It was all about the money.

After seeing and hearing all the crying, the screaming, my only survival was escaping in my mind to Rock that one night, so many years before, on the beach in Monterey. I remember during one of my sessions of meditation, we were taught to find the happiest place in our mind and start visualizing, feeling, smelling, concentrating on taking one's self there. This was so easy for me to do, as I had been there in my mind so many times before.

I was given so many drugs that pretty soon I built up a tolerance to them and could almost function as a normal person. By week two, I began working on crafts. They had me make collages from magazines to show what I was thinking about. I was so proud of mine, all on fashion and makeup. I also enjoyed shooting pool, but it became gradually more difficult to hold the pool stick without shaking. I couldn't read books any longer, because the words were too blurry from the drugs. It was also becoming very hard for me to eat my meals. My hands were always shaking, a side effect of the medicine I was told. The medicine was making me feel better and I didn't seem to have a care in the world. I must be getting better and was certain I would be able to go home soon.

In therapy I would not show any emotions when talking about my dad, the loss of my grandmother and my silent hidden secret, the loss of Rock, who could never could be replaced by anyone else, and I would just have to learn to deal with that in my own private way; escaping through music of *The Sea*, where he could remain in my heart and soul forever. But the counselors did point out something of interest to me, and that was that a loss could mean many things. In therapy class, we were each given a note pad and pencil and told to write down if we had lost any pets, aunts, uncles, or friends. Did someone we were close to move away? Did we ever move from our home to another? And so on. When we each realized that each of those things caused some type of grieving, no matter how small the loss might seem to someone else, we would each deal with losses differently, and over time, they can start to add up, and one day something small can trigger all those suppressed feelings and have them rise to the surface. I had never spoken of all the losses I had had in my life. I lost track of how many times I had to move. But this session made me start thinking, and in my mind, look at what a long list of losses I already had at still such a young age. It made me cry myself to sleep that night. Just missing my high school friends alone when my family took me out of school, was a deep loss. I knew now why they made me start at the beginning of life, from my earliest memories, in order to try to solve the mystery of why I felt the need to be here.

The staff shared concern that I was incapable of showing emotions like anger, so they made me spend the day in my room making the bed with square corners, and then they would come tear everything up and throw the bed linens in a big pile and have me make it again, over and over, hour after hour, for the entire day, and they still could not get me upset. That alone troubled them because whatever was bothering me was so well hidden they couldn't get it to the surface. For me, it reminded me of what our soldiers would have to go through in order to become a stronger person, so I took it as a challenge of my temperament, and I did need to learn how to be stronger, to be a survivor, when times would get bad and not feel the need to sleep to escape.

I had a surprise visitor. It was my mother and my close friend Joe from the desert. Joe was one of my favorite friends who worked at our local grocery store in Desert Hot Springs, where Michelle and I had met him. Joe would hide in the refrigerated section of the store where they kept the milk, and when Michelle or I would go to get something out of the case, a hand would appear from the other side and try to catch us. We would be caught off guard and Michelle and I would shriek with laughter. He loved to hang out with Michelle and me and tell us funny stories. Mom thought he was just what I needed to help me get well.

As it turns out Mike never told my Mom what had happened to me and never would allow her any information during these past three weeks of my hospitalization. So my Mother hired a private investigator to search for me, who followed Mike, which lead him to the hospital in Brea. Since I was not allowed to make a call or have any contact my mother, she had been beside herself. How cruel Mike was to cause her so much concern and expense. But that is what he was really like. She was so happy to see me and I was so happy to see her. Both Mom and Joe noted that I had lost a lot of weight. I told her I was feeling much better and I felt I was ready to go home, that finally I had lost all the baby weight and was back to my modeling size for clothes, and would really like to have some new things to wear. Mike was very tight with the money. Even when I had a hole in my shoe, he asked me to go a little longer until we could afford new ones. When I questioned Mike during his visit later that evening, I asked him why he would do such a thing. He said it was because of everything she said to him when she called him while she was drunk and he didn't want her to upset me anymore. I suppose that could have happened knew it was entirely possible, but seeing her that day, and knowing all the trouble she went to find me, I felt blessed that someone could love me so much. I often believed that my mother didn't know how to show love, but this time she did a great job!

When Mike arrived the following night, he brought Michelle with him. When I went into the visiting room, I could see her through the glass window in the entrance area. But Mike would not allow her to come inside to see me. I cried so hard over how mean he was and the things he said to me about how my children needed me, of how I needed to come home, and he would not let me talk to Michelle until I came home. All I could do was look at her through the glass, putting my hand up to the glass, with her holding her little hand up to mine on the other side.

That's all it took for me to be determined to get out of that place. I asked the nurses if I could pack my bags. I wanted to check out in the morning. They told me I would have to wait to meet with my doctor and tell him my request to be released. The following morning couldn't come soon enough! I met with my doctor and told him I needed to get home to my daughter. He told me they were not ready to release me, that there was still more work to be done. I told them that I had checked myself in and now I wanted to check myself out, but was told that was not how it worked. I had to be checked out by a doctor, or moved to another hospital. And my doctor was not going to allow me to leave. It was going on four weeks. I finally started showing my anger.

Later that night after everyone had gone to bed, I was so angry, I got dressed and took off running out the door into the fields to try to escape to get back to my daughter. I hid in the dark behind trees. I planned to hitch hike my way to her if possible. But it wasn't long before I was found when they put the big spotlights on. I was brought back inside and taken to a private room where I was drugged again, and kept knocked out for the next couple of days. When I woke up, there was some crazy woman sleeping in the bed next to me, masturbating. I hadn't heard anyone come in, then later found she came there a couple of days earlier. Now, I knew I had to find a way to get out of this place! When Mike came to see me I told him I was ready to come home, but that they wouldn't let me come home permanently yet, only for weekend visits.

It felt like the best day of my life. Mike arrived early at the hospital, although he came alone. I was hoping to see my family, but he promised, not until later that night. He had the whole day planned for just the two of us. First stop was Laguna Beach, where he took me for breakfast and a walk on the beach, followed by shopping where he bought me a white crocheted bikini to show off my new slim figure, new tennis shoes and stilettos, dresses, jeans, tee-shirt tops, lingerie, cosmetics and more. He apologized for how he had been so mean, making me wear shoes with holes in them. Even though I was also working and bringing in money, he was in control of the finances, which in some cases, was probably a good idea, since I was never able to hold onto money very well. I would never try to get attached to anything that could be taken away from me again. The pain was too great. The same feelings went for all my personal possessions as well. Anything of any value whatsoever I will give to others. Giving away to help others, my form of buying love, seemed to work and make me feel great about myself.

The most important gift was sharing in my children's lives and getting home to them as soon as possible. Finally, it was off to home and time to be with my children, to finally hold Aaron in my arms while looking into the face of my sweet daughter. I did feel much better. I was more energized. I felt happy again and slept with both my children that night, never wanting to spend one second less than I had to without them. It was such joy, looking at them both, studying their sweet innocent faces as they lay sleeping.

I asked Mike to make arrangements to move me to another hospital since this one was never going to let me go, only wanting to keep me there for the money they could bring in. I insisted he find one that didn't put me on drugs. I wanted to come home and I needed a clear frame of mind. It took a few days but I was finally released to another hospital, Christian Therapy Center. When we arrived, it didn't look like a hospital at all. When we entered, it immediately felt very warm and welcoming. The woman who greeted us was filled with laughter and happiness and it made me feel good just to be around someone who was so pleasant. She explained that no drugs were given here except the ones my personal physician would prescribe in my case, Tagamet and low-dose Valium. They believed in the healing powers of God. The food served each day would be more plant-based, making me healthy for my mind, body and spirit, with exercise to help strengthen all of me. A Bible was given to me along with a prayer book. I would not be allowed to watch TV or read newspapers but was expected to have complete personal conversations with God as He would help guide me to become what He desired me to be. He would teach me to share with others. I told Mike goodbye, that I would see him the following weekend. I needed this time alone to get well so I could come home once and for all.

I was led to my room, down a U-shaped hallway that was all windows and doors that led outside to the pool, which was surrounded by flower gardens and seating areas for meditation and reading. The food was vegetarian and I started to feel healthier than ever before. We met with our counselors each day and mine requested that my mother come up from the desert and spend a few hours speaking with her about me. She also met with Mike. This therapy was much more intense than what I had previously experienced. They were quick to strike a nerve and bring up uncomfortable issues. Then they would have me read verse after verse together from a small book I was given, telling how me how I was never alone no matter how bad things might seem. All I had to do was call on God to give me strength. Then it was off to exercise in the pool, where it felt good to get some sun and exercise on clear days.

Here, there were no people walking around in a drugged state, and everyone supported one another. What a difference the place made! Had I come here first, there is no doubt in my mind I could have come home in three weeks or less.

What my mother told me after her long interview with them, was that the other hospital report said I was ill and had delusions of grandeur, as I would speak of my life in Pebble Beach, the referral to Jilly and Frank Sinatra, the Secret Service, and many more stories that seemed impossible, coming from a woman like me, married to a police officer. After the long interview with my mother, who explained that these stories were true, and going into the details of my father and his death, and how neither of us were prepared for his death, I started being counseled directly on my issues about death. After two weeks and feeling healthy in my mind, body and spirit, I was told I was going to be released. I was allowed to call Mike and let him know he could come pick me up.

I was called into the office for a long meeting and was told that at first they had followed up on the other doctors' reports and my delusions of grandeur condition, and after speaking with Mike and my mother, that they knew that this was not the case at all. They were able to pin-point that the real problem was not dealing with the death of my father and grandmother, and the fact that there had been three assassination attempts on my husband. I had to try to protect my children from gang murders, and it put me into a state of total helpless depression, and the only way my brain knew how to protect me was to try to shut down any unpleasant thoughts and suppress all feelings I had no control over.

It was advised that I first to speak to Mike when he arrived to pick me up, and let him know that it was recommended for right now that I do not return to the same situation and home living environment that could cause a set-back. If I felt the need for them to speak to him, they would be happy to do that, but I said no, I would tell him myself. Then they suggested I take a college course on death and dying or EMT, something that would help my feelings of helplessness in case of an emergency, and give me power to at least have some idea of what to do. It all sounded great.

When Mike finally arrived, I told him I had signed all the necessary papers and was finally discharged from this hospital, which really felt more like a beautiful hotel. I was free to leave and my suitcase was packed and waiting inside the office. But I needed to have a talk with him about their findings, and their suggestions for what I needed to do to assist in my complete and full recovery. We sat at a small table in the lunchroom and I told him all of this, and that I thought it would be better if I took the kids for a week or two to stay with my mom in the desert and not and come back so quickly to the home that would remind me of being in danger. It would give us time to find another place to live that wasn't in the city where he worked. I told him I knew it was my fault for insisting we move to Chino. These things would never have bothered me so much if I hadn't been so afraid of losing him to the murder of the gangs.

Mike said to me, "If you do not come home with me to our home right now, I will see to it that you never see your children again." With that thought and with that controlling attitude, I slowly reached for his glass of ice water and dumped it over his head. He got up and left the table and told me to find my own way home.

So here I was, checked out of the hospital, suitcases waiting by the door and not a penny to my name to make a call. So I went back into the office and explained to the receptionist what had happened and asked if I could use the phone for a short personal call. She felt very bad for me and gave me access to the phone and I called my mom and asked her to come get me. It was at least an hour's drive for her, but there was nothing in the entire world that was going to stop her from getting to me as quickly as possible. Thank goodness she had already visited and could find her way easily. I just sat and read my small handbook of prayers and knew everything was going to be all right, and just like the poem about footprints, I knew God had never left me but was holding me now to give me strength and help me to get to my children.

When Mom arrived and I explained everything that had happened she also felt it was better and safer for me and the children to come stay with her at least for a short time while Mike found new living arrangements for us. We drove to the house in Chino and Mike came to the door, saying the kids were not there and I was never going to see either of them again. I left and went to the police station where he worked to complain about his kidnapping my children. They advised me it was a civil matter and that I would have to work it out some other way than through the police department. Mom and I drove back over to the house so I could speak to Mike again to try to reason with him, and when we pulled up he took two large green garbage bags and threw them out on the front lawn. He said because Michelle did not belong to him, he didn't have any say over her, so he let her come out and get in the car with me. But he said I would never see my son again, and to never come around here again or I would be arrested.

So off Michelle, Mom and I went to the desert without my baby boy. At least now I had a safe place to stay and was reunited with Michelle. My poor mother, now taking in her daughter who only had a small suitcase of clothes, and her granddaughter, with two green garbage bags filled with her belongings. She made us feel right at home and said everything was going to be alright. At least we felt we were home again and safe. I just needed to find a way to get to my son. No one could keep me from him. Not even Mike, in spite of the control he felt he had over me. As Michelle and I lay in bed that night, we said our prayers, praying for Aaron to come home soon.

CHAPTER 14
Divine Intervention

You're kidding, right? I did not have a dime to my name. I had a small suitcase of clothes, Michelle, and her two green garbage bags of clothes, no car, no job, and had burst into my mother's life, who was drinking again after the loss of her husband and mother. Please just pinch me. Have me wake up and still be at the hospital.

I can't imagine why Mike would have threatened to take away my children. Was this a nightmare and was I still drugged? Would I wake up soon from a bad dream? I wasn't crazy. I had been very depressed and just wanted to sleep. I acknowledged something was not right. I first went to the Church for help, which landed me in that terrible place in Brea where they just wanted to keep me drugged and not get well, so a steady amount of insurance money would keep flowing in. Even when I wanted out, they wouldn't allow it, like I was actually crazy. Nothing could have been farther from the truth. What I had been through in my young adult life seemed to be overwhelming, and I didn't blame myself for just wanting to curl up in a ball. Knowing how all this started due to the love of a man, a man who was a musician, saddened me. The sound from his lips when he would even just say my name was enough to have my heart pounding out of my chest. And yet, here I was, just released from not one, but two nut houses. This will look good on my resume.

It really was a blessing to have found the Pomona Christian therapy unit, where drugs were not allowed and God was the healer. But I think if Mike could have handled it differently and allowed me to go to my mom's with the kids for a couple of weeks, it would have given us a chance to move out of Chino where he was working to find a safe place for us. That would have been the smarter choice. Looking back, I can see that his parents poisoned him against me. I'm certain they were constantly grinding it into him that he should not have married me.

But all that was behind me now. I needed to figure out, with all the odds against me, how to get my beautiful little boy back. I missed him so much while I was away and now that I was free, I had nothing except the word of God to help guide me. It was early in the morning and for the next two hours I locked the door of the bathroom and sat on the floor crying. I had brought the small prayer book with me and in between the tears I would try to read the daily prayers asking for help. I looked at the bottle of Valium and Tagamet on the sink and instead of opening the Valium to make life a little more bearable, I decided to take a walk before it got too hot outside. I walked only a few blocks up the hill when I noticed a Catholic church directly in front of me.   Morning mass was just getting out and the doors were open. When I was sure everyone had left, I went in and sat in the front pew. I knelt down, looked up at the statue of Jesus behind and started asking for help. Please Jesus, please help me to be strong when I am weak. Guide me to do the right things to keep my daughter safe and please send my son back to me. I must have spent an hour crying, but undisturbed, I slowly got up and walked to the altar and got as close as I could below the feet of Jesus and prostrated myself, arms outstretched, begging for help and guidance. I felt the presence of the Holy Spirit going through me. I rose up and walk out of the church and headed straight home. I walked straight to the bathroom and opened both bottles of pills and flushed them down the toilet. I knew I did not need either ever again.

I then went to the phone book to look up the number for a local attorney. I think there was only one that spoke to me and he was kind enough to see me right away. At the appointment, I explained exactly what had happened and how I ended up in the desert the day before and wanted help to get my son back, explaining I had no job or money, but that I would go immediately to search for some kind of income, and that I had a license to do hair. He told me that he was leaving on vacation at the end of the week but he would make a call to a colleague knew in Long Beach, if I could find a way to drive there. I said I was sure my mother would allow me to take her car for the appointment. He said he would get back to me. So I walked home to wait for the call. It was mid-summer, and I wasn't used to walking in the 110-degree temperature, but it wasn't very far and at least I knew I had done what I felt I had been directed by Jesus to do. Surely, He was looking after me.

The following morning I received a call from Mr. Meyerson's secretary saying he had an opening on Thursday afternoon at one o'clock and would that work for me? Work for me? Are you kidding? This was fantastic news! I might soon have an attorney to help me. I didn't know how I would pay him, but Jesus was doing the driving this time.

It was a two-hour drive from the desert but it was nice to be in the cooler climate in Long Beach. I hadn't waited long when Mr. Meyerson came out to greet me. He was a gentleman in his late fifties with slightly graying hair. He escorted me to his office where a tall younger man stood who was introduced to me as Frank. He shook my hand and pulled out a chair next to him for me. Mr. Meyerson said Frank was a new intern in the office and was sitting in on all his meeting that day. He asked if I would mind speaking with both of them. So I told them my story, explaining I had no job or money, but that I needed help with my precarious situation. Mr. Meyerson and Frank both took lots of notes about my case. When finished, Mr. Meyerson said he would be happy to take on my case pro-bono, and that we'd be filing for divorce and full custody of Aaron. Tears just poured down my face from gratitude. I was so relieved to know I wouldn't need to worry about how I'd pay the legal fees, and that I would get all the help I so desperately needed.

The papers were drawn up and sent to me for my signature, filed and served on Mike at work, which I'm sure came as a real shock to him, especially, knowing he left me with nothing. But he had forgotten about the power of The Almighty who I had come to know personally during my two weeks in Pomona. Mr. Meyerson suggested I find a job, any job, to show the courts I was working. I found an ad for a maid in a small hotel within walking distance of Mom's house. It wasn't a lot of money, and only five hours a day. Since I had no bills, that much money each week looked really good. My mom helped to buy me a pair of pants and a fresh white blouse to wear so I'd look good in my new maid position. She also bought me the most beautiful three-piece suit to wear to court when the time came. My mother really came through for me. She helped with Michelle and the two of them were always doing things together and found a special bond. At lunch time, my mom would have one glass of wine, then take a nap, and it never seemed to be a problem or concern. She knew she had to be strong for me and I think it made her feel great knowing she was needed.

It did not take very long to get a judge to hear the case, less than one month. When the day finally came I went alone with my two attorneys, which I'm sure, looked very powerful! I think Mike and his family were taken aback by their presence and wondered I how pulled this one off. I was alone, but Mike's parents came to support him. I wish I could recall most of the questions asked as Mike's attorney pummeled me at great length. Then Mr. Meyerson questioned Mike. Then Mike's attorney questioned his mother, then his father, and then they brought in the priest who had come to the house the day he suggested I go to the hospital for help. He told the judge that during the time he was at my house and speaking with me, I had been crying, and when Michelle and Aaron came in from outside and said they were hungry, I gave them a yogurt to eat when it was dinner time. (I was shocked to hear his version of this event! It wasn't dinner time! It was snack time!) He said he felt he couldn't help me any more than he had tried, with the sessions he had with me and I needed further professional help and why he made the suggestion I go to the hospital. Then Mike was questioned by his attorney about my mother and her drinking, and being in law enforcement, did he feel it was a danger for his son to be in that environment. Of course Mike said yes, and gave an example of a domestic case he had as a policeman. He also spoke of how my son Aaron would be living with not only his father but that he had moved back home with his parents, so not only would Aaron have his father, but also his grandparents, having a male and female influence on his life. They spoke about my not having an education and how Aaron's grandfather was an elementary school principal for many years and they would make sure he'd have a great education. Aaron's grandmother had quit her job and was now a stay-at-home-grandparent able to be there whenever needed. At the end of the day's session, the judge said the case would continue in two days and he requested that I bring my mother and daughter.

All I could do was pray and have faith that God was on my side. Mr. Meyerson had done a fantastic job of representing me. I felt everything that was said on my behalf proved me to be a great mother.

Very early on the morning the hearing was to continue, I received a call from Frank. He said that during the night Mr.

Meyerson had a heart attack and died. He said since the case was at one o'clock that afternoon, if I liked, he would be able to continue for him and felt confident that even if this was his first case he would be able to do his best representation for me. I was in shock to hear of my attorney dying the night before final argument, and I had never heard Frank speak, only take notes, but faith is what I had and now was the time to prove it, so I said of course. I told Frank that I knew he'd do a great job and thanked him.

I'm sure once Mike and family learned my attorney had died they thought they were going to win the case. My attorney called up my mother and they had a talk about my father dying and the recent death of her mother. They spoke about how she had the new house after moving from the Monterey Peninsula recently, and how we each had our own room, and that there was a school nearby for Aaron to attend. She spoke of how she enjoyed cooking and sewing as her hobbies and had been busy working on a new quilt. My mother's closest friend Elizabeth came to court with us for moral support and it was not intended, but she also ended up being questioned by Frank. Elizabeth worked for the local Catholic

Church and would also help to make sure that Aaron was kept in the same denomination, if that was wanted by the court. The judge then excused himself and asked to have my daughter Michelle brought into his chambers for a meeting. He spent about one half-hour with her and when court resumed, he said he would take everything into consideration and notify the attorneys of his decision.

It was a few days later when I received a call from Frank saying he had the judge's decision and wanted to let me know that I could make arrangements to pick up Aaron at any time and bring him home with me. The judge also went on to say that I should not be punished from realizing something was wrong and seeking help. He also felt that in time I would be making more money and in a higher position than Mike. I couldn't believe what I was hearing! Me! The girl that just got out of the nut house, with no money, no car, and working as a maid cleaning hotel rooms without air-conditioning in the middle of summer, dripping wet each day while walking home from work, will now will have her children! Thank you God!

I made the call to Mike a couple hours later to make arrangements to get Aaron. Michelle and I went to the grandparents' house and Mike came to the door holding Aaron and handed him right over to me. I must admit that Mike and his parents were exceptionally nice to me. I wondered if what they heard in court made them realize that I had the ability to be a great mother, and that the final decision for my depressed state of mind stemmed from the fear of the death of someone close to me, and from having suppressed all the losses, including the fear of losing Mike. He filled my mom's car up with everything that could fit. He would be getting Aaron on the weekends for visitation and would bring the rest of his things on Friday.

The next day I asked my Mom and Michelle if they would stay home with Aaron for a few hours while I went out to look for a job. I knew that in August not many places were hiring yet, but I needed to try to get a better job. I had huge responsibilities and was so excited to create a better life for all of us. Just the fact that the judge said he believed in me gave me the self-confidence to know I was going to do great things one day. I took my mom's car to the closest mall in Palm Springs where the main anchor store in the center of the mall was called Walker Scott. I went right to the cosmetic department near the entrance and I asked to be directed to the office. I rode up the escalator and found the gift wrap area and cashier and asked if they had a job application. A lady there said she was the assistant manager. They were not hiring in August, but I could fill out the application and she would keep it on file until the new season hiring starts. While I was filing out the application a tall nice-looking gentleman passed by and complimented me on my handwriting. I told him they aren't hiring now, but I want to be first on the list when they do. He introduced himself as the store manager and sat down beside me and asked about my past job history. He said he would love to have me in the cosmetics department but all spots were taken at this time. He asked if I would be interested in selling Junior clothes until something opened. I wasn't quite sure what was happening, but it sounded like I was being offered a job! He said it pays $3.50 an hour and would be forty hours a week. Plus, when a cosmetics department job opened, I would get commission on my sales. I was so excited and said, "Yes! Thank you so much. You won't be disappointed." I was to start the following Monday.

I could hardly wait to get home and tell Mom and Michelle the exciting news. How would I get to work and back? Mom needed her car. I had seen where there was a local city bus that went from our home to Palm Springs. I would have to check the schedule. I had to make arrangements for daycare for Aaron and Michelle. I couldn't expect my mom to handle all this. The local YMCA had a program Michelle would be able to go to every day and make crafts and swim and make new friends. There was a special pre-school program for Aaron who was going to turn four in a few months. I could walk to the bus stop and back only two blocks away. Mom could drop off and pick up the kids and everything was just falling into place.

CHAPTER 15

Resilience

The year was 1979. The Album of the Year was *Saturday Night Fever* and the top Billboard songs were *Heart of Glass* by Blondie, *My Sharona* by The Knack, *I Will Survive* by Gloria Gaynor, and *YMCA* by The Village People.

I felt I finally had my life back. I could breathe. I was able to get out of my toxic marriage and had custody of both my children. Living with my mom wasn't always easy, but she needed me and the kids as much as we needed her right now. I started working full-time, riding the bus each day. I actually enjoyed riding the bus. I'd see the same working people daily and the same driver and because it wasn't very crowded, we were social and I felt very safe riding to and from work.

I loved the job in the department store selling clothes to all the young teens, and it soon became the in-place to hang out and try on clothes after school. I enjoyed being a part of setting the trend for being the cool place to shop. I also liked the discounts I received on some very nice clothes, household items, and special things for my mother and children. But most of my income went into savings so I would have enough for a down payment for a car.

It didn't take many months before I was able to buy a small economical Chevy with stick shift, sunroof, and cassette player. My family was excited the day I came home, loaded everyone in, and off we went driving through town with the sun roof pulled back as we sang. This would be the first of many fun adventures, also giving us much more freedom. My mom loved it when she was included in family outings and loved being around young people. At home, I did all the cleaning and gradually completely redecorated her entire house to look fresh, light and bright with deep textures brushed on some of the walls, while others were mirrored to give a more open feeling.

Since my mother's close friend Elizabeth worked as the secretary for the local Catholic Church, my place of refuge on the day I flushed the pills down the toilet, I chose to attend church there with Michelle. Mike had Aaron on the weekends, picking him up on Fridays, returning on Sunday evenings.

I remembered what I had been told when I left the hospital. I needed to take a class at the Red Cross to learn how to do CPR and give myself tools to not feel so helpless in case there was an emergency, and to also learn more about the dying process. So I went to our local college and studied the list of all classes offered. I was really excited to sign up and take the class called EMT, Emergency Medical Technician. I had no idea I could take college courses considering I had never finished high school. It was a chance to go back to school without my dad doing my homework, and now that I was older, I seemed to crave knowledge.

No previous medical experience required. I got my CPR certification from the American Heart Association. I learned basic life support, how to make and use a spine board, and steps for medical and trauma assessments. I also learned how to make and use splints, how to stop bleeds, and how to treat diabetic, cardiac, respiratory, heat and cold emergencies. Plus I learned how to lift patients, use different types of equipment, and I learned about patients' rights, confidentiality, and filling out forms. I devoured anatomy and physiology, a very in-depth course to give me exactly what I needed to get well and never go back to such a dark place again. I had to do so many hours as a volunteer working in the hospital emergency room, the fire station and as a ride-along in the ambulance.

I really had come a long way. Now it was time to do my practical work in the ER where I had to spend my volunteer hours, helping to take vitals on new patients coming in. Some were ordinary broken bones, cuts, and sickness from flu-type illnesses. But occasionally we would get a gunshot or car crash victim with excessive bleeding. I would have to help apply pressure and try to calm the patient before the wounds could be tended to.

I soon learned the importance of what the "golden hour" meant, and how getting the right care from the right doctor in the quickest amount of time could make the difference between life and death. It was the care the first responders made before getting the patient to the ER that was critical. The hardest part for me was little children coming in completely traumatized with open wounds. Being in the ER helped me come to realize I was not meant to work in the hospital environment. Once the crisis was over and controlled, and I started talking to the patients, my emotions kicked in. That's when I realized I work best under stressful situations where the adrenaline is pumping, and I have no time to think, but remain calm and react as needed.

Next it was onto doing my hours working with the paramedics who drove the ambulances. I was the third person to ride along. In the front seats were the paramedic and an EMT, so I rode in the back where the patients would ride. At first it took me awhile to get used to not feeling car sick with the stuffiness, and smell of blood, vomit and other smells. But I suppose because my adrenalin would kick in the minute we were called into action, that I quickly got over it. It was the unknown of what you will witness the minute you arrived that kept you hyper and your heart racing. When we would get to a car accident the first thing was to do a triage to determine who was hurt the worst and needed care first.

I assisted and comforted patients in the back of the ambulance as the paramedics were in conversations with the ER doctors, giving patient information and being directed which IVs to begin to help keep the patient alive until we arrived at the hospital. I loved everything about being able to work under the pressure of not thinking about the personal interaction with patients but the actual emergency work of saving lives.

My dream was to get so good at this that I automatically knew what to do and could react quickly. It was a very powerful feeling knowing I could help in case of a real emergency with my own family or friends, should one arise, and to be able to react and keep my emotions in check.

My third and final practical hours were at a fire department. I thought it would be easier if could do my hours close to home. The minute I got off work I drove straight to the fire station and asked to speak to someone in charge because I needed to do some practical hours so I could get certified as an EMT. The fireman I was speaking to looked me up and down and smiled as if to say, really? You, in your high heels and false eyelashes, want to be a fireman? I'm sure that was what he was thinking. All right - show me what you've got. The man who greeted me said his name was Captain Rod Phillips and he would like to help me. (I just bet he would, laughing to myself) He went on to explain that this was a volunteer-run station. I asked how the volunteers know when to respond to a call and he said the volunteers have a device which is signed out to them called a Plectron. When the alarm goes off in the fire station it also goes off at your home at the same time. If our volunteers are available they will write down the address the dispatcher gives, and dress in the appropriate clothes for the type of call, get in their personal cars and drive straight to the location, most times quicker than the engine can get there. You take training classes each week until you finish learning what is required to be a fireman. The captain also said they currently have ten volunteers including two women, which was very unusual since women were not known primarily to be firemen. While the Captain was explaining things, the alarm went off and he asked how I would like to take a ride in the fire engine and observe what happens. Sure, I said! So he replied to the dispatcher and copied all the information given. He helped me up into the beautiful big red fire engine with my high heels and all. My adrenaline kicked in, and I was filled with so much excitement and anticipation about what would come next as the huge garage doors opened and we pulled out of the driveway with the sirens blaring, sounding the alarm to other motorists to pull out of the way and let us through to get to the emergency. This call was a car accident on the main street in town. The captain asked me to remain in the engine and observe and we would talk later.

Upon arrival, I observed a car had run into the wall of an unoccupied building. No one else was around but a few witnesses. As the captain quickly left the truck to go check the victim, a few more cars pulled up to the scene with what must be volunteers. They helped grab the first-aid kits from the fire engine and one started taking the patients vitals, while the other helped direct traffic as the local sheriff pulled up to assess what had happened. I watched the volunteers help get the victim from the car, onto the gurney and put in the ambulance. The vitals had been given to the EMT who passed them onto the paramedics who communicated with the ER doctor Once the patient was started on IVs, the EMT got in the driver's seat while the paramedic jumped into the back with the patient.

It was from this one observation that I knew this was my calling and I wanted to learn everything possible to start saving lives. I could see how working in this field would not only help me in lifesaving skills, but I could actually make a big difference in the community where I was now living. I could hardly wait to get home and tell my family.

Certified Emergency Medical Technician

Now, onto becoming a fireman! Since women didn't belong in this field yet, I, along with the group of two powerful women in the volunteer group of men was about to use the term "firewoman" for the first time. Here I was, a very feminine woman who wore skirts, silky blouses and high heels and never left home without false individually applied eyelashes, working daily selling cosmetics, doing makeovers on women, teaching them how to apply eye shadow and lipstick, a shock to most men to even think of a woman like me able to handle such a job. I was a female version of Clark Kent! But thanks and gratitude to the captain, who believed a woman was capable of making firefighting history. He was a pioneer of women coming into this field. It was hard, and not just a little hard. It was physically back-breaking hard work. As a woman you had to do twice as much, never complain and prove yourself over and over again. Certainly never have them see you cry. I found the captain would rarely let me out of his sight, and always made sure I was protected, wearing the safest gear. If he caught any of the men speaking badly about the women, he asked the offenders to come into his office he would speak to them about respect. The captain definitely took women under his protective wing and made us feel respected.

I was constantly learning new emergency procedures working with hazardous materials, operating apparatus and equipment, maintenance of equipment, public relations, and of course, how to fight a fire. There were weekly volunteer training classes and tons of paperwork to study nightly. The training was grueling and physically exhausting. I was happy I had established a healthy study pattern for myself, and my family knew I needed quiet time at the end of the day. My Mother was a huge help, always having a hot meal prepared for us with and home-baked bread. When I walked in the door, the aromas were most welcoming after a long day.

I had to always be self-motivated and focused on saving lives and property and it was the adrenaline pumping through my veins that saved me. I was so busy concentrating on what to do and react to the situation that I never had time to think of the person or feel their pain. I needed to give them the best I was able to give. Often times that meant watching people die in front of me, and sometimes they were already dead when I arrived and I'd try and try to resuscitate, giving mouth to mouth and chest compressions. I also learned how to operate the Jaws of Life, a giant "can opener," or very powerful "scissors," to help extricate a person from a car. I will never forget the first time I was issued my uniform and took the oath of a fireman, promising to demonstrate concern for others, a willingness to help those in need, and the courage to perform the job's duties. Then I was handed my badge to pin on my uniform. I was officially a trained volunteer fireman, as well as a certified EMT, who had studied and practiced long hours to reach this goal.

It was time for celebration at home. My family was so supportive for me and they loved it when the captain would come by unannounced in a fire engine and park it in front of the house, and come in for a visit with my family and me. Mom would always make him something good to eat or a nice cup of coffee. Mom adored the captain as we all did. We were in awe, I suppose, of this real-life hero

One night there was a call of a structure fire. I jumped out of bed, pulled on my turnout clothes and wrote down the address of the call. My mom, Michelle and little Aaron three years old were at the door waiting for me to leave the house. Mom had my hair brush and Michelle had my lipstick, handing them to me quickly as I left the house. I handed my mom the address of the call. They were able to listen to the scanner, to what was going on at the call. When I arrived, I was one of the first to meet the engine, and had to grab the fire hose and try to create a firewall of water between the house and the carport where I needed to prevent the vehicle in it from exploding. Windows were breaking from the pressure of the fire. We would call these intense heated fires "a real ripper." We were told an elderly woman was inside with her dog. I was allowed to be the first to go inside and do a search. As we got the door opened far enough for me to crawl inside at ground level, I felt the body the body of the dog, charred and lifeless. I picked him up and carried him outside and laid him by the fence surrounding the house. As I looked up, there was my mother, son and daughter, standing outside their car watching me. I'm sure with the home totally on fire they were feeling many emotions of how proud they were of me, how frightened of the danger I was facing, and learning from others watching that someone had died inside. The woman was unable to be saved. The call came in at about midnight and mop-up was not finished until sunrise. The old woman was found dead in her chair, apparently having fallen asleep while smoking. The cigarette must have fallen, causing smoke inhalation, and that explained why the dog died so close to the door probably trying to get to fresh air. My family left to go back home once the fire was under control, but I did manage to go give them all a big hug, even if I did smell like smoke. After a fire, I always had to take off my clothes in the garage where there was a robe waiting for me. Every inch of me smelled like smoke. Time for my shower, get a couple hours sleep, and get ready for my day job looking well-turned out and ready to make my customers look beautiful!

CHAPTER 16

He Deserved Better

Aaron was becoming very emotional and was crying a lot. It was very typical of a little boy of three. If I went from one room to the next, he had to go with me. If I went to the bathroom, he would scream and cry at the top of his lungs, kicking the door. The screaming was a shrill sound that would go right through me, making me want to pick him up to comfort him, even though I knew I should let him have his tantrum. He was very demanding and I understood it was a difficult age. I knew that with all my schooling and hours at work, that when I was at home, he deserved everything I had to give. Michelle spent hours playing with him and tried to entertain him after school until I got home. Mike came on the weekends to pick up Aaron, but when he would return him on Sunday nights after a weekend of fun with his family, Aaron would cry and carry on for his father and reach out for him, and I was forced to close the door so his dad would be able to leave. I kept remembering the court case and how I was able to win custody of Aaron, but was I really the best choice for this little guy? Mike was living in a nice home with his Mother and Father who had great values, integrity and loved Aaron as if he was their own. If I let Aaron live with them, he could have a complete family with a male and female influence. All his needs would be purchased instantly. I would always have to wait for my pay check. His grandfather who was an elementary school principal would see to it that Aaron received the best education. I thought of how I lived with my Mom, and Michelle, trying my very hardest to just make ends meet. This went on and on in my mind, when finally I told Mike that as much as I loved having Aaron with me full-time, I had made the decision to give him custody. It seemed the right decision for my son. I would be the one to have him on the weekends and give him that quality time filled with nothing but love. When it came down to it that was what I could offer my son. Unconditional love from a mother to her son, that no one could replace. Mike and his family were thrilled I would do this, even though Aaron had been awarded to me. I did not feel that I had failed. I knew I was doing what was the best for my son. So from that moment on, Aaron lived with his dad, and his grandparents. He would be getting a really great education, going to church each

Sunday, making friends, and getting to spend each weekend with his mom and sister. He had the best of both worlds. He would become totally loved and provided for.

I loved my weekend visits with Aaron. My son and I would do something different together each week. We enjoyed going to the park, swimming, or just watching cartoons together. It didn't matter. What mattered was having quality time instead of quantity. I spent so much time with Aaron, my work and volunteer work that I started feeling I needed to also be doing more with Michelle so I signed up at Michelle's elementary school to be a Girl Scout leader for a junior troop. I wasn't sure exactly what to do, but I knew I needed to start spending quality time with Michelle, and what better way to do that but to get involved in something fun? Girl Scouts become self-confident, strong and compassionate. The girls were taught to respect themselves and others, make good decisions, be open to new challenges, and to use their talents to make their world a better place. Michelle would learn to build strong friendships, be a leader, and put her values into practice in her everyday life. The best part was on the weekends when we had special events I could bring Aaron with us and he could be surrounded with lots of girls just spoiling him. A win win situation for us all.

A dozen signed up and just getting to know each girl separately and as a group was fun. I started out having them earn a badge in cooking. In order to pull this off, I needed to call in the help of the captain at the firehouse. I asked if on Tuesday evenings for the next few weeks, my Girl Scout troop could use the kitchen to cook dinner for him and the volunteers along with the mayor and city council. Of course he said yes. How could he refuse one of his own? I set up a meeting with the editor of the local newspaper, Chris, and told him how involved I was in helping the city. Chris was also a very charismatic gentleman, much like the captain, and had a smile that lit up a room with a personality to go along with it. During every event the girls were involved in, he was going to have the newspaper photographer there to take a picture and do a story. He said that this town needs a Sharon in it to make it special. With words like that, any lady would be flattered, I'm sure. Chris had one of the most beautiful wives (inside and out).

It wasn't long before the Girl Scouts became known in the city. The paper ran stories with photos each week of them doing special events to help others while earning the badges. The dinners and the cooking badges were earned without anyone getting ill. The fire station grew in volunteer turnout each week as the meals became announced. Soon there was a car wash to raise money, and of course, it was held at the station so the picture in the paper was all the girls climbing up on the engine washing it with Michelle wearing my turnout jacket. My volunteer work as a firewoman, a Girl Scout Leader, a mom and a full time cosmetic sales person was really keeping me busy.

Sometimes the calls at the fire station were just plain funny which made up for the more tragic ones. I was working at the station one Sunday when the alarm went off, Man Down - it was at the local gas station. The captain was the driver, and I was standing up on the back of the engine holding on as we went code red, sirens blasting as we went down the streets. As we pulled into the gas station and saw the victim lying on the ground. The ambulance pulled up just about the same time. The captain jumped out and went straight to the victim as I got the bag with blood pressure cuff and chart to document the readings. I kept hearing the captain asking the man what had happened and the man kept saying he ate poo. You ate poo? The Captain would ask! The victim was put in the ambulance for drug testing and then whisked off to hospital to determine if he was insane. I have to admit that when the adrenaline is flowing, and you think it's a real emergency, then you find a druggie saying he just ate poo, it's hard not to laugh about it when the call ends!

The Captain and I also went on tragic calls, too, like the one where a man had skin cancer, but the cancer had eaten away half of his face and he was dying. It was an image I will never forget. The captain and I discovered we had become very close and found comfort in each other that no one would understand unless they lived through it. That is what started to happen between the Captain and me. When you share emergency work and what you see is almost unbearable, it is your co-workers who then become your support system. No one else could begin to imagine the feelings and emotions that you go through. A silent bond is created, especially for someone like me who never saw a dead person till my Dad. And now I was seeing bloody death from accidents. Watching people die in tragic ways is very difficult and we formed a special bond. The captain and his wife were separated but they remained very close friends due to their children and grandchildren together. He had never wanted to file for a divorce because she would get half of his retirement. So they had both chosen to live their own lives with her dating and him dating with no mention of divorce.

After six months the Captain told me he was falling for me and that he had just moved closer to me rather than living a half hour away. I was surprised in a nice way since Michelle, Mom and Aaron also were becoming more and more attached to him as I was. Rod rented the biggest guest suite at a nearby hotel which had two bedrooms, a full kitchen, and large living room. He didn't want to mention it to me until he was moved in. I had never mentioned the story of my court case and how this hotel was where I had been a maid one summer, so I had to smile when he took me to show me his new place.

I had been doing very well at my job and the money was helping me to provide for my family, but now I felt it was time for change. I was at the top of sales in the cosmetics department, and Robinson's Department Store had their eyes on me, hinting that if I was interested that I should contact them. Some of the cosmetics companies I represented also had accounts at Robinson's and I started hearing more and more chatter about how I should go apply for a job over there since it would pay a lot more money. I had gotten so involved in my emergency work that I almost felt that was the direction I should go in. But what if I could sell cosmetics part time and also do emergency work part time. That would be really nice to have income doing both jobs that I loved. So not only did I take the job at Robinson's but I also took a job working for the local ambulance company.

I gave a two week notice at the fire station since my free time would even be more limited now. The captain always had encouraged the volunteers to spend the night in the fire station, so we would be quick to drive a rescue truck while the county paid fireman drove the engine. When I would find out what nights the

Captain was sleeping at the station they became the nights I would volunteer to stay in and drive the rescue truck. We were to bring our sleeping bags to the station. Our beds were the sofas in the living room. We put our sleeping bags down and brought a pillow. And just like at home, when the call came through we would jump into our turn out gear or wear our uniform to the call. I always wore a white t-shirt and brought some shorts to sleep in. Which I'm sure drove the Captain crazy since I didn't wear a bra to sleep in under the white T, and I once had caught him out of the corner of my eye watching me as I took off my uniform slacks wearing only my panties as I put on a pair of shorts. He, on the other hand, had his own bedroom/office with twin bed. It was for the Captain or the paid person on duty. On this one special night when he was in his room and I was getting ready to crawl into my sleeping bag, I heard my name called. I went to see what he wanted even though I had a feeling he wanted the chance to kiss me under some false pretense. He said, he wanted to know if I needed any extra covers since it was a little cold. I said that would be very nice and he held out his hand and took me into his bedroom. He asked if I would mind if he kissed me and I asked, "What took you so long?" He pulled me close to him for some long passionate kisses. I knew where this was leading and I wanted sex as much as he wanted to give it to me. I told him I didn't think it was a good idea we did it in his room. What if we were caught? He took my hand and led me out to the garage. He said I have always wanted to do this. Captain Rod Phillips helped me climb up on top of the fire hose bed at the back of the engine. This turned out to not only be exciting, not uncomfortable and filled me with a wild sexual adventure, just knowing the alarm could go off at any second. I needed that sex. I needed everything about it. It made me feel not only good physically but mentally and helped to give back that feeling of being a desirable woman after the past few years of living a nightmare.

Early one Sunday morning the alarm at home went off announcing a drowning victim and location. CPR had been started and every second counted. It wasn't far from my home so I quickly pulled on pants and my uniform shirt and out the door I went, praying it wasn't a child. I was the first volunteer to arrive with the ambulance coming in right behind me. Other volunteers and the engine would soon follow. It was a man in his sixties, very overweight, pulled from the hot tub after an apparent heart attack. I started mouth-to-mouth on the man and soon another volunteer started the chest compressions to help me out. After a short while the gurney was wheeled over and the man was loaded onto it with CPR continuing. A large crowd had gathered since this occurred at a hotel hot tub. I happened to look down at my shirt to see if I had tucked it in and came to find I had not only not tucked it in but hadn't even taken the time to button it! Black lace bra for the entire world to see! (Thank goodness this wasn't during the time of cell phone cameras!) When I asked why someone didn't tell me, one guy said we thought if the guy was revived he would take one look at you and think he had died and gone to heaven. So as embarrassed as I felt, I couldn't help but laugh and smile each time someone would call me "buttons" the rest of the week.

The only brush fire I was asked to go on was in an area close to San Bernardino where a plane had crashed into the mountains. The captain was in charge of a team and he asked if I would be interested in going for the next twenty-four hours, that it would be good money paid by the state. I would get a chance to see what it felt like to be on the fire lines and how to get an idea of the flow of our system. I was home from work so off I went, and for the first time I was away from home and the family would not hear from me for the next twenty-four hours. But they were excited for me. When I arrived I was given a tour and immediately the battalion chief in charge had me placed in the command center which meant I would not be fighting fire out on the lines at all, but instead would be working inside a large trailer that was fully set up as a command post. It would be my job to write the statistics down on paper, photocopy them, and deliver the information, while driving a big truck along the fire lines, handing out the current information as to weather report, loss of life, structure losses, and any other important information needing to be shared. This was before cell phones so direct notes worked the best.

At night it was very cold and I was shivering so hard that for the first time in my life I could say I actually drank a full cup of hot coffee to warm my body up. I had never tasted coffee before. They had a bonfire at fire camp for warmth, with tables, big barbeque grills, steaks, potatoes and stick-to-your-ribs-type food was being served to all the firemen coming off shifts on the fire lines to eat and get a few hours' sleep before going back out again. I was given a paper sleeping bag and slept on the ground. I must admit it wasn't bad at all and it really did keep me warm the entire night. The following day I awoke early to a big harvest hand-type breakfast (as my mother would have called it) with steak, eggs, potatoes and biscuits. Then I grabbed a sack lunch and hit the road with the crew. By then, they had finally been able to reach the pilot killed in the crash. Most of the fire had been contained and by 4:00 P.M. that day, my twenty-four hour shift was over and I went home. That was my first and only chance to fight a brush fire and I didn't get the chance to do anything but hand out flyers and follow all the current statistics as they happened.

CHAPTER 17
Buttons

There has been a few times when my EMT skills came in handy personally. Like the time Michelle and I went to pick up Aaron for his weekend with his Disneyland Mother and sister (as Mike would describe me, since we only had quality fun time). Each week when we picked up Aaron, there was always the protocol I had to endure; come in for a few minutes to visit and get Aaron's things, then fifteen more minutes of talking at the car. All I wanted to do was get my son and drive back home. But this one night was a little different. Mike was in good spirits and asked if he could take us down the street to Coco's for a little dinner before we drove back, and I agreed and Mike led the way in his car with Aaron and Michelle in my car. We came to a stop light and right along the right side of us in the soft shoulder area, came a speeding car, bumping into many cars along the way, then turning right, going up a street into a housing development at full speed. Neither Mike's nor my car was damaged, but this was a hit and run driver and Mike, even though off duty, decided pursue the vehicle. His cop instincts took control.

We followed in the dark and when we came over a hill and spotted Mike's car we pulled up right behind him. Across from him was the hit and run car with the driver sprawled out on the asphalt, face down, his hands outstretched. Mike's car door was open and he was kneeling on the asphalt with his gun pulled on the man. He called to me to tell me to have a neighbor call 911, to tell them that an off-duty police officer had a hit and run driver down on the ground and to send the ambulance.

I then saw where blood was pouring out onto the asphalt around Mike. He said he had been shot. I took the white "Members Only" jacket that Michelle was wearing, locked the car doors to protect the kids and ran quickly to a couple standing outside watching what was happening and they said they had called 911 when she heard a gunshot go off. I then ran close to Mike, and then crawled, lowering myself to the ground so I wouldn't get shot in case this man rose up from the ground. I could tell Mike was in big trouble and there was no time to be wasted. I quickly wrapped the jacket around his leg, not too tight, but enough to help me control the bleeding. It was taking forever for the ambulance to arrive, but the sheriff arrived, taking control of the scene, while Mike told him exactly what happened.

It seemed Mike was able to get the car to stop. As he was pulling his badge out to flash the guy with it, he also pulled out his gun, which got caught on the door handle and he accidently shot himself. The hit and run guy heard the gun shot go off and hit the ground not knowing Mike had been shot. He thought Mike had shot at him so he wasn't about to move. Finally the ambulance came, loaded Mike and took off. The kids and I went back to the house to tell Mike's parents what had happened. They quickly got in their car and we followed them to the hospital ER. Waiting for word on Mike's condition took forever. The kids told Mike's parents the entire story of what happened. Finally the doctor came out and said he was going to be fine. The bullet had gone in one side of his leg and out the other. The doctor said I had helped not only save his life, but his leg. My children were so proud of me and even Mike's Dad had to say thank you along with his mom. There were days of recovery and I made a couple trips back up to check on Mike. Knowing what to do in case of an emergency paid off and I knew I would no longer feel helpless when it came to emergencies.

My last week working as a volunteer had me reflecting on some of the hardest calls I had, most having to do with infants. There was one when a baby was not breathing and I took him from the crib and started baby CPR while holding him. But the baby was already gone, and in spite of it, the driver drove as fast as possible to get to the hospital. This one was due to the parents being unable to afford to see a doctor when their baby caught a cold and it suffocated from mucus build-up. Another baby died from crib death while the babysitter was in charge. It couldn't have been prevented, but I'm sure to this day they blame themselves. It was always difficult for me to bring someone in who had already died and was pronounced dead in the ER. Then the family might come in their own car, following the ambulance as quick as they could, only to learn the fate of their loved one. I often saw these families with the looks of shock and disbelief on their faces, knowing that their brains would now take over and the natural protection of shock would set in, helping them deal with the inevitable.

When I started working for the ambulance company I was always partnered with a man, although there were two other women working for the company. The men treated me like a guy. It was a rough existence with twenty-four hour shifts, often sleeping in the ambulance in the middle of the desert somewhere in between calls. In Indio or Palm Desert, they had a small office with a bathroom but no shower, and a bunk bed so we could crash there. The guys didn't care if I was female or not and would sleep in their boxers, while I slept in my uniform pants and at least was able to take off my uniform shirt and sleep in my bra and tank top. They were respectful. Being an EMT, I was always placed with a paramedic and learned quite a bit on each call. It was so much harder than being a firewoman. There were terrible car accidents, suicides, murders, and many other types of calls I had never been on.

The worst I saw was when we were the first ambulance on the scene of a school bus accident. The bus collided with a big rig on Highway 86 (known to this day as" Killer Highway") and we saw dead children lying on the ground and could hear the sounds of children crying in the bus, and asking questions about their siblings who were also on the bus. We quickly did a triage, figuring who had a chance to live. When all the other emergency service workers showed up, in my eyes they were the angels coming to help. We loaded four very badly injured children into my ambulance on beds resembling bunk beds, and off we went while many more ambulances were coming to get the injured the help needed as fast as possible. The highway patrol closed the highway, covering bodies with sheets. One of the four children in the back with me kept asking questions that I couldn't give an honest answer to, but kept giving her hope. I knew her brother had died at the scene. This became known as one of the worst school bus accidents to ever happen in California.

Along with working for the ambulance company, I knew my bigger income would come from selling cosmetics. Joining Robinson's was a huge pay raise for me. I was given top lines like Clinique and Borghese, and major fragrances, and on each of those lines I made good commissions each month. Even though I was part-time I was making double what I had been making before. My Girl Scouts were doing well. I was seeing Aaron each weekend and brought him to all the fun events so the scouts could all spoil him. My mom was happy and the captain visited her sometimes while I was at work, just to check on her and Michelle. He asked Mom if she would mind if he brought Michelle and me to live with him, explaining that he was busy working out a plan where he could offer us a good life. Behind my back this was all settled. Michelle was excited because where we were going had a big pool, where she could have her friends come over. But for me, it meant that soon I would have to move again. Whew! I really didn't want to leave the one home where I felt safe and secure, but I also realized I had to try one more time. Maybe if I just pretend he was Rock? "If you can't have the one you love, then love the one you're with."

CHAPTER 18
Love the One You're With

The Captain

Moving in with the Captain was fun; Jacuzzis each night after a long work day, barbeques and pool parties with friends coming over. It made for a great social life. With his magnetic personality (especially under the influence of alcohol), other volunteers, Girl Scouts families, or friends made along the way were always welcome. Soon after moving in with him, I noticed his excessive drinking. He confided in me that he used to come over to visit my mom and had a bottle of whisky hidden in the garage that only he and my mom knew about. They would also have some beer for a chaser. No wonder she loved him and they got along so well! They had become best drinking buddies! We still went on a few calls together, but that soon ended when I started working on the ambulance and didn't have free time for volunteering any longer. When Aaron came on the weekends he was always excited because the captain always paid special attention to him and would often take him to the fire station. I'm sure, without question, he made an impact on my sons life.

I started not feeling well, with cramping and heavy bleeding during my periods. All the heavy lifting was not helping while working my shifts on the ambulance. It was no longer the call going off in the fire station, jumping into my turnout clothes and rushing to the back of the big red fire engine, climbing on while holding onto the bar on the back of the engine as we went code red down the streets to accidents, fires or medical aides. During those calls, my adrenaline was high and it could help me lift anything. But working for the ambulance company was completely different. I was sent on daily calls with no code red. I will never forget the non-emergency of a three-hundred-fifty pound man on the second floor who had to go to go to hospital for some testing and couldn't drive, so we had to load him onto the gurney and take down a flight of stairs. Just getting him from the bed to gurney was hard for me. At this moment my wanting to be Linda Carter as Wonder Woman ended. I do not know, to this day, how I didn't drop him. Fear of killing him from the fall, I suppose, gave me the strength. In any case, all the heavy lifting couldn't have been good.

I went to the doctor who told me I needed a hysterectomy. I was told I needed to consider giving up the ambulance job because I would not be allowed to do the heavy lifting for a few months, if ever. I went in and had the surgery, but since I do not take any meds, I didn't do well on morphine, and it turned me into a werewolf hollering at the staff, which was out of character for me, but nevertheless I was told I wasn't very nice. Later, I was told, I even made some calls, one to Mike asking him to pick me up and take me home, which I guess the captain stopped right away. I was to stay in the hospital for a week, but that was soon shortened to a few days. I just wanted to get out of there, and was driving everyone nuts, I'm sure, so I was released before they had to put me in a straight jacket. The captain took responsibility to give me the care I needed.

Upon arriving home I found the apartment filled with flowers and special gifts. I couldn't stand up straight. I went straight to bed. In the middle of the night I awoke to the sounds of a woman moaning. I got out of bed and literally staggered into the living room where I saw the captain and the landlady in charge of the hotel in a mad passionate embrace. I said nothing and went back to bed. The following day after the captain left for work, I got busy on the phone making my plans to leave.

As crazy as it sounds I never felt anything. I never got angry. I knew I had to pick up and move on. The truth was he had never been in the center of my heart and could never be. He was fun, but only another time-filler of my life. I think I was always trying to fill the empty feeling, the void. I found a small single story motel room for Michelle and me to move into. They rented out by the month at a price I could afford. It was a studio complete with kitchen, dining room, living room and swimming pool right outside our front door. The captain moved everything I needed, and we always remained on speaking terms. He taught me a lot and I am forever grateful. Our time spent saving lives and the special bond of friendship can never be broken. I had already learned that if they hurt me, just smile, wave and walk away. I started forming a pattern of everything being disposable. Don't hold on too tight or have much faith in another person. They will only let you down. Just move on and don't look back.

If I wanted to do something or go somewhere and didn't want to depend on a man I would be creative. Take for example, the New Year's Eve concert at the Palm Springs Convention Center, in the heart of downtown. The event, "Rockin' the Night Away," featured Sonny Bono, Dion, The Mamas and Papas, Donovan, and Jan and Dean. I wanted to go to that so badly I could taste it, but tickets for the sit-down dinner were expensive and I wasn't about to go solo on New Year's Eve. So what to do? I got to thinking… they must need servers! So I called the Convention Center and got appointment for an interview. I convinced them that I had years of experience waiting tables and serving drinks and they believed me. I got the job! Not only would I be paid by the hour but I would get a percentage of the gratuity paid by the twenty-five hundred persons attending. The uniform was easy, black pants, white blouse, and they provided the cummerbunds. Sonny Bono had just opened a restaurant in town and there was speculation he was going to run for Mayor. Jim and Tammy Faye Bakker were in the front row. Sonny introduced his daughter Chasity and they did a duet together with Chasity singing all her mother's parts in the Sonny and Cher medley. I wouldn't have missed that night for anything. I managed to serve drinks with no problem, luckily, since I was assigned to the tables in front of the stage. I was able to make a few hundred dollars in tips and watch the show up close and personal. It was a night to remember!

I started going to my favorite gay bars to dance the night away, so I never had to worry about any fake pickup lines. By this time I had learned Palm Springs was nothing like Monterey. This is where men came, gave a girl a line, flashed a rolled up wad of bills, and these silly girls fell for it every time. I used to have fun playing right along with them, thinking they had it made, telling me their planned and practiced lines, then saying "bye-bye, this is on behalf of all those you have played so many times before." The funniest thing was that the next time I ran into the captain it was at a gay bar. He appeared to be having the time of his life dancing with a girl he brought along. I think that was one of the things I loved best about him. No prejudice against anyone. He had a good heart and was a kind soul. He still had some wild playboy left in him. My not drinking may have cramped his style.

It was really a good thing that I learned how to be strong when it came to life and death and after all, isn't that what my doctors in the hospital had suggested? Learn about death and dying. It is a natural part of life. The bad part for me was feeling like I lost my softness, my feminine side. I rarely cried or showed much emotion because of mastering the technique of suppression. I was now feeling as if someone could die in front of me and I could take care of the body without the slightest emotion.

My secret to not feeling emotions was to escape to Rock's music in my mind and to that one unforgettable night with him the night he gave me my most cherished gift of *The Trilogy*, including the vinyl record album, *The Sea*, and the song, *While Drifting*. It is always playing in the background of my mind, constantly bringing the feelings and emotions, that would live on and on, after all the others had gone away, my time-fillers as they are known to me now. It had been years since I moved from Monterey. How could one man have affected me so deeply that I turn to him so often, sometimes daily? I loved that Rock was still bringing pleasant thoughts to my mind, knowing it was impossible to see him again. I wondered where he was now. Performing all over the world? Or just in my mind? I could only dream of him, make secret birthday wishes to him, and have a vision of seeing him at the end of my rainbow one day. Thinking of Rock was the only pain medicine I had for my heart and soul. If only I could find someone who had enough edge to them, enough of something different to offer, that it could help me focus on them instead of on Rock. But in the meantime if I can't be with the one I love, then …

The Preacher Man

The Lord must have been preparing me for the future, for when I would need the strength to handle the worst of situations, but for right now I needed to forget death and sickness and get back to living. The man who really stepped up to show support for me was Chris. He said if there was anything I needed he would be right there to help, especially if it was Mom, who he had come to know and share a few stories with. His wife had Bible classes at their house each week and she invited me. I loved the idea of sharing Bible stories with the women, while the men went into their own room doing the same study. It was special bonding time for all.

The mayor and his wife also attended.

It was time for me to return to work. But this time there was an opening at a high end specialty store named I. Magnin. It was only two weeks after surgery but I needed to start making some income again. I was given the job being a full time cosmetic sales associate. Standing on my feet for eight hours was at first difficult especially since we needed to wear high heels. But I managed, and started to make really nice money, more money than I had ever made. It was 1980 and I had come a long way and lived in many locations, not only since the day I was born, but since I moved to the desert. I had lost track of how many moves I had made.

I was able to move us out of the motel, but let me first say, that motel room was a lot of fun. As long as Michelle and I were together with Aaron coming on the weekends, life was very nice. With our small sleeper sofa and a swimming pool outside our door, we didn't need any man to lean on for any reason. The scout troop would come over for a swim and picnic and we truly enjoyed ourselves.

Chris called and asked if he could come over to talk to me. When he arrived he told me he had accepted a very big job at a large Church in Orange County. The service was to be broadcasted every Sunday. He would be the personal administrator to the pastor, while at the same time training to go into the ministry himself. He and his wife would be moving during the next few weeks. He told me how much he had come to care for me and that I could expect calls from him because he wanted to stay in touch with me. He also said his relationship with his wife was friendly, but not romantic; that it had been that way for years (isn't that what they always say?). He told me he found me to be very sexy, inspiring, motivating, and exciting. He kissed me goodbye and left. Now I have to admit, I was a little smitten. Chris had a very powerful personality. When he spoke you wanted to listen. He was a brilliant man who had graduated from college at age seventeen. During the 1960s he was one of the top ten radio personalities. With his distinctive voice, I really enjoyed listening to his stories of when he used to have a PR management company. Chris had managed one of the top #1 music groups of that time. So off he went, back into the world of the rich and famous. The newspaper editor gig was apparently just a way of keeping busy while taking a break in Palm Springs where no one knew him and he could have something of a normal life. But Chris enjoyed living life large and this temporary gig was just that. However, his newspaper really did contribute to the huge growth spurt in the small city that no one would likely realize unless they lived there during that time. This area was a well-kept secret where the Hollywood elite could escape to namely the hidden spa resort of Two Bunch Palms.

Several months went by when I received a call from Chris. He wanted me to bring both of my Girl Scout troops, the junior troop and my Angel View Crippled Children's Girl Scout troop to appear on television for a special day devoted to the disabled. Of course we will, I told him. He made all the arrangements through the children's hospital. It helped that they knew him as the editor of the local paper, before his new job. He gave us a song he wanted me to teach them. The other scout troop would wheel the Angel View scouts up on the stage. A special bus would come to pick us up and we would be spending the night before there, with dinner at a five-star restaurant for all of us. It was a dream comes true. The

Angel View girls mostly ordered steak; most saying they had never had it before. I suppose in the children's hospital everyone is on a very restricted diet for calorie control due to limited amount of exercise that get do. But for this very special occasion, bring on the crème brulee! The following day I wasn't to be involved at all, except coordinating the girls, who was to do what, where and when. A half-hour before the service, Chris came to me and told me he wanted me to go up on the stage and lead the girls in their song. Keeping in mind that I sound like Minnie Mouse when I speak and have never been able to carry a tune, I looked at him, in this huge house of worship seen on television in front of millions all over the world, and I said without hesitation, "Yes." It was a moment all of us involved will never forget. God filled my soul. I had no fear, and it went off flawlessly. It was so real, so unrehearsed and heartfelt. It was seen over and over again during the years in reruns since it affected so many people and reached into their hearts, and I'm sure, their wallets. The newspaper clippings, some of which I still have, will remain among my most treasured belongings. I loved being a special part of it. Helping to inspire people and turn their scars to stars. When we were leaving,

Chris told me he knew what I was capable of doing. I just didn't know my potential myself.

This was one of the last special events I was able to do with the Girl Scouts over a two year period of time. I now had to start focusing on work and making a better life for my children. As the years would continue the only time I heard from Chris was when he wanted to talk sex as he was calling me from his desk in his very prestigious offices. Later years he became a pastor himself.

Life had its bumps in the road but we were okay. Michelle and Aaron were doing really well and we were having a great time together and I was able to move us once again. I was now able to manage a large duplex with Jacuzzi, and my only responsibility was to make sure the Jacuzzi was kept clean, and make sure the room next door was rented.

CHAPTER 19
Don Juan's Green Card

Within 6 months I was promoted to becoming a cosmetic department manager. Jill, who was my Estee Lauder sales person, said she was planning a girlfriend weekend getaway down in Baja Mexico at the resort town of San Felipe, and would I like to join her and some other girls. I said, "Yes, that sounds like lots of fun." I asked if it was Tijuana, close to San Diego but she said no, it was a small beach community off the Mexicali side of the border. It was a four hour drive and we would stay in a lovely hotel, right on the water, and the water was warm for swimming. Food was inexpensive and the weather amazing.

The drive down was so easy, smooth, and a straight 2 lane road. It took two hours to drive from Palm Springs to the border town of Calexico, connected to the Mexicali crossing; leading to another 2 hour drive of straight stretch till you started seeing views of the Gulf of California (Sea of Cortez) in the Mexican state of Baja California. What a short drive to end up in such a different world. I was fascinated by all of it. The small population catered to tourism. An international airport served the area. At times the population can increase by as much as 5,000 due to the presence of Canadian and US part-time residents and vacation home owners.

Upon arriving at the hotel, we were greeted with doors opened wide, leading into the massive lobby, filled with fresh cut flowers. After check in I walked to my room, through beautiful walkways lined with rows of bright red colored hibiscus flowers, and a luscious green lawn. I looked out over the Olympic size swimming pool, complete with full service bar in the center covered with a canopy of palm leafs to protect the guests while sipping on their fresh frozen margaritas. On the other side of the pool were small steps leading to the beach filled with sun bathers. I could hardly wait to get to my room, unpack, and head to the beach. I was looking to bask in the sun, swim in an ocean filled with 70 degree water. Fresh shrimp were abundant since this is how this small town survived through selling these large kilos to tourist as we would head back home when the weekend was over. Being without Michelle and Aaron felt a little strange and I could hardly wait to return with Michelle. Mike wouldn't allow me to take Aaron into Mexico, but I knew this would be one of Michelle's new favorite places.

I was transported that weekend to a secret hideaway, a safe haven. No sense of danger, loving people in the shops, restaurants, on the beach. The staff catered to us like we were royalty. Music at night was in a nightclub on the property, complete with hanging disco ball. The girls from work and I danced the night away. Freshly tanned, toned from swimming, and rested, we hated to leave our new found paradise in San Felipe. Once back home I looked forward to each time Michelle and I would continue the trips to San Felipe. Michelle was turning 12 soon and she loved it as much as I did. I always allowed for a girlfriend to come along so Michelle had someone her age to do things with. The three of us would go into the town shopping at the rows of little trinket shops filled with souvenirs. The girls loved to buy fireworks, because each night after dark the beach always had families showing off the day's purchase of rocket ships, sailing through the air sending off bright lights of color, sparklers and Michelle's favorites a little box called "snaps" that she and her friends would throw in the hallways and snap on the cement walls creating a loud pop then run fast as not to get caught.

We always requested the same room on the second floor, the last room on the end that had a full open view of the ocean. Each morning early in the day around 6:30am, the tide resedes almost as far as the eye can see. We were able to walk far onto the same sand that within hours would be filled back up with the ocean. We looked forward to the early morning walk, picking up bags of sand dollars during our weekend jaunts. The manager of the hotel, Ernesto and his wife Sara became like family. They always made Michelle and I feel like we owned the place. I completely understood why. During the day, Michelle and her friends would get go to the hamburger shack on the property and order the daily hamburger and fries. Total bill would be $4 for both girls. Michelle would always leave a five dollar tip, larger than what they had ordered. When I would get the bill at the end of our weekend stay, I always had a few surprises. But compared to what this type of luxury in California would cost, this was inexpensive. We would bring my Mom down to San Felipe with us sometimes, and she loved to sit on a lounge chair, under a thatched hut in her bathing suit with hours of reading material. She loved to read the current gossip newspapers she picked up at the news stand as we left town. If she wanted anything brought out to her, Michelle would place the order and a handsome young man would bring her drink and food on a silver tray. She would always tell me it was some of the best times of her life.

Michelle and her girlfriends loved to go ATC riding on the beach. Michelle even fell in love for the first time at 12 years old. She and her girlfriend were flirting with two boys while out on the beach having ATC races against them all day. One night after the fireworks, Michelle asked if she could stay out another ½ hour by the pool before coming upstairs. I said sure, it was dark but still early and on this most special of nights for my daughter she had her first kiss. Michelle wasn't the only one to fall in love in Mexico. I also started flirting during the last several visits with the hotels food and beverage manager Bert. He was at least 15 years younger and always went out of his way to make me feel special.

He had that Latino gigolo charm. He would see to it we got seated before others when we entered the restaurant. He would come over to surprise us with free desserts to win Michelle and her friends over. On Saturday nights the disco was open with a DJ, so Michelle, her girlfriend and I would love to go and dance. Bert would come out and dance with us all. Laughing, dancing and singing along to the music. For me, finally, I didn't have a care in the world. Having a wonderful job, living in a tropical Mexican paradise on the weekends when I could get away and now finding a man who didn't know me. He didn't know where I lived, where I worked, and sincerely seemed to care about me when I walked out of the water in my black swimsuit, no makeup and no façade. He just liked me for me, I thought to myself. He also made Michelle feel special with all the attention. Of course at that time she was also high on love.

Bert never inquired about my past loves and I never offered to reveal. After all these years, finally someone found value in me the real me without knowing anything about me. When summertime came, Michelle and I looked forward to taking my two weeks' vacation in San Felipe. She could bring her girlfriend like always and we would have the vacation trip of our life. Always staying in the same room, when we checked in this time there was flowers waiting and a love note. From the first day on I was wined and dined. Fresh flowers were picked each day and left at my door when I opened it in the morning. Bert had my undivided attention for two weeks and if he set out to capture my heart he did. All I ever wanted was for someone to really love me for me, romance me like Rock did so many years ago. It might be Mexican music playing this time around but I love music and new sounds would bring newness into my life. After two weeks Bert asked me to marry him. I was shocked. I know we lived 4 hours apart and it would require us going back and forth for a while, but I'm such a hopeless romantic, I decided to say yes. Well, when I did you'd think they entire hotel was going to celebrate. We would have singing, dancing, tequila and love. The hotel manager Ernesto and his wife Sara were going to watch the girls for me while Bert and I slipped away to California to get married in the courthouse in El Centro, CA. two hours' drive there and two hours back. A wedding party was being planned for our return later in the day.

But as luck would have it a large storm came in during that four hours and the road to travel was too dangerous due to the flooding and we would have to stay in Mexicali for the night. We had a difficult time reaching the hotel to let them know where we were and Michelle and her friend were to be watched by the management. I'm sure this must have traumatized Michelle being without me during a storm in the hotel alone with just her and her friend. But the second day light came the following morning we would head back to the hotel. It might have been my wedding night, but I couldn't enjoy it because I was separated from my daughter. We had a nice dinner, a glass of champagne and since I had never slept with him before, this wasn't the time to consummate this marriage now. It was too stressful being separated from Michelle. Bert was fine with that.

The road was washed away in one spot but I managed to go around into the hardened sand and get back as fast as I could to Michelle. The minute she saw me she was so happy. I got to hear all the exciting adventures the girls shared with me about the storm. Now the sun was out and all these girls wanted to do was get on an ATC and ride the beach, going boy hunting I would imagine. Later that night the hotel staff gave Bert and me a big party with cake they made and lots of dancing and celebration. I stayed in a separate room with the girls than my newly married husband, but I did manage to sneak away long enough to have some sex time that was disappointing but I figured it must be due to the alcohol from the celebration.

Once we returned back home Bert didn't come back with us. He was planning on catching a grey hound bus to arrive in Palm Springs in two weeks and spend a few days with me while we decide what to do to make this marriage work. My co-workers at I. Magnin's could tell my excitement when I returned to work with the news of the wedding. The manager of the store and all the associates chipped in for the best wedding party that could be thrown at our local Mexican restaurant. Bert arrived and got to see where we were living, got the entire desert tour. He had already met my mom and she was so happy to welcome him to the family. The store associates at the big party greeted him with open arms and we danced the night away. We were serenaded by mariachis.

That night there wasn't a sad face in the crowd. This was a celebration that finally I found someone who loved me.

We continued over the next two months taking turns to come see each other. One evening after work I called and the operator at the hotel called his room and a girl answered. She handed the phone to Bert and I said is that a girl with you? And he said yes, there were two girls in his room. I told him I didn't think this marriage was going to work if he still wanted to be with other women and he said, "You didn't think I married you because I wanted to spend my life with you. I married you because I wanted my green card." I'm sure we can work something out when you come to visit me this weekend. He had to go then and ended the call.

I did drive down alone the following weekend and he was just as wonderful as always to me and as I sat across from him I told him I would need to get a an annulment and he smiled and said I'm sure we can work something out. I told him I never wanted to hear from him again. I was so desperate to end this marriage that I went to Aaron's father Mike and told him the truth of what I had done.

He immediately contacted his lawyer, who got all the information that was needed from me and because it was international law, no annulment was allowed and it took 6 months to process the paperwork to make it legit. Finally, I could put just one more mistake in my life behind me. I already had trust issues with men and as much as I wanted to believe and trust, I would from that time forward have a wall up to protect my feelings. The hard part was the low self-esteem. I would rise above this when I went back to work and joked with my co-workers at how stupid I was. They laughed with me and life went on. It felt good knowing I never shed a tear but would I ever trust anyone again?

CHAPTER 20
Cosmetics

Working at I. Magnin in Palm Springs will always be one of my favorite jobs. They taught me great customer service which I still use to this day. I was given the counter manager job selling Clinique and the very high-end line, La Prairie, along with some fragrances, including a new one that was just launching, "Oscar de la Renta." My personal favorite fragrance of the time was "Joy" by Jean Patou, then, the most costly perfume in the world. We were given many samples and large full testers. These companies knew how to take care of their sales staff! When a rep came into town they would always take us out for either a beautiful lunch or dinner, wining and dining us, while they would talk about how to grow the business.

I was responsible for a huge percentage of sales in that cosmetics department and I knew how to do all the tedious paperwork. But I also loved working with the customers. I was trained by the toughest cookie in the cosmetics industry, "Miss

VV." In the very beginning, when Revlon and Max Factor were the rulers of the industry, it was VV who believed in a woman named Estee Lauder and she put her products in I. Magnin, and the rest is history. If you were a company wanting to get noticed in this industry, this was the woman you needed to know. You sent her extravagant gifts, bought her furs and trips around the world, just to get prime locations at one of the counters. How all that works is a completely different book in itself... so maybe another time.

As for now, I was trained by the best. I had an amazing staff of sales associates and I spoiled them like crazy, always sending them home with goodie baskets of testers and samples. We also had fun contests and created special events for them to invite and entice their clients to attend. We became very social together. Meeting at nights, sometimes for dinner, for no reason, but just because. There was never any bickering because they all got along so well. Richard was a very outgoing personable gentleman that was the Chanel counter manager. Oh my goodness, did he ever make us laugh! He had a partner whom he lived with who was very conservative, but we called Richard the floozy of our group because he went to the gay bathhouses to get it on with all kinds of other men. He always joked about it… at least he couldn't get someone pregnant! In 1982 Palm Springs had one of the highest populations of gay men anywhere in the nation. Richard did things that shocked us; things that as women we would never dream of. He was just a little tramp and proud of it! Richard had followers all the way from San Francisco, where he used to work, who would come to see him whenever they were in town. His stories of his escapades gave us belly laughs each and every day. Eventually, Richard started to not feel well and this continued to get worse and worse. He was diagnosed with AIDS. We hadn't heard much about AIDS before that, but knew it was an epidemic that was spreading throughout the gay community. Richard was one of the first one hundred persons to contact this supposedly contagious disease.

They placed Richard in a hospital room that was completely isolated. Only his partner and I, and one of his closest customers came to see him. Everyone else feared of catching this from him. We were made to put on a disposable bodysuit, hair-cover, gloves, booties and a facemask, looking like something out of the Twilight

Zone. There was no question in my mind whether to go see Richard or not. I would never have left his side during a time when true support and friendship was needed. I watched him become a skeleton of just bones and flesh very quickly. I held his hand and told him what a beautiful a place he was going to. I read him Bible verses and he would pray with me. I assured him that I knew God loved him, because he loves everyone that has faith in Him. It wasn't long, a matter of a couple of weeks, when by the grace of God, Richard went quietly to sleep and that was the end. But I do hope to see him once again… that cute little tramp.

I needed not only to run the business, but to help sell on the floor. Our store had the highest percent increase in sales in the company. I attributed that to knowing the stock and getting the right stock mix we needed for our customer base. Back in those days ordering was not done by computers… we didn't even know what a computer was. All orders were done by hand in stock-keeping books that had pages and pages of items that required a hand-written count of each piece in the store.

I.Magnin used to lay off most of the cosmetics sales help for a few months each summer. That year I had them take vacations, but no lay-offs. I also made sure we had stock and started to do some great special events with lots of handwritten invitations sent out to customers who stayed in town, helping to build up the largest client base of cosmetics shoppers in the desert. We continued with that high percentage of increased sales all summer. When it came time at the first of the year to do inventory, we had a great one. We had good sales and good inventory and that made for a very happy store manager.

One Christmas Eve I was waiting on a handsome Italian gentleman who had come in to buy his wife some perfume. I asked him to tell me about her and he said they were "semi-separated" but still on good terms. While asking about her personal style, he said she was a very strong outspoken woman. They were both from New York and he introduced himself as "Vince." I gave him a few fragrances to choose from and he chose the one-ounce bottle of Opium. I gift wrapped it, and it was obvious to me that he was flirting. There was definitely some chemistry there, but I didn't want to be involved with anyone who was married. I wasn't into any more "time-fillers" at the moment. He left the store but later that night when I was on the road heading home, I noticed a Rolls Royce riding along next to me, not an uncommon occurrence in the desert. We came to a stoplight and I looked over and it was him! He motioned for me to pull over and I did. He wanted my phone number but I wouldn't give it to him. I told him if he was ever single to come look me up and home I went. The following day he had his Rolls waiting for me at the back door of the store to give me a ride to my car which was parked two blocks away. I once again turned him down. The day after that I was not there but had heard he was faithful and was waiting. When I came back to work Vince was there again, this time in an Excalibur, but I turned him down. The following day he didn't come but had a chauffeured limousine waiting and I accepted the ride to my car. There were roses inside with a note that said he won't give up. He went all out, sending me roses at work, doing everything possible to get my attention, never failing to be there waiting in an exotic car of some type. I learned he owned a vintage car dealership, hence, all the fancy cars. This went on for a couple of weeks when finally I started to allow him to drive me to my car. Vince said he was in the process of getting a divorce and he wanted to start taking me places, but explained he didn't want problems with the money settlement, that no kids were involved with the divorce, but he wanted to see me and keep our relationship quiet for now.

I waited another couple of months before giving out my home number. When I finally did, you would think I gave him the key to the city; at least he felt he had the key to me. He bought me expensive jewelry, diamonds and gold. Anything Michelle wanted, all she had to do was tell him and he would buy it for her. That wasn't unusual; men always tried to get to me by buying things for her. We laugh about it even to this day! Get to the daughter and you stand a chance of getting to the mom. He often took us out for dinners to an Italian restaurant in the small town where we lived since he knew no one would likely recognize him there. After spending time getting to know him I was starting to become more involved and I found myself willing to try one more time to find happiness. With all the attention he was giving to Michelle and me, and how well he got along with my mother, it seemed like a safe risk to take.

He told me the divorce was almost final, and said his wife had moved out of their home. She had gotten a new place just as nice. He was living in this huge house and invited me to come over to spend some time with him. I knew he had a romantic rendezvous planned because when I arrived the candles were lit, the fireplace was burning. The home tour included appetizers and champagne served poolside. Once I had a couple of glasses of champagne in me he decided that now was the time to make his move to get me into the bedroom. I was ready to take this big step, and even if it was for just a night of great sex without me being emotionally involved, I could do it. I could slip away to Rock in my mind and imagine it being him, if needed. Vince, like all the rest were not Rock, but maybe this time I wouldn't have to close my eyes and I could have a chance of actually being a couple with someone who really cared about me and wanted to spoil me with all the material things I never wanted or needed. Somehow perhaps, I could relax and enjoy. I did the whole seduction thing of slipping off my pink St. John knit dress, letting it fall to the floor, with just my pink lace bra and panties showing as he grabbed me around my waist telling me how beautiful I looked, lowering me to the bed, passionately kissing me from head to toe while removing the lacey items.

Then Vince heard his wife knocking at the door and jumped up, threw on some pants and went to the door to stop her from coming in and finding me there. Here I was, naked, and there was this huge fight going on with her accusing him of having someone in their home. Since she was trying to force her way into the house with Vince trying to hold her back, I didn't have time to get dressed, so just grabbed my clothes and ran out to the living room. As I hid under the bar counter top in between the bar stools I reached up and grabbed the phone. I called the police and told them about the fight, that I was hiding under the bar naked and I needed them to break up the fight and get her away from the house in order to give me time to get out of there. Well, needless to say, not one police car showed up, but several. They broke up the fight, had her leave, and came inside offering me a hand to help me get up off the floor, as I held the clothes, panties falling to the ground, I had to bend over to pick them up since I knew they sure weren't going to help! I made it to the bathroom with my naked backside in full view, as the talking stopped for a moment. I quickly dressed, combed my hair and made my last appearance of the night, as I vanished out of sight hurrying to my car. I doubt his wife ever did find out what happened that night.

Vince started an apology campaign, sending me all kinds of gifts, but it really wasn't a big deal for me to be naked. I was raised loving the human body and all its beauty, but was more embarrassed for him as a businessman, and in a small town where you knew these cops were going to start talking. I enjoyed the gifts, although what I loved the most was the sincerity of his heart. He moved Michelle and me into a beautiful two-story condo that had a balcony overlooking the entire desert floor. The view at night was filled with the twinkling lights of Palm Springs. He was paying the rent and although he didn't live there he wanted me to know his intentions. Vince often spoke of being raised in New York. He loved his mom and dad back in New York, who had been married many years. He had a single sister still living at home with his parents. I would make huge basket s of perfumes and cosmetics all shrink-wrapped and ready for him to mail to them, since he told me he had told them about me and they were looking forward to the day they we would meet. He would always tell me how much they enjoyed the gifts. One day I received a call from him saying his father had died and he had to leave to go back to New York and prepare for the funeral and take care of things. When he returned a few weeks later he asked me to fly to New York and stay with him at his mom's home. I had never been anywhere like that so that was going to be a really a special trip. Mom would watch Michelle, and work allowed me some vacation time for the week.

It was a long flight from LAX to New York City, but there I was ... In the Big Apple. Vince gave me the best sightseeing tours. I had never eaten a White Castle hamburger so that seemed like a big deal. He took me to Little Italy for dinner and I found that to be one of my favorite places, especially since it reminded me of the food Frances and Jilly would make in their kitchens. It also reminded me of the slang and the way Jilly spoke to his fellow Italian brothers. Vince's mom and sister were still shaken from the death, and my compassion skills came in really handy, as I enjoyed my one-on-one time with them in the kitchen. I did not sleep in the same room as Vince and it was never even an option. Instead I was given a tiny room on the top floor. It was a three-story town house that appeared straight out of *West Side Story*. It made me want to stand outside and start singing *Tonight*.

Vince was planning on taking me downtown to Broadway for front row seats to see the musical *Cats*. I felt like the day couldn't get any better. When I was ready to go I had a few moments free to visit with Vince's mom and sister while Vince was out running an errand. I mentioned the baskets of perfumes I had sent them. They had no idea what I was talking about. I told them about how I made these beautiful gifts and Vince said he sent them and how much they loved them and how they couldn't wait to meet me. They told me they had never heard of me before and was still a little uncertain who I was and why Vince brought me and why his wife didn't come. Wife? They said yes, she was just there with Vince for the funeral. I was so shocked I couldn't speak. There was no sense in my telling them what a rotten lying cheat he was. Instead I excused myself to go to the bathroom, still shaking, thinking what should I do? I was so far from home with nowhere to go, and didn't know a soul in New York. I needed to go home.

Now!

When Vince arrived he was all ready to go to the theater and I didn't say a word when we walked to the kitchen to kiss his mom before we left, and she and his sister wished us a great evening. When we reached the foyer, I said, "Your mom and sister just told me you are still married and you brought your wife here with you two weeks ago; that you slept in the same room together." Then I hit him in the stomach as hard as I possibly could and walked out the door. It was just starting to snow. Vince was still in shock from what had just happened. I suppose his worst nightmare had come true. He followed me down the street and insisted I get in the car and we go to the show, and give him a chance to explain. We did end up going to see *Cats*, which I absolutely loved. The night was filled with apologies and the next day he arranged for us to fly back to California. It was starting to snow much harder and wouldn't you know, the flight was canceled and we were sent to a hotel, compliments of the airline, until we were cleared to fly. So Vince and I were together in a hotel room. By now the shock had worn off and I realized he was just another time-waster and I would make mad passionate love to him, but it wouldn't really be him I was making love to, but Rock. This time I was using him for sex, instead of the other way around. No bad feelings, no bad words, but time to say goodbye and move on.

Chapter 21

Beverly Hills Here We Come

How would I break the news to Michelle? Upon returning from New York with Vince, I knew I would have to move again soon here we were, where Vince had taken care of most of the expenses. At this point I knew I never wanted to have anything to do with men again! They must all look at me and see an easy mark; "She'll fall for anything. She will give me her heart, and I can step all over it, chew it up and spit it out just for fun." It would be best for me not to trust men any more. I needed to concentrate on what in the heck I was going to do now. Please don't tell me I have to move us back home with my mother again; the poor lady was always rescuing us. Luckily she could laugh with me at all my adventures, and she never tried to make me feel bad about myself quite the opposite. She taught me that I could do anything, and that something better was always ahead.

Work was going great. At least I had a job that I loved. We might not have a roof over our heads soon, but I had a job, thank

God. So it was back to work as usual, with co-workers asking how my New York City vacation was. I try never to speak badly of anyone no matter how much the pain hurts my heart, so I just said it didn't work out. I wasn't the one for him. No one ever brought it up again and I refused to look back. That's the way life had always been for me. God has carried me through the tough times and He never failed me. I just needed to keep the faith.

I was called into the store manager's office and was offered a job to be the new cosmetics manager at I. Magnin in Beverly Hills! It was the second largest store in the company, San Francisco being number one. It was where the very rich and famous shopped. There would be thirty to forty sales associates in the cosmetics department alone. I was used to only ten in the Palm Springs store. I thought to myself, Wow! God, you did it again; you've given me a job with enough salary to help give us a new start. The company was paying for Michelle and me to take a week's expense paid trip to Beverly Hills to look for a place to live. This, too, was perfect timing. It was during the summer before Michelle's sophomore year, so at least I didn't have to take her out of school. Since I would be working in Beverly Hills, I wanted to make sure we found a place to live within the school district so Michelle could go to Beverly Hills High School, which was within walking distance to my work. Michelle and I checked into our hotel and I got all the local newspaper ads and we started hunting. The first place I called was on North Hamilton Drive, one block east of La Cienega, close to the corner of Wilshire Boulevard. The apartment was just what we were looking for: a one bedroom and bath, comfortable living room for a sofa sleeper to accommodate Aaron's weekend visits, a dining room, and a nice kitchen. The rent was affordable, and for us, it was the best location possible.

1984… What a year it was! The Olympics were to be held in Los Angeles. Fashions were all about GUESS or emulating Madonna's look. The top billboard songs belonged to Madonna.

Michelle started school and I started my first day on the job. The store manager held a morning meeting in the cosmetics department to introduce me to all the new salespeople. I have to admit, I was ever so nervous. There weren't many smiling faces and most had prima donna attitudes. I knew right away this was going to be a tough crowd to please. It would be a challenge just to learn their names and the cosmetic lines they represented. I was given an open to buy dollar amount and had all the vendors coming to me to write their orders. That was much to my advantage, because I was able to get them to create special in-store events that other stores didn't have the chance to do. I would have the major companies like Lancôme, Estée Lauder, and Clinique give morning breakfasts where they would cross-train everyone in the department to sell their products, not just the ones she represented. Friendships were built and it wasn't long before we started having fun together and I felt I had won over the divas!

Our store was always chosen for personal appearances whenever a new fragrance came out. Hubert de Givenchy himself paid us a visit. Max Huber, the creator of Crème de la Mer, used to come over to the apartment and hang out with Michelle and me, bringing us his miracle crème, having us taste it each day and rub it in our eyes. Saying it would help us with better eyesight.It was loaded with vitamins and healing properties. He was just a friend, but he would take me to the finest places to dine in Beverly Hills. I learned a lot from him, and he definitely showed me the finer things in life, not because he wanted to impress me, but because he was just a beautiful man who enjoyed life, and had I been open to it, he might have wanted to share a life with me. He was right there in front of me and I didn't even see it! He could have been the right one!

The only man I actually got interested in was Chris, who called me out of the blue and asked to take me to dinner. He was staying in town for the night. We had a wonderful dinner, like two old friends, and he confided in me about some unethical things going on at the church, and that he was in a difficult place trying to make the best decisions. His integrity was being tested. He turned to me as a sounding board, because if nothing else, we could always confide in each other.

On the weekends I would go pick up Aaron and bring him back to Beverly Hills. I was usually off on the weekends since I was required to be in for my meetings during the week. Michelle, Aaron and I had a Sunday morning routine. We would drive down La Cienega to the Donut shop and get a special treat, while I would pick up my Sunday *Los Angeles Times* and then we'd head home to have our quality time together. We shared stories, and there are moments that no matter how old my children get, they will never forget. These were priceless, precious, moments a mother spends with her children. Beverly Hills was that time for us. Some Sundays were spent at Venice Beach, where we ate at a wonderful health food place, helping to make up for the earlier donut fix. Or we would go to the Beverly Center for pizza.

Aaron learned to break dance and would get a piece of cardboard, go out on the sidewalk in front of the apartment, set up his boom box playing his favorite music, then put his cap out just in case anyone felt compelled to drop some money in it. This was when Mike first started to deprive Aaron of our weekend visits as punishment if Aaron did something wrong during the week. He knew how much Aaron loved us and our weekends together. To use us as his weapon of punishment is something I will never be able to forgive, and as years went, although I have tried, it still haunts me with sleepless nights.

Michelle excelled in school and made some great friends. One of her best friends got her license to drive and off they would go, both really good girls. I could always trust my daughter and she had never given me any problems. Michelle became a Beverly Hills varsity cheerleader. She was a popular girl and became more outgoing. Each school morning I woke her at 5:30 with a tray of breakfast in bed to start her day off happy and healthy. We listened to D.J. Rick Dees on the radio. One morning she said, "Mom, I think I would like to go meet Rick Dees and do a cheer for him representing my high school." I told her that sounded fantastic and we would take some fresh baked chocolate chip cookies to give him. By 6:30 the following morning, we were at the studio. He invited her in and let her give a cheer over the air. This is just an example of one of so many things Michelle and I would do on the spur-of-the-moment. It's just how we roll. When I'm dead and gone, this daughter of mine is going to have many memories that will bring a smile to her face.

I appeared as a contestant on a TV show called "Anything for Money." I won five-hundred dollars and some free commercial products. It was a blast. Michelle is always encouraging and inspiring me to do it all and never limit myself.

I opened a Neiman Marcus charge account and the next two Christmases we spent one-thousand dollars on gifts for others and ourselves. It would take a year to pay off but was such fun having a mother-daughter shopping day. It was more about not having so much that made it really special. It was decadent for us to just have a cup of hot chocolate and dip our buttered toast in it.

The only time I felt bad about our being poor by Beverly Hills standards was when one of the cheerleader mothers had a meeting at her mansion to discuss fundraising ideas. (All the girls lived in mansions!) Her staff served beverages and appetizers and took care of our every need. It was suggested we meet once a month and be social. Thank goodness I wasn't the one chosen for the following month! I was so concerned Michelle would be as upset as I was thinking about these high rollers coming to our little one bedroom apartment. But instead she said, "Don't worry Mom. If they don't like us as we are, then they are not going to like us even if we lived in a mansion."

That was easy for her, not to give it a second thought. For the rest of the night we laughed so hard about what we could do to pull off the best party of the season; perhaps have Aaron to do some break dancing for entertainment, or get some Venice Street entertainers for the front lawn! We could always throw down a red rug for the red carpet effect. I know I could make better appetizers and I could get some of my sales people to do free makeovers on all those face-lifted women. Luckily, my turn never came up and I never went back to another meeting. But I never missed a game, and Aaron was in awe of his sister as he watched her out on the football field doing her cheers.

Cosmetics sales people in a store the size of the one where I was employed had the opportunity to make very heft commissions. The hard part was that they were given monthly sales quotas and if they were not able to make it three months in a row, they were automatically terminated. Over a two-year period I had to let twenty people go. Some terminations were due to theft, but most were for not making the quota. I worked long hours each day. I was stressed from always striving to meet the department's sales quotas, and it made it less and less and fun. I was getting burned out.

That would mean going back to Mom and starting over once again. Michelle was okay with it. She didn't mind the idea of spending her senior year graduating with kids she had gone to school with. Plus, her best friend Maria still lived there. If she did mind, she never let me know. But I'm sure she didn't really want to leave her new friends. This had been such a fun social time for her; she learned to drive, and she was enjoying going to teen dance clubs with her friends.

Well, we went, we saw, and we had the best time living life large in Beverly Hills on a beer budget. We never had much but we felt like we had it all and would be leaving with some wonderful memories.

CHAPTER 22

Are You Kidding Me?

Once we moved back to the desert Michelle always came home with the funniest ideas of what she would be getting herself into next, like the time she came home from high school and asked me to sit down, that she had something important to tell me. I thought to myself, better brace myself; this can't be good. She was so serious! She said, "Mom, I want to join the Marines." Whew! That was a relief! "The Marines," I asked? "Yes. They came to my school today and gave a speech in my Social Studies class and this is what I really want to be. Would it be okay if the Recruiting Staff Sergeant come to our house to speak to you?" Sure, make the appointment. If this was something she felt she needed to do for her country, then I was one-hundred percent in support of it.

Meeting with the Staff Sergeant was great. I could see why Michelle was interested with all she would be able to do for her country. Not being at war was a big plus for me, and she had a chance for a better education than I ever could afford to offer her. We were invited as the Staff Sergeant's guests to attend the graduation ceremony of other recruits in San Diego. It was only a couple weeks away and he would drive us. We did go, and it was amazing to see and feel the pride these very young men and women displayed through their words and actions. These recruits go through so much to be able to protect this beautiful nation of ours. The Staff Sergeant would take Michelle to meet with other potential candidates; use her beauty and her motivation to help enlist other young people. Michelle was very interested until she found out she had to get shots. Michelle had a phobia about shots. Once when she had to have a cavity filled at the dentist, I actually had to hire a psychotherapist to walk her through it. At that time she could faint right in front of you at just the sight of a needle. The subject was never brought up again. But we always smiled each time we would receive recruiting mail from all the different armed forces.

I had found a new clothing boutique to work in. Aaron had come down for Mother's Day weekend and Michelle asked if she could drop me off at work that day so she and Aaron could go out shopping for my gift. That afternoon a Palm Springs police officer came into the store and asked for me. He said my children had been in a car accident and were taken to the emergency room and offered to drive me there. I had someone take over the store for me and the policeman drove as fast as possible to get me to the hospital. He did not tell me if they were alive or dead but that a car driven by teenagers had pulled in front of Michelle to make a left turn, from a far right lane, forcing her to drive into three parked cars. I can't begin to tell you how I felt at that moment. I had seen many mothers and fathers arrive at the ER to learn that their child had died. What was I going to see when I arrived?

Aaron, who had hit the windshield, was lying there with his front teeth missing, bleeding and crying. His father had been called and was being flown in by a friend in a private plane to pick him up and take him for medical help closer to home. Michelle had been unconscious when they found her. She had hit her head very hard and needed to be watched very carefully over the next forty-eight hours, but could be released and brought home. She had temporary amnesia and when she spoke, moments later couldn't remember what she had just said, repeating everything over and over. Mike came and got Aaron and the police drove them back to the plane. Aaron had told the police his dad was a policeman in Chino, so that explained why I was given VIP treatment to get to my children. The police also drove Michelle and me home, since my car was now totaled. This was one of the worst days in my entire life. I will never forget the feeling of not knowing the fate of my children.

Now I had no car, and my mom's was a twenty-year-old classic that she loved because she could push a button and the rear window went down. It was a big monster and gas hog, but I had no choice for now but to drive it. The insurance money from my car was going straight to the hospital to help cover the cost from the accident. This was the only car in the family. While I had been in Beverly Hills, mom would write her weekly letters and always raved about her mechanic, "Al." She said he was always very helpful and never took advantage of her. He managed the gas station where she bought her gas. Mom told me that she often brought him homemade goodies. I asked Mom to take me to this gas station and let me beg this mechanic to do whatever he needed to make sure her car was in perfect running condition so I could depend on it to get back and forth to work until I could go buy a new one. I couldn't help but notice that Al was a handsome man of Middle Eastern descent, Iranian as it turned out. He had that lovely dark color to his skin that reminded me a little of Rock. He spent a couple of days fine-tuning my mother's clunker. The first day I drove the car to work, I pulled into the parking structure, put it in park, and the entire steering column fell into my lap. I tried to compose myself, before I walked into the store and greeted the customers as if it were the best day ever. Once inside, I called Al the mechanic and asked him if he remembered me, that I just had him fix everything possible on the car so it would be safe for me to get back and forth to work. I told him what happened. He said that I needn't worry about a thing. He would have the car towed back to the gas station and would lend me his car.

Al showed up at the store, took my keys, and handed me the keys to his Thunderbird. He said the tank was full and I shouldn't worry, that I could use it for as long as it took him to repair my mother's car. He turned out to be a lifesaver. After two weeks of using his car and finding out (from my mother) that he was single, I invited him to dinner to thank him for the use of his car. He lived forty-five minutes from my work, so I chose a restaurant in his town. We were seated in a private booth reserved for couples only, where a curtain was drawn for a candlelight dinner. It was very romantic to say the least. Al was a charmer.

He told me he was recently separated and his wife and two daughters, aged two and nine, lived in a home close by but went to her family's home in Glendale on the weekends with the two-year-old, leaving the older daughter with Al. After a month and a few more dinners of appreciation, I still had Al's car. They no longer made that classic part mom's car needed. But by now we were officially dating. I couldn't get over his kindness. If I needed anything, he was right there to help. If Mom needed anything, he was right there and she loved him like a son. Sometimes I'd spend the night at Al's apartment and it didn't take long before his separated wife found out about me.

Al was in the shower once when the phone rang and he asked me to get it. It was his wife, and she asked me who I was. I told her and there was no reaction when I told Al she called, so I assumed all was cool. On the weekends when his wife left town to go be with her parents he would invite me to come stay at the house with him. I was able to get to know his nine year old daughter Shelly, a very sweet girl. Everything was great the first year. His wife eventually got a job working in Glendale and Al moved back into his house. It was too long of a drive for me to go see him very often, but somehow we made it work.

Al never was able to get the part for Mom's car but he was able to sell it for her as a classic and she bought another car he found. Cars were often given to him when a customer couldn't afford the repairs.

In the meantime, Michelle had a fantastic senior year. She fell in love for the first time. She entered beauty contests and won the city title, then another, and another, followed by becoming a Princess at The National Date Festival. Being a Beverly Hills High School cheerleader helped her gain confidence so she could get up in front of a large crowd and speak. She made it to the Miss Southern California beauty pageant and that was another opportunity, a great experience for her. She didn't win, but that was at a very different level than the small pageants she had experienced. A young lady had to have a lot of money behind her to make her dreams come true in the world of pageantry, or else have big sponsors. It was all I could do just to afford the clothes required, let alone the hotel, food and entrance fee. But it was the opportunity of a lifetime, and the experience she gained was priceless.

Michelle started working after school at a shoe store and soon bought her first car: a red Sprint. One of her closest girlfriends was part of the Hearst family, so Michelle spent some unforgettable times at the famous Hearst estate in Palm Springs. Once while visiting the estate she was in the driveway washing her new car, wearing a bikini, her hair in large curlers, and a masque on her face, when a tour bus came by, and stopped at the house, giving details and history of the Hearst family. She ducked behind her car quickly. It was a most embarrassing moment she will never forget.

Once she had a chance to run back into the home her girlfriend's grandmother sat her down and explained the story of the Hearst family.

It took a while, but I realized that Al was an alcoholic with issues. What is it with me and alcoholics? Many times he drank so much he'd end up crawling on the floor to the bathroom to throw up. He began accusing me of things that never happened, forcing me to defend myself, and we had numerous breakups. After a week or so, I would convince him I was innocent and he would allow me to return to his life. When I returned it was like a honeymoon. He was sweet and loving and always bought me makeup gifts, but before I knew it, something else would happen. This became a pattern. Al said once he spent the day at marriage counseling, something the divorce judge had ordered, he drank and cried about how hard it was, and how angry he gets just being in the same room with his wife. He said he had a few more counseling appointments to go before it would all be over.

Aaron was still coming for weekend visits, but his time with us was more limited. Mike was using me as Aaron's punishment, not allowing him to come see me or speak to me on the phone. Mike had always been so controlling and sadistic, getting pleasure from our of pain of separation. When I actually did get to see him, we shared quality time.

Aaron and I loved to go to the baseball games at Palm Springs Angels Stadium. One evening we went to the Palm Springs Stadium to watch the Triple-A teams. The team bus was parked in front, the driver standing nearby. I asked Aaron if he would like to ask any questions of the driver, a very nice-looking older gentleman. Aaron and he started up quite the conversation, and before I knew it, the driver asked us to be his guests for the evening and watch the game in VIP seating. That was the beginning of a nice relationship between the three of us. His name was JC and he lived in San Bernardino close to where the home stadium for his team was located. It turned out he was one of the owners of the team, and he just loved driving the bus all over the state from game to game during the season. I would pick up Aaron in Riverside and take him to the home games in San Bernardino.

JC was single and a gem of a guy. During the games we could

talk for hours about our lives. Aaron didn't mind. He was too focused on the game, being in VIP seating and having barbecued steak served to him for dinner. JC always had our gas tank filled and made me promise to call him the second I would get home. He also was concerned about Al's excuse to cause an argument so he could stay away for a few days. Al would go on a drinking binge, find reason to fight with me, and then makeup, all the while making me feel like I was the problem. He was verbally abusive. Once again, my self-esteem was spiraling into an abyss.

I had told JC I was so tired of being treated this way after all these years. I told him I made the decision to buy a car, a Toyota Corolla, give the Thunderbird back to Al, and walk away from it all. The next time I went up to take Aaron to the game, JC took Aaron and me to the Toyota dealership, paid cash for my new car, and gave it to me as a gift. He said he never wanted me to be tied to someone like Al just because of not having a car. JC brought a briefcase filled with fresh bills and counted it all out in front of the car agent and he had the title put in my name. The car would be ready to pick up the following week and he would come to Mom's and drive me to pick up my new car. His generosity was overwhelming to me. I felt very blessed that someone so kind would find worth in me.

I remember once mentioning to Al that I would like to write a book about my different life experiences and he just laughed and said everyone has stories and that he doubted anyone would want to read mine. The following week Al and I broke up and I gave back the car. Mom finally was able to meet JC and fell in love with his personality and could tell he cared a great deal about me. He was wonderful to all of us.

After graduation Michelle went to work for Marriott's Desert Springs Resort and Spa as concierge on the VIP level of the hotel where she mingled with the rich and famous as they relaxed and enjoyed the open bar, chocolate-dipped strawberries, an abundance of appetizers including trays of fat shrimp and fresh fruit and cheese platters. By the time Michelle turned twenty-one she thought it perfect timing to make a change. David was a top chef at Marriott and had been offered a great job in Las Vegas. Michelle and David were always doing fun things together, like driving across the country and back. They were best friends, but nothing romantic. So, when David had the chance to move to Vegas he asked Michelle to be his roommate. They went to Vegas and found a fabulous new condo, and she was able to land a job as cocktail waitress at the newly-opened Excalibur. Michelle could be trained in time for the grand opening. JC gave me a card and when I opened it, there was one-thousand dollars in cash. He told me to go spend a few days in Vegas with Michelle while he was on a road tour with the team.

Michelle was starting to dislike the way she was treated at the Excalibur, so she left that job and became a bartender at Sharkey's. This girl made so much tip money that her dresser drawers were filled with nothing but bills that she would toss in at the end of her shifts. She had planned to attend college there, but by the time she got off work it was often four in the morning. It was not conducive to waking up early to attend classes.

While Michelle was away, I continued to see JC. I also concentrated on my work managing the stores. JC invited Aaron and me to a game and said he had a gift for me. He put a cigar band on my finger and asked if I would consider marrying him. He said he would take me to pick out the ring of my choice at Tiffany's or Van Cleef & Arpels on Rodeo Drive whenever I was ready. He said he knew he was much older and we hadn't had sex, but he loved me and wanted to spend the rest of his life with me. I asked him to give me some time to think it over and he told me to take all the time I needed. From then on, no matter what city the team tour was on, he would send me a gift from that town and he sent flowers to me every week. The problem was I wasn't in love with him. I actually wasn't in love with anyone, nor did I think I was worthy of love.

Michelle was getting burnt out living in Vegas and was ready to move home, and nothing could have made me happier. She came back to live with Mom and me and went right back to work at the Marriott in Palm Desert. Before long she became the boat dock supervisor, then the lead concierge, bringing her to the top of the pay scale for that position. A new restaurant, Morton's of Chicago, a high-end steak house, was opening directly across the street from the resort. She applied for a part-time job as dining room hostess and was hired. Michelle entered another contest to become a Bob Hope Classic Girl, and was one of three chosen out of dozens who applied. She wore the "Hope" name on all the cute outfits they provided. Wherever Bob Hope would go during his famous golf tournament, these three girls would be right by his side. Former President Ford played in the tournament, along with many celebrities and top PGA golfers. All the media attention, autograph signings, and personal appearances each year for the three girls chosen was a very big deal and a great life experience. Thanks for the memories, Bob Hope.

Michelle soon became a server and it wasn't long before she was elevated to catering director and became very successful at bringing in large parties and special events to the restaurant.

Al and I bumped into each other and he noticed the new car. I told him it was a gift from a man I really cared a lot about. He told me the only difference between that guy and another is that he could afford to give me champagne instead of beer, that it didn't mean he loved me more than he did, but JC just had the advantage of showing it with material things. He confessed how much he loved me and how he might not be able to offer me all the material things but he could offer marriage if I would consider. He couldn't get married right then because he was just purchasing a Chevron station in Palm Springs, but before he did, he'd like to take Aaron, Michelle and me to Hawaii for a week's getaway. I asked if we could also take his daughter, but she was in school and couldn't come this time, but maybe next. He piled it on so thick with his love and not wanting to live without me that I went back and told JC that I had to end it. Looking back now, this was one of the worst decisions of my life.

Aaron, Michelle and I had a great time in Hawaii. I paid all the expenses for the kids and my flights, and Al and I went in halves on our week's condo. Al asked me if I would move back in with him when we returned. Al had found a beautiful place for the two of us to live in Palm Springs. He even told me to pick out a wedding dress. He said his divorce was now final. He bought me a small diamond ring and when I asked which finger he wanted it put on, if he wanted it on my left hand. He said that in his country it is worn on the right hand so it really didn't matter to him. I moved in with Al, and he really had changed. Perhaps our time apart changed him. It was without a doubt one of the happiest times of my life. I felt I really did have it all the passion, the love, living in a great home with pool, enjoying my work, and Al's new business going well. I was actually very happy.

Aaron didn't come to see me very often now. He was a teenager and doing sports and seemed to always be busy with his own agenda, which I thought was very normal for a young man that age. When Aaron did come down he enjoyed his time with Al. They were building a special bond between the two of them.

Michelle and I planned a nice day of lunch and shopping with my mother. As we were driving along, she started saying things that didn't make sense. She was calling the different streets we were on the names of streets from the Monterey Peninsula. Going into stores made her very anxious and a little sick to her stomach, so we took her home. She had already been diagnosed with diabetes at this point and needed to be on medication. We thought perhaps that was the problem. She no longer drank since the diagnosis. As the weeks passed, we both checked on her often. She had been living alone ever since I moved away. So I decided to spend a weekend with her. I noticed a number of disturbing things. Every single day my mom drove to the grocery store down the street, choosing whatever she wanted to cook that day. One morning she had a hard time remembering how to get back home. She had the store call me to come get her. She told me she was scared and knew something was wrong. She admitted she was afraid to drive the car any longer, for fear she might hurt someone. So she gave me the car keys and asked me to have Al sell the car for her.

I got her to the doctor the following Monday where she had all kinds of tests. The doctor suggested she go to a memory clinic for further testing. The tests proved her memory was fading fast. I noticed she kept repeating questions she had just asked only moments before. It was the beginning stages of dementia, or most likely, Alzheimer's Disease. Not much was known about the disease and my mom was only 72, which seemed too young. All types of tests were done at the hospital. There was no sign of a stroke and Alzheimer's was confirmed as her diagnoses. I was so proud of my mom for voluntarily giving me the car keys and selling the car as soon as she sensed something wasn't right.

There was no way I could continue to live with Al now, or consider getting married. My mother needed me and she was my priority. Life went on. I tried to never let anything get me down. I just tried to take one day at a time and stayed positive, suppressing my emotions. My mantra was "tomorrow is another day," and what seemed like the end of the world could change very quickly.

I started going to Alzheimer's support groups at the local hospital. But the more I attended these meetings, the more I learned what was in store for me. There were women in the group that were taking care of their husbands. Their husbands, who had been the bread winners all their married lives, didn't even recognize them any longer. The once wonderful guys often became mean and angry and would accuse them of stealing things when they couldn't find something. They had no idea what to do. They were afraid they would lose their home and all the security they had, due to all the medical bills. The husbands had just barely enough memory to qualify being placed in a nursing home, but wouldn't allow a stranger - a caregiver - in their home to help with their bathing and cleaning. These women really needed this support group to remain sane. Fortunately, my mother went completely in the opposite direction, becoming the most docile, sweet women in the world. She became the mother I had always dreamed of having, but it took Alzheimer's to create that person. I loved spoiling her. She was so appreciative of everything and became a kind, loving, gentle soul. She was nothing like the fiery redhead who raised me.

Over the next four years I devoted myself to my work as a cosmetics/accessory manager for a large department store in Palm Springs and to Mom. She kept the same daily schedules, and as long as I had everything prepared for her with notes to follow throughout the day, she was great. We had breakfast before I left for work, and Meals on Wheels brought her lunch each day. She enjoyed all her favorite TV shows, and her two little lap dogs kept her company. I always had things prepared for her in the refrigerator in case she got hungry. She could phone me at the store if she needed me. As long as she remained on her schedule, she did quite well.

I was able to still see Al on occasions and he would check on Mom for me if I asked. Mom loved Al and he could do no wrong in her eyes. On my mother's birthday, I wanted to do something really special for her. Mom loved Willie Nelson and called him a Good Ole Boy. His recording of *Stardust*, the song that my parents used to dance to, was her favorite. I bought front row tickets for Mom, Al and me to go see him in concert. Michelle arranged for a beautiful birthday dinner at Morton's of Chicago. As a hair stylist since I was sixteen, whenever I lived nearby, I had been doing Mom's hair and nails for years. I made sure she had the best-looking clothes and accessories, and tonight, her special night, she looked stunning. Dinner and dessert were amazing. Mom said goodbye to Michelle and off we went to the theater, just fifteen minutes away.

By the time we arrived at the theater, Mom no longer remembered the dinner. She enjoyed her Willie Nelson concert, especially when he came down from the stage, as I'm sure he felt her energy, and took her hand and kissed her cheek. She was all aflutter and feeling on top of the world, like a radiant young school girl. After the concert she got in the car and we drove twenty minutes to get home, but by the time we arrived she no longer remembered Willie or the dinner. That night taught me so much. It was about giving her as many wonderful moments as I possibly could during this new journey. There would no longer be memories, only moments.

From that night on, life as I knew it had to change. I realized she needed to have more care now. I hired a wonderful lady to spend a few hours with her in the afternoon until I got home from work. While Mom took her nap she helped with cleaning and made sure Mom was given a nice hot meal. It made it much better for me.

Al understood that my mother had to come first. This was part of his culture and gave him greater respect for me. He introduced me to his parents. They had heard good things about me and when they met me they brought me precious gifts from Iran. Al said his divorce was final and he moved from the home we had shared to a home he owned. He wanted me to treat his house like it was mine because, as he said, someday it would be. I took some furniture and clothes to the new place, deep cleaned it, tended to gardening, and tried to make it feel like I belonged there, even though I couldn't spend much time. His daughters were only a couple of blocks away, so it was nice that they could come over to see their dad anytime they felt like it. As the girls got older I got to see more of them on my infrequent visits. Al had this huge piece of land with a beautiful garden filled with fresh crops of corn, grapes, all kinds of vegetables, and fruit trees. Some of my most enjoyable moments were working in the garden with Al, getting my hands in the soil, reminding me of gardening with my father. Al was an awesome cook and made wonderful Persian meals, both of us enjoying the fresh, healthy fare from the garden. When the hired caregiver was able to spend the night, I was able to get a little private time for myself.

CHAPTER 23

Day Spa and Deceit

By my fifth year working at the department store, I was busy caring for Mom, trying to run the cosmetics and accessories department. Each cosmetics counter manager was responsible for creating special events to bring their customers to the counter. My beautiful Clinique counter manager helped me created the perfect event. We named it, "Take the Day Off." In the mall, just outside of our store was a small empty store. The mall management let us use it for three days. We had the visual director go into that store and decorate it like a tropical island, complete with spa music, faux palm trees, and a mural of a tropical island. Chilled Perrier and bowls of fresh fruit were served. If a customer spent forty dollars in Clinique, she was given a free manicure, Clinique facial, and a complete makeover. I was able to find a manicurist but couldn't find anyone to do the facials so I thought to myself, wait, I'm a licensed cosmetologist, but I really had no idea whatsoever how to do a facial. In Beauty College we practiced mostly on fake dummy heads to learn the technique the hands and fingers should make on the face. I used Clinique products years ago when I was counter manager for that company. So at least I knew the products and as long as I made sure I used the mildest of each product, such as cleanser, scrub, toner and masque, I knew they wouldn't likely have a reaction. I had the store provide a lounge chair along with pillows, fresh sheets, and a pretty tropical blanket. Over the next three days I did sixteen facials. The entire time I worked at this, I couldn't help but notice how relaxed and de-stressed I became.

I knew it wouldn't be long until I would need to become self-employed as it was almost impossible to keep up with my mother's needs when I was working on a salary and had to invest long hours in my job each day. Sometimes Mom would call me at the store to ask me a question, and a few minutes later she'd call me back and ask me the same thing. From that special event the seed was planted. I was going to open up a small place where I could do plain manicures, facials and makeovers. I went out searching for just the right location and found the most perfect spot. It was a one-thousand square foot room, with a small kitchen and bathroom. I spoke to the landlord and explained the situation with my mother and my idea for the business and he loved it. His name was Mr. Goldring, and he wanted $1,000 a month, first and last month's rent, and a year's lease. I showed the place to Al and he thought it was nice space for the price. Al said he knew someone who was great at construction who could build the treatment rooms I required.

I had been going to the same manicurist for the last five years and told her my plans. She said she was going to be leaving the salon where she has been working to open her own. She was getting a large loan and would be happy to loan me $15,000 to get me started, with a fair percentage rate. I agreed and told the landlord I would take it. I gave my two week notice at work and a replacement was found right away. I was very excited! In cosmetics when training any new sales associates I always told them to treat each and every customer as if they were a guest coming to visit in their home, so it was only appropriate that I named the new business "The Guest House."

Two weeks had passed, it was mid-July and almost my

birthday. On the morning of my birthday I was going to officially meet with Mr. Goldring and sign the papers. I was excited, yet nervous, starting a business that I really knew nothing about except doing sixteen facials in three days during the store event. Now I was giving all that security away so I could be flexible with my mother's needs. At nine o'clock that evening I received a call from the girl who was going to loan me the $15,000 startup money and she said she had changed her mind. So here I was with no job, no startup money, and no idea what I was going to do. I had no business plan, and I had only done sixteen facials in the last thirty years, yet I knew that that was what I wanted to do more than anything. I tossed and turned all night. Al wasn't much help, telling me what a mess I was in and how I shouldn't have given up my job; nothing but negativity. When I woke up the next morning I knew exactly what I was going to do. It was my birthday and I was going to sign the lease at nine o'clock. I had $5,000 in savings and great credit. So over the next thirty days, I spent close to $45,000, most of it charged. That included some spent on newspaper ads to run a special promotion to get a facial for $35 and a free manicure.

On opening day and the phone was ringing like crazy! I felt sorry for my first few clients. I was faking it, but the ad brought in lots of business. At least it was enough for one person to handle in this one-thousand square foot space. Perhaps these first customers might never come back, but at least I had enough business to pay the rent and utilities. I hadn't done a manicure since beauty college some thirty years earlier, but how hard could it be? I had the visual director from the department store come and help me design the business. I bought an indoor waterfall and tons of plants, beautiful fixtures, massage table for facials and three manicure tables and chairs since I knew my business was going to grow. I also learned there was something new in the industry called a "day spa" and that sounded very inviting. I didn't have any real competition, only two small day spas, The Spa Hotel and Casino, The Ritz Carlton, and Marriott Desert Springs Spa. That was it. I had searched everything possible about day spas on my computer and found a trade magazine called Day Spa Magazine, which became my new Bible. I devoured it, reading it cover to cover. I learned I was on the cutting edge of this incredible field that was just starting to take hold elsewhere, not just in my area. Day spas at that time had a ninety percent failure rate. Of course I didn't know that. It's a good thing. Mr. Goldring was the best landlord I ever could have imagined. There wasn't a morning where this sweet 95 year-old retired jeweler didn't come to see me, pull up a chair and visit me for a few minutes before going home. If it was slow, he would say, "Don't worry honey, they will come. Just give them time to know about you." When the rent was due, he would say, "Why don t you just give me $500 this month. Next month it will be much better." He was always encouraging me not to give up. He eventually lowered my rent to only $500 a month and always gave me advice on how to run the business. The first month I made a number of changes. I went to the local Beauty College, made friends with the manager and told her of my dilemma with my mom, and trying to create a business I really knew nothing about. She said she would come teach me how to do a facial and a manicure, pedicure for $100, so I set it up. She was awesome and, oh, what a change it made when I did my treatments. Next was to hire some professionals to come in to help do facials and manicures. It was to be on an on-call basis with a sub-contractor and I offered a 60/40 split, the business getting the latter. I received many calls from the ad, and found just the right esthetician and manicurist. This was a huge help, because now I would begin working on marketing the spa.

If I have learned anything it was how to create special events, promotions and things to get the business in the door. My business was only 1000 square feet. I changed the marketing wording to "Private Day Spa." My ads began targeting visitors who might be bringing girlfriends to the desert for a weekend get-together. They could have the day spa all to themselves, completely private. Lunch was provided and they were served tropical frozen margaritas. I changed the name to The Guest House Tropical Day Spa. The internet was our friend. I hired a team of webmasters that helped me create my website. I ranked number one on the search engines for Palm Springs day spas.

A year later I hired a spa director; she really helped me with internet marketing, making appointments from all who called in from our website to book. She would describe the treatments and up sell them on bigger packages. It was a tremendous boost to the business and income.

At the same time I learned how to help teens get rid of acne, doing a special series of treatments to clear their skin. One of my first clients was Al's daughter Shelly, now close to eighteen years-old. She came to me twice for this treatment and it really helped her skin. One day after her treatment I took her out to lunch. I mentioned that it was too bad she wasn't able to come to Hawaii with her dad, Michelle, Aaron and me. She said she didn't know how to tell me this, but she thought I should know that her mother just filed for divorce from her dad because she found he had written a love letter to an old girlfriend in Iran and had sent her $15,000. It was a girl he almost married instead of her mother. They had never been legally separated. I learned when we went to Hawaii he told his family he was in school in San Diego for that week.

I realized that for 9 years when he pretended to be mad at me it was so he could leave because he needed to go home to family. His family knew me as a friend and never as a girlfriend. He asked me to marry him, bought me a diamond ring, and even a dress for our wedding! He was married the whole time and had no intention of getting a divorce. It was his wife that found out what a lying, cheating, two-timing rat he was. Not with me but with his old girlfriend in Iran. How many more might there have been? Could I ever trust another man? I should have learned by then never to do that. This was a blow to my already low self-esteem. I never said a word to his daughter, just thanked her for telling me the truth.

I drove straight to where I knew her mother and, his wife, worked and went in and introduced myself. I told her how very sorry I was. I explained all the lies and exactly what the real truth was. She was kind and grateful and understood how we were both played as fools. From there I called Michelle and her boyfriend Kevin to come to Al's house and help me load my things and get the heck out of there, never to look back. By the time I got to Al's he was sitting outside at the picnic table having a beer and enjoying the afternoon sun. I calmly went and sat down and told him very gently what I thought of him and that I knew he had been lying to me for the past nine years. I told him that Michelle and Kevin were on their way up with a truck to help me load my things and I asked him to leave while I did that so there wasn't a scene and he complied. He was extremely close to my son Aaron, so I never mentioned to Aaron what had happened and just said we broke up. When Michelle and Kevin arrived, we quickly loaded everything. As Michelle and I did a final walk-through of the rooms to make sure I didn't forget anything, Michelle made me go back in and take all the toilet paper "so he couldn't shit on anyone again." We still laugh about it. For the next year-and-a-half I did not date, not daring to trust any man. My main focus was my mother.

Michelle taught me many things about running my business for which I am forever grateful. She made sure I was a member of the Convention and Visitors Bureau and the Palm Springs Chamber of Commerce. The CVB kept me in business for the following year and this is exactly how it happened. I made sure all the staff of the CVB was treated to complimentary treatments of choice. Travel writers from all over the world come often to do stories about the desert. They get a free trip from the company who sends them and it really brings a lot of attention to the resort area. The top travel writer Carl Simpson worked for a highly-circulated newspaper and was coming to town to do a special article called *Pampered and Pumped*. He would be experiencing the many exciting activities available throughout each day. At the end of each day he went to a spa selected by the CVB and receive treatments, then reported on each of these experiences. The rep from the CVB involved in this was Elaine, whom I had given complimentary treatments and loved The Guest House. Elaine put together all the activities and spa packages for the journalist. She asked if I would be interested in hosting a spa evening for him after his day of chosen activities, and I immediately agreed. I asked who else would be doing it. Elaine mentioned the top resort hotel spas. I was thrilled to learn I was the only small business to be considered, such a small place compared to three major hotels with massive spas, but I felt up to the challenge of being the little giant!

I came up with a plan. When I read the journalist's itinerary which had been faxed to me, I noticed that he was staying all four days at the Hyatt, right across the street from The Guest House. That was the best news ever. I also noticed that on his last day out of the four he was to come spend his evening with us, but according to his itinerary he barely had time from when his last activity ended to get showered and arrive at my spa. I sure didn't want him to be tired, hungry and coming into a little tiny place after all the giants. So I called Michelle and asked her opinion and she suggested we bring in a catered dinner from Morton's of Chicago. Perfect! So when "Carl" arrived in town, I called over to the hotel and said, "Hi Carl. My name is Sharon and I own The Guest House Tropical Day Spa where you will be visiting on your last day here. I noticed on your itinerary that you don't have much time to get here for your treatments after your activities that day. I would like to have dinner brought in for you that night. Did you come alone or with someone?" He said his partner had come with him. So I suggested they both come together for the treatments and asked what they'd like to eat steak, or seafood. He said they would both enjoy seafood. I suggested salmon and they both agreed. Then I said, "Picture this: you are both sitting side by side, relaxing, getting your pedicures. What drinks would you like in your hands?" He said, "A Martini!" I said, "Vodka Martini, shaken, not stirred, like James Bond?" That seemed to break the ice as we both started laughing.

When Carl and his partner Andy arrived, Michelle had gone way over-board and totally blew the roof off the place as she not only brought huge trays with the meals, but acted as the private server just for them. I made sure I was doing one of the pedicures so I had that half-hour private time with them while they ate to answer all the questions about the business and how it all started.

The day the two-page article came out in the paper, I was given very high praise. The *newspaper source* is syndicated and the article appeared over the next six months in locations throughout California, generating lots of new business for me. That one special evening paid off tenfold and saved me from failure. At the start of the article Carl talked about all the things he had done over the past few days. Then it went on to say:

Actually, rock climbing is easier than it sounds and more fun than, well, golf. Lessons are reasonable, and the guys working there are friendly and helpful as you cling to the tiniest rock, literally hanging on by your fingernails.

And even those poor, tortured fingernails get the just reward in

Palm Springs. Last stop The Guest House Tropical Day Spa in downtown Palm Springs, where fingernails, toenails and almost everything in between will be soaked, massaged, trimmed, buffed and otherwise pampered as only you, Olympic God, you deserve to be pampered.

Or at least that's the way Sharon makes you feel. Her new establishment is a tiny, not particularly fancy when put up against the mega spas at Marriott's or the new Givenchy. But Sharon makes up for what her place lacks in size with a delightful combination of personal attention and friendliness. And great deals. In a city not known for its low price, Sharon's spa offers terrific, full on mega blasts of pampering like you haven't had since you were, oh, 2 years old. The foot treatment, a foot bath, a half hour of reflexology, a paraffin treatment (your foot massaged with oils and then sealed with layers of warm paraffin which are then peeled off and a pedicure is just part of one spa package. Sharon will even call you the day before your appointment to find out what cocktail you'd like to have with the cheese, crackers and fresh fruit she serves.

Foot quivering on the gas pedal as I drove back to Ontario for the flight back home, legs aching and toenails shining inside my shoes, I reflected on all the activities I'd had, and started planning a vacation. I think I'll take up golf.

I started my marketing campaign to out of state guests with things like: "From the moment you enter the room, you are in a tropical setting with lush exotic plants, flowers, and a gentle waterfall creating the beat of the tropical rain on broad leaves and hanging vines, all to help provide you with the sounds of nature. Refreshments including champagne, fresh fruits and your personal requests will be on hand for your arrival. Your bodyguards are welcome and limousine parking is available. Are you ready to feel spoiled and pampered? Are you ready to leave your cares behind?"

It was a pretty bold press release from a person that still didn't know much of what she was doing, but always loved creative marketing.

The spa was decorated so beautifully that when a movie actor decided to get married they chose my spa to do it in. No paparazzi,

No interruptions. Just romantic candlelight love. A night time ceremony in a tropical room illuminated with nothing but candles. I was just a big crying mess. This was the ultimate romantic wedding, so private and so unplanned and yet a moment in time remembered by me forever. My son Aaron drove down to be the photographer for the event. Though many years have passed I will always feel they are family to me.

Soon after the wedding, my spa director was given an offer for another job she couldn't refuse. I loved this girl. She really made the business grow strong and represented the spa well, as she would travel door to door to every hotel in town leaving our spa menus, getting the front desk staff to come in for a free facial so I could win them over, then go back and send their hotel guests.

My son Aaron graduated from high school went onto college where he specialized in fire science, becoming a paramedic and went on to become a firefighter for the next eight years. I saw him every few months, with his girlfriend Tina. Soon Tina came to live with my mother and me for a few months, helped me at home and took over the spa director position.

Oh my goodness, Tina and I had fun! We decided on the eve of my fiftieth birthday that I should go to Vegas to celebrate. We traveled the dark back roads of the desert that night, driving through a thunderstorm we will both never forget, I'm sure. We stayed in a suite at The Venetian. By the time we went out for a drink it was almost midnight and my fiftieth birthday. We were at The Bellagio Hotel Fountain Room and I will never forget us joining the table with the owner of one of the NFL football teams and him buying my first birthday drink, a pink martini, before he had to fly out that night. The following day we went shopping at Neiman's where I bought a spur-of-the-moment sexy white suit and Stuart Weitzman stilettos, and we went back that night and played until 4:00 A.M. The men went crazy for Tina; she was a gorgeous-looking model-type with a great personality to match. After a while I think my son figured out we were having way too much fun and he missed her terribly, so she had to return to him. But it was fun while it lasted.

During my spa days, Michelle fell madly in love and married the greatest guy, Kevin. They were married in California at

Kevin's family home, outdoors, high above everything overlooking what seemed the entire view of southern California. When the ceremony was over they took a limousine to LAX and flew off to Bora Bora for a two-week honeymoon where another island wedding was catered just for the two of them. The marriage in Bora Bora is not recognized in the USA, so they needed to be married here first to make it legit. The second wedding took place in the late afternoon two days later, complete with Tahitian dancers, fire dancers, and live island music. Michelle was brought to the edge of the island by boat, then lifted high and carried to her throne where Kevin was awaiting her arrival. She was given a headband of fresh flowers to wear and dressed in a long white sarong. The wedding guests were all guests from the neighboring hotels who came to witness this special take-your-breath-away event. They stayed in the honeymoon suite over water bungalow. It was a complete fairytale wedding. I loved watching the videos when they returned. I hope in my lifetime I will also get to go one day. It is on my bucket list.

Michelle received a job offer she couldn't refuse and became the catering director for a top Country Club in Palm Desert. After the first two years, she became pregnant but continued to work for the first few months. I encouraged her to come be my new spa director and run my business. She could have a nice income and wouldn't have to work so hard. She accepted.

Michelle taught me to get a binder with clear plastic sleeves and go out to every place that was anywhere close to doing my type of services, get a copy of their menu of services and put it in the book. Soon I had everyone's services offered, the description of each and the prices they were charging. I saw where everyone was doing massages also in the day spa business along with pedicures. So I slowly started adding in massages. I had an additional room added, so now one room could do facials, one room could do massages, while in the front area where the waterfall was you could have a manicure and now pedicures. I had seven massage therapists on call, as that became a very popular treatment. One of the biggest, most profitable changes came from how I did my menus. I looked at everyone else's and they all seemed boring; deep cleansing facial, European facial, Swedish massage, deep tissue massage, etc. I wanted mine different. I knew I was marketing to people all over the world who were searching to come to a spa in Palm Springs while they were on vacation. I wanted to transport them to a tropical island in their mind while just reading my descriptions of available treatments "Rainforest Massage (Swedish massage) Relax in this tropical atmosphere while having warm oils massaged on your body as you drift away into a relaxing sleep." Whereas the other spas would say, "Swedish massage," period. We had so many cool names. Our spa pedicure was called "Hang Ten." Then I started adding spa packages where one could choose from a combination on all treatments creating a package if you had them all called "Over the Edge."

Next I wanted to have my products and cosmetics become private label with my signature logo. I had a photographer come take a signature picture, where Michelle was the model lying on a massage table with fresh orchids placed close to her head on a pillow. In the background was the tropical waterfall. Very colorful, very relaxing, a place you wanted to be. I paid my massage therapists to give me classes on doing massages and my estheticians on how to do facials. Then I started creating my very own personalized signature facial. I took the best from each person and put it all together into one treatment. First I would cleanse, scrub, tone the skin, put the steam on, and while they were lying there with the steam I would massage the neck and shoulders, hands and arms, then apply the masque and while relaxing more, put warm steam towels on the feet followed by massage of the feet and legs. By the time I had finished with a 15-minute foot massage they were already feeling like Jell-O. I would then take off the masque with warm steam towels, tone the skin and add eye cream, throat cream and moisturizer. Once the relaxing facial massage was finished, I would turn them over onto their tummy and do a warm oil back massage complete with hot stones. After this 1½ hour signature facial I created, the guests had a hard time walking out of the room. The guests were completely under the influence, so relaxed, and the word soon spread about this signature facial.

One of my favorite and most memorable experiences began the day I started the building of the day spa. I worked alone at the beginning - a one woman show. Outside my building towards the back was where the dumpsters were for all the adjacent businesses. This also happened to be where several of the local drunks hung out. They would go buy the cheap beer across the street at a liquor store, hard liquor if lucky, then come back and join their friends behind the dumpster and drink until they would pass out. I would go alone to put my trash out and due to the filthy dirty conditions and the no shower stench, it was often more than I could handle. I was slightly scared and would go home and have some nightmares, praying for an answer of what to do. One morning shortly after awakening, I knew exactly what I was going to do.

I went to work in my jeans and T-shirt instead of spa clothes and opened up the doors to the garbage dumpsters and started pulling both of these large things out of there. Then I brought a shovel and started shoveling all the old cardboard boxes, trash, debris and attached a hose for water and started hosing down the place, making it spotless and putting everything back just like new. Then I went and got fresh cardboard boxes and cut them open to lay flat. Right about that time about four of the street homeless showed up for the daily meet, drink and sleep. They asked what I was doing and I told them I was making their home nice for them. I invited them in to sit down with me on the cardboard and I got to know each and every one of them. Later I had pizza delivered for them. Well, they never forgot my kindness and from that moment on they were very protective of me. One time one of my new friends said I gave him the reason to change his life. He went to the local church where they helped clean him up and he went to AA and actually got a job. He found a beautiful shell while he was away and came to bring it to me as a gift of thanks. I will treasure that shell forever.

One night I was in the spa alone. The last guest had just left. I blew out all the candles but somehow missed one that was in the bathroom. It was one of those half coconut shells filled with wax and a wick. I had it sitting on a wicker shelf. It had burned to the bottom and I didn't realize the flame was still burning. I was in the front of the spa doing paperwork when I started smelling smoke. I walked around the corner and there were flames coming out of the bathroom heading towards the big open vent that would take the flames into the attic and completely take the entire attached building down, including the bar at the end with all alcohol. Oh My Gawd! I grabbed the fire extinguisher and tried to knock it down which it did for a second while I grabbed the phone to call 911. Now, mind you, the fire department was next door to me on the other side of the wall. But because I was on a one way street and they didn't know I was right behind them, they completely missed the entrance to get to me and took a moment to realize it. In the meantime I had to resort to grabbing as many small bowls of water possible and start throwing it on the flames. By the time the firefighters got there I was able to let them know I had put it out. They came in and double checked it for hot spots. Thank goodness I don't break under pressure and can react quickly due to my experience as a firefighter in previous years. But now what to do? Things in the bathroom were destroyed and business insurance had that all cleaned for me, fixtures replaced, and so on. Then it was time to paint it all like new and all my homeless friends got together and sobered up long enough to come and completely clean and paint my business in one day and we made a party out of it. Pizza and beers for everyone! I thanked them so much over and over again. You know what they said to me? "We just wanted to make your home nice for you."

When Michelle came to run the spa for me during her last few months of pregnancy everything changed. Overnight, she took what I thought was doing well, to making it great. I had been paying all the sub-contractors 60% and the business 40%. Her first order of business was to hold a meeting. It was announced that the percentages were now reversed. The business would now take 60%, since we did all the marketing and paid the rent and utilities. Of course we added on 18% gratuity to each service. Every single person chose to stay. They believed in her and they believed in this little spa. Most massage therapists made close to $1,000 a week. Not too shabby! Michelle did massive marketing. The website got upgraded. More services were added and she went for the big money in doing private parties. It became the social thing to do among girlfriends and they had a blast. We added the "after-hours" for couples only; side-by-side treatments that took 4½ hours, bringing in $450 a couple. The Guest House was now known as a romantic place to go and was featured in a major publication given to celebrities to know the hidden spots not to be seen, bringing in some never-can-tell names where the limo drivers would drop off and pick up without anyone knowing.

Meanwhile, my mother continued to get worse. The caregiver that I depended so much upon went back to college to get her nursing degree and had to leave me. I went to our local agency and they sent a very nice girl the next morning. She was very fun loving and a great help to my mom right from the start. They had a special bond and I always felt my mother was safe when she was there. Nothing was more important to me than knowing Mom was taken care of while I was at work. The minute I left the spa it was straight home where I became the caregiver doing all the spoiling. I just loved it. But at the same time it made for very long days and never a day off for many years.

Since Michelle was doing marketing, I thought it was the right thing to do to take her to all the hotels and introduce her to the front desk people who were already sending us business. So we made a special day just for that. Michelle was now about seven months pregnant and I took her to one of my favorite hotels which happened to be "clothing optional," the nicest of many in Palm

Springs. They had called me several months earlier to see if I could come do a facial in the room for one of their guests. The money was not an issue for the client so I loaded up all my facial equipment and showed up at the hotel. After ringing the doorbell and announcing who I was through the intercom, I was greeted by the naked owner. He was the nicest man who greeted me with a big hug and welcomed me in and thanked me for coming over. They already had someone who did massages poolside under a special gazebo area, but this client wanted a facial. Tom gave me a tour, introduced me to his nude wife working at the front desk and then showed me the pool area completely occupied with nude couples lying around sunbathing. I felt very comfortable and thought what a great place and wished I was a couple so I could come spend time there. I was escorted to the room and greeted by a naked woman waiting for her treatment. The facial went fine, I was paid well, and as I was leaving, the owners asked if they could use my services again if given enough notice. I said I would love to do it and told them to just add $50 traveling fee to the services on my spa menu.

I also was invited to come lie out poolside anytime I wanted for the daily fee. I started doing this for my relaxation at least once every couple of weeks and being nude in front of others who had the same mindset as I did of how beautiful the human body is was really nice. My favorite part was every day at happy hour, the lobby was set up with carafes of wine, fresh fruit and cheese platters, and always, the naked owner would carry a tray of fresh fruits and wine down into the pool for all of us raft floaters to be enticed and invited us for happy hour. I would often get out of the water, have a glass of wine and go relax in the hot tubs for a short time, while savoring the moment of complete relaxation. I would often get a massage poolside and it felt so free and so relaxing not to be covered by a sheet during the treatment. So I never gave it much thought when I took Michelle to introduce her. She didn't seem bothered by the idea, or at least she never mentioned anything. Again the naked owner greeted us and I introduced her and she was given the same tour around the pool. She seemed very comfortable and had perfectly adorable manners when being introduced to all the nude friends I had met along the way. She was smart, especially knowing every time I went there to do a treatment it was good money for the business. We left, and as soon as we got in the car Michelle broke into unstoppable laughter with tears were pouring down her face. Then we were both hysterically laughing. She had to call Kevin right away and if you could hear how she described her shock and how she had to control the laughter from the moment the owner opened the doors. She had me laughing even harder. A moment in time I know neither of us will ever forget!

CHAPTER 24

Never Trust the Handy Man

I started to have a problem with the caregiver helping Mom several months later. Sometimes she'd forget to show up and I'd have to call to check on her. I began to suspect she must be on drugs, so I called the agency and came to find out they never did a background check on her. I had to let her go and it would take one extra day for them to find someone to replace her. Early the following morning when Michelle arrived at the spa she found the front door broken with glass everywhere. She called 911 and then called me, telling me she was waiting for the police to arrive in order to go inside to see what damage had been done. I contacted the agency ad they said they would have someone over within the next two hours. Mom was doing great. She had just ate her breakfast and the TV was all set for her morning shows, so I left right away to get to the spa to check out the damage and to make sure Michelle was okay. When I got there, the police had arrived. No money had been taken, and it didn't even look like anyone went inside, so all I had to do was clean up the door glass on the floor and have the glass company come out right away and replace it. The charge was only three hundred dollars and I couldn't help but think how much worse it could have been. After the door was repaired, Michelle stayed and I went home to Mom and was able to be there in time for the new caregiver. I got her all settled with Mom's routine, and then I went back to the spa for a few more hours to make sure all was okay.

Everything was good at home and in the morning I went to call Michelle from the landline and couldn't get through. I called the telephone company from my cell and they had me go outside to the grey telephone company box in the backyard and open it up. When I did, I saw where the phone lines had been cut. I was starting to get very concerned. A broken door at the spa, phone lines cut at home, so I called Aaron and he said to hang up and he would call the local police and report it for me. It wasn't but a few moments later when I saw a police car pull up in front of the house. That was fast!

The officer came to the door and asked for my mother by name.

I thought that was strange, but I let him in. He said a person at the local Bank of America was trying to cash one of my mother's checks. The check was in my mom's name, but the bank teller felt something wasn't right and went to check on my mother's signature. It didn't match and she called the police. In the meantime the woman who had tried to cash the check had left the bank. They had no cameras on in the bank so I will never know 100% who it was, but on the recovered check there was a notation on the bottom of the check that said "caregiver services."

I couldn't believe it! The police hadn't arrived because of my son's call, but because they had a tip off from the bank. The police asked me to check where my mom's checks were kept so I could see if more were missing. We had a joint account for twenty-five years and the checks used were from that. The checks were always kept in the top drawer in my bedroom and Mom hadn't signed a check for years. Yes, all the checks were missing. The bank was notified to put a stop on the account. They found over one thousand dollars had been cashed in the past twenty-four hours. The worst part was I discovered all my jewelry had been stolen.

Every sentimental piece that my mother and I had saved from both our lifetimes was now gone. The bank reimbursed the money used in the fraudulent check scheme and the home insurance paid for the jewelry, but no amount of money could ever replace the personal value. I was at least grateful that I had already passed down to my daughter and my son the things I wanted them to have from me, diamonds and the more expensive pieces.

I now knew why the spa's glass door had been broken. They didn't want anything from the spa. They wanted the distraction to get me out of the house so they could take exactly what they wanted. They cut the phone lines so mom could not call the police. I believe to this day it was the caregiver I had fired. She knew I would have to leave to check on the day spa and also knew my mother, and knew her two dogs so they wouldn't bark. Nothing could ever be done to prove it was she, but who else would know to write a note on the check for caregiver services? Just another lesson on how people get jobs to be caregivers as a way to cheat and steal from the elderly, especially Alzheimer's patients. Poor Mom would never be able to tell me even if she realized what was happening.

I guess I should be grateful no one hurt my mother. The first police officer was ready to leave to go back to the bank for more information, when a female police officer showed up. Now this was the one my son had called about to let her know the phone line had been cut. The two officers talked about the case and the connections to both the spa and home. The female officer was very nice and understanding. She said I should do what she had recently done at her home and that was have motion sensor lights put around the home, and not to wait too long to do it. I asked who did the work for her and she said she was referred to a gentleman that the local real estate offices used for all repairs to their properties. She gave me the handyman's name and the number to the real estate office. I called right away, and they referred me to him. I called him and within fifteen minutes he was at my house. I told him what had happened and he said he would go right away and buy the fixtures, and lights and install them on the front and back of the home within the next few hours. The charge to me would be forty dollars in labor and the cost of the fixtures and bulbs. I couldn't believe how kind he was. I couldn't help but notice he was very handsome and extremely muscular, of foreign nationality with a huge smile showing white teeth against his tanned skin. Or maybe it was because I hadn't dated in over a year and a half since Al, and now, here was someone also concerned for our safety. He did an excellent job over the next few hours and left me his number to call him right away if there were any further problems. He said he would stop by the following day to check on us.

The cost for Mom's care was growing higher, but as long as I was working, I could afford her private in-home care for now. The nights were still with me alone. I would get her dressed for bed in her nightgown, but by morning she somehow managed to take off her clothes. There was always a naked mom in the morning for me to check on. One night Mom fell in the bathroom. The noise awakened me from a sound sleep. I jumped out of bed and ran to the bathroom to see what had happened. Mom lay naked on the bathroom floor and wasn't able to lift herself up. She was complaining of pain in her arm. I tried to put some clothes on her and get her to her knees in order for her to help me get her to her feet. I called my son who was an hour away and told him what was happening. As a firefighter-paramedic he asked if I could get her to the hospital and if I couldn't, to call the ambulance and he would meet me at the hospital. I was able to get her into the car within the next half-hour and my son must have broken all speed limits because he arrived immediately. We learned she had broken her wrist.

As luck would have it, it was her right wrist and she was right handed. Her personal hygiene would suffer, if you get my drift. I soon found I would have to do much more for her than before. Now she needed physical cleaning and the expense got much higher since I now had to hire a nurse in order for me to go to work. This accident was when I really noticed a change in her Alzheimer's. Her memory suffered a rapid decline.

The handyman Ricardo did follow-up on his promise to check on us. Since his pricing was so great and he had told me about his business and that it wasn't a one man business but he had teams of workers he sent out to jobs every day, I asked how much it would cost to paint my mom's home. He said he would do it for eight hundred dollars. I had recently got an estimate for fifteen hundred dollars so I told him I would love to hire him to do the outside. He showed up with a team of four, including himself. They worked over the next two days. One day they did all the prep work, the next day, the actual painting. The job was fantastic. I was very impressed. Over the next month, I found quite a few jobs I needed done and the price was always right. He had built up a great friendship with my mother, new caregivers and me. I found myself being more attracted to him. Looking back I'm sure it was because for the first time in my adult life I was scared a little and there he was. The fact that he was so handsome and strong was an added bonus.

Once my mom's hand was healed, she was able to start doing more things for herself again. I always tried to give her as much assistance as I could, but at the same time to let her feel independent. She didn't like anyone to go to the bathroom with her. She just needed help up from the sofa and to start her on her walk, heading her in the right direction. It wasn't long before she fell again, this time during the daytime in the living room. Luckily, she did not break anything this time, but her balance had become more unstable. It was so hard to take her to a doctor's appointment. She didn't have patience now. She would sit in the waiting room for a few minutes reading, then tell me she had to go to the bathroom. I would take her to the bathroom. I would bring her back sit her down again in the waiting room and after a few minutes it was a repeat of what she had just done. She told me she needed to go to the bathroom. I would tell her she just went and she would say no she didn't and needed to go right now. She would try to stand up by herself, and I had to be so careful she didn't fall and we would go back to the bathroom. And this routine would continue again until her name was called. Then once she was taken to her exam room, she kept asking me," When is the doctor was coming? I want to go home now. I have to go to the bathroom." She would say in a loud voice to the nurse, "Where is the doctor? When is that dumb cluck going to get in here?" It was so difficult. The doctor couldn't help but overhear her. By now it had been eight years since she was first diagnosed. Her doctor told me the time had come for me to start looking for a place for her to go. It was going to continue to get much worse and with her falling. She was going to need more round-the-clock care.

Since I was working, I couldn't be awake all night caring for her. Michelle and I went to quite a few facilities in our area for inspection. All were private pay and the cost very high, about $5,000 a month. My mother's income at the time was only eighteen hundred dollars a month. Even with my help I knew we would not be able to afford them. I found a facility that specialized in taking care of Alzheimer's patients. They offered to take her income and help me fill out the forms for state funds that would make up the difference. It was more of a hospital setting. It had over 100 residents and complete nursing staff.

My mom had made me promise to never put her in any kind of a nursing home. I wanted to respect her wishes as much as I possibly could. At one time, Mom had taken a college course and became a certified nurse's aide. She could never forget all the things she had seen during her training and made me promise to never do that to her. There was no way I would ever get her to go of her own free will either. Since Mom had been spoiled and pampered like a princess all these years and her mind was still in tune with her surroundings, I had to make sure that she be placed where she couldn't tell it was a nursing home. Until I could find the right place, I had to continue to give her the best possible care I could afford at home. The costs grew and grew. It took everything I made at the spa along with her income to cover the costs. I had to start paying lots of bills and expenses on my charge cards. The bills kept getting bigger each day.

One night I was home alone with Mom in the living room. She was on the sofa and I was at my desk. She said she needed to go to the bathroom, so I helped her get up and walked her to the bathroom. When she was finished, she came back and sat down again. Everything seemed fine. About 20 minutes later I asked if I could get anything for her. She asked for a glass of water. As I walked over to get her glass I felt the carpet was wet. I went and opened the bathroom door and water came pouring out, flooding the living room, down the hallway and into the bedrooms. She had put a stopper in the sink when she washed her hands and forgot to turn off the water. Now it became impossible for me to keep my mom there that night.

The rest of the night was a nightmare because Mom had to sleep in my bed in my room and had to use my bathroom since she would fall if she tried to walk to the other part of the house. She got up and down all night to go to the bathroom but couldn't figure out where she was. This was the beginning of many difficult days to follow. Poor thing; I felt so bad for her.

Michelle had just given birth to my grandson Logan, so I couldn't take her there. My son Aaron was helping his dad take care of his very ill grandmother. Aaron did surprise me in a good/bad way. He said," Mom, you know how you and Al broke up a long time ago? "Yes." Well, he and I have remained friends all this time. We go water skiing all the time. So I called Al and just told him what had happened and he wants you to bring Grandma up there to stay with him until everything is fixed at home. Is it okay if he calls you, and you decide after that?" Al and I spoke for about a half hour and he was right. I needed help and now wasn't the time to bring up boyfriend- girlfriend issues. So under the circumstances, I felt humble and so grateful that I had a place to take my mom. It wasn't a time to be mad and upset at my son or Al at that point. They were both right there for me when I needed them. For that I will be forever grateful. Al was the most gracious host and during our stay there, it was very trying. I had to walk Mom everywhere because she would lose her balance and fall easily. She would go to the bathroom, come back, sit down and ask to go again. She did eat well for us and she loved Al to pieces, and he was especially kind to her. Too bad he was a liar, cheater, and I could never trust him again. But he really did have a kind heart. One night we were able to have a talk about us and what had happened. He said the reason he had to lie was because he didn't want to lose me, that I was the best woman ever to come into his life, blah, blah, blah. He started buying me gifts and bringing them home each day in hopes of winning me back into his life again. I had lost that loving feeling and once it's gone, it's gone. But he was sure there for me when I needed him the most.

Moving an Alzheimer's patient in later stages is the hardest thing to do. It took two weeks for all the carpet to be pulled up and the work to be done well enough to bring Mom back into her home. During those two weeks I was not able to work at the spa.

The doors had to be closed for business. Michelle was now busy with her new baby, and there was no one else I could depend on. I often thought of selling the spa, especially since it had been making a nice amount of money, but the problem was, it was my hands, my facials, after all was said and done, and Michelle's marketing that made the place. There was really nothing to sell. But right now I had to come up with Plan B to make this work better.

Finally, I was able to bring Mom back home. Things were able to get somewhat back to normal. One day the handsome handyman Ricardo stopped by when he saw my car parked outside. He said he was concerned about us and wondered what had happened. I told him all about the water damage and having to stay somewhere for two weeks until it was repaired. He made sure I knew that he was there to help me and that I'd never have to call the insurance company again if something happened. He would make sure all the repairs were completed by him. He started bringing Mom and me flowers and before long, invited me out to dinner and a movie. He began leaving flowers at my door early in the morning, and he made it very clear he enjoyed spending time with me over the last few months while he was doing work on the property. He was hoping that I would allow him to come over more often and take me out.

Over the next few weeks I was actually having real dates again. It felt wonderful. He made me feel like I was the most beautiful woman on earth. He said he had a plan to help bring a woman to give additional care to my mother. She didn't speak much English, but would make sure everything was clean, and she could cook very well. The cost to me weekly would be very small, since the woman would be so grateful to have a beautiful home to live in. It sounded great. At this point there wasn't anything I wouldn't do to help my mother. I wanted to honor her wishes and keep her in her own home. The business was barely making the caregiver's costs but I knew I couldn't do it alone. My hands were tied, so I told him, I would welcome the help. About two weeks later he brought the most loving, kind woman to my home. Her name was Stella. Finally, I had a little relief just knowing another helper was there with me.

Ricardo invited me to go away for the weekend, just the two of us. I needed to get away. I made sure Mom had all the coverage she would need. I had the spa back up and running and in great shape, and had someone come in to do facials while I was gone Friday, Saturday, and home on Sunday

Beautiful days of sun including horseback riding on the beach, dinner, dancing and a wild night of making love - what could be nicer? The following day, Saturday, was equally beautiful and come Saturday evening, after dinner, while sitting outside having cocktails, Ricardo said there were some things he needed to share with me. First, he wanted to let me know that he was in love with me. He had never met anyone like me who was so kind and generous, loving and forgiving. He started telling me about his childhood and what it was like being poor, with parents who would beat him, how he would go to sleep hidden inside a Laundromat at night, just so he could stay warm. By the time he was a young boy, he didn't have much of an education, and the older boys would always get him into trouble. Before long, he was hanging out with the bad boys because they always had food at their family's homes.

If he didn't have shoes, his friends would find something for him to steal and that would earn him the shoes. Over the years these friends became adults and soon became part of a drug cartel. In later years they became the biggest drug dealers around. Money and women were unlimited. He told me he was no longer involved in any of that. He wanted to marry me, and he wanted me to know about his past.

Now, to know me personally, would be to know I trust everyone. I love almost everyone I have ever met. I do not believe I am here to be the judge of anyone. That is for God to do. Even if you are a sinner, and who isn't, who am I to judge you? I have made a lifetime of mistakes. But I have to believe God puts people in my path for a reason. Ricardo had always shown himself as being devoted to me and my mother. At this time, Michelle was busy with her husband and new baby. Aaron was helping his father with his very ill grandmother. Ricardo was becoming my strength, someone I could lean on who was actually able to be there for me. The fact that I found him sexy and handsome didn't hurt either.

Ricardo continued to go on with his story. He told me he had been in prison before twice for six years each time, so a total of twelve years. The last time he was to appear before the judge he was to receive a ten-year sentence and his cartel friends paid off the judge $6,000 cash and his sentence was dropped to two years. He ended up staying six years because he had company business he had to do while in prison. Since a lot of the drug activity business is run from inside the safe walls of a jail cell, Ricardo's job was to follow behind the car carrying drugs across the border. He was to report the shipment was received. If there was any problem of any kind, he was given orders to kill the person who messed up the delivery. If it wasn't killing the person himself then it was arranging for a member of that family to be killed. I now realize I am in the company of a murderer, a cold-blooded killer who wants to marry me.

He continued with his confession as I ordered another drink. Now, for some reason, as he told me he served his sentence, paid his dues, was no longer working for the cartel, was retired, and was not on parole, I was still trying to not be judgmental, because after all, he was being completely honest with me, something most men

I had known had never had the guts to be. But Ricardo was here confessing his deep love and loyalty to me. For a moment it even felt nice to know I would be protected and no harm could come to me. Looking back it was truly a moment of complete disbelief that this loving, kind man could kill someone. He confided in me how he was able to retire from the cartel in order to win his freedom. Which he did and the more he kept talking the more I knew I was learning too many things I should never been told. We spent the rest of the night talking and talking, me learning more and more about the life he led, details I should never have been told. But all he knew was he wanted to marry me and we could live anywhere I wanted. He would make sure my mother had the best of care and for the rest of my life I would have anything I ever needed. He had a great legitimate business, and worked very hard building it. He had lots of cash stashed away and he could build a home for me, anything in this world. He never had a woman, especially a woman like me, a real lady, who believed in him and made him feel like I did.

CHAPTER 25

And Then What Happened?

We left to drive home the following day and when he dropped me off at home and left, I called both Michelle and Aaron and asked them to meet me at the spa in the morning. I had something important to tell them.

By the time I arrived at the spa, both Aaron and Michelle were waiting for me. I told them Ricardo wanted me to marry him. I have always been 100% honest with both of them. I also told them some of what I had learned about Ricardo the day before. I kept some things from them for their protection. This meeting with my children didn't go very well, as you could imagine. The bottom line was NO, you cannot marry him. You cannot ever see him again. My son was literally crying from anger; he was upset and mad. Michelle was in such shock that she was speechless. They insisted I go home and end this right now.

So, after the brief meeting with my kids as I am driving the half hour to get home, I'm thinking about Ricardo the murderer who believes I went to tell my kids my great news and that I will come back and tell him I will marry him. I have a Mother that I do not know what I am going to do about her now that I have to deal with all these things on my own. I have a day spa that is doing great. I loved working there. I was so proud of where it started and what it was now, and the potential for the future. But I had to concentrate only on telling Ricardo goodbye. I called him when I got home and asked him to come over. Stella was in the kitchen, making some great food for Mom and me, and I let the weekend caregiver leave.

Ricardo came right over. I asked him to go sit outside with me. He asked how everything went with Michelle and Aaron. I told him it didn't go well at all. They were against the marriage and wanted me to give it some time, since so many things were going on right now with the business and Mom and asked me not to make any quick decisions. About that time Aaron called me and was still very upset. He asked to speak to Ricardo. I gave the phone to him and I could hear Aaron telling him to stay away from his mother, that I was loving and kind and that he didn't want him to screw up the rest of my life, that he needed to leave me alone and never come back. He told him he was only going to create a bad life for me no matter how good he thinks it will be, that he knows the person he is and the things he has done and he doesn't want any of that brought into his mother's life. If he continued to see his mother she would never see her son again. Aaron remained calm, cool and collected throughout the call. He handed the phone to me and Aaron told me to tell him goodbye and end this right now.

Hearing those words from my son, hit me like a brick. I knew he was right. As much as Ricardo tried to convince me he would give me the world, this was not negotiable. Nothing and no one is going to keep me from my son. I told Ricardo we should never see each other again. He gave it all some thought. Michelle then called. She asked to speak to Ricardo. She told him she didn't feel good about this relationship and she hopes that it would end. Ricardo asked her if she would never see me again, also, and she said no, she would always see her mom, nothing would change that. But she didn't feel he was the best person for me to marry. Again,

Ricardo was very calm. I left and went inside to check on what was going on, and when I came back outside Ricardo said he had enough respect for me and my love for my children to say goodbye and to leave my life. But there were certain conditions I had to agree to: 1) I was to give him back every picture we had taken together, so he could take them in the middle of the desert, tear them up and throw them away as if we never existed. 2) He wanted back any gifts he had ever given me. 3) He gave me a large dollar amount of money I needed to pay him. 4) He was going to take Stella back. Those were all of his requests. He needed to have the respect he deserved. He knew it wasn't because I didn't love him, but because of the wishes of my children. So there was nothing broken with us. He just needed to make sure I gave him the respect for the man he is and for the time spent together.

I was happy and relieved to give back everything. I didn't have all the money he was asking for but I wrote him checks dated over the next six months for him to keep cashing until my debt was paid in full. I was wearing an expensive gold and diamond bracelet that had been given to me by someone else. I went to the bathroom and took it off my wrist. When I came back Ricardo had told Stella she would be leaving and he was putting her suitcase in his car. Since I couldn't speak her language, I looked into her eyes, with tears in mine, and I gave her a big hug and slipped the bracelet into her hands and motioned for her to hide it. It was a moment in time I will never forget. She was a beautiful loving woman with such a kind heart. She touched my soul and took very good care of my mother.

I didn't sleep very well that night as you can imagine. But I had bigger problems than Ricardo to think about now. I had a business to run that I couldn't afford to be away from, and a mother who was getting worse by the moment. The one blessing through all the confusion she never knew anything to be wrong. She would never remember anyone that had been in her home besides me, and I continued to spoil her every second I could.

The following day, I spoke to both Aaron and Michelle and told them it was all over and how it ended. They were very relieved and if it was just a matter of money to be paid off, that was better than what it could have been had Ricardo been left to stay in my life.

The day Aaron met Michelle and me at the spa and became so upset, he left and drove straight to Al's home. It was Al I later found out who was going to make sure that I was okay. He didn't care about the fact I was with another man, because he knew my heart and he knew how easily I believed the best in all people. He just wanted to make sure I was safe. Al called and asked me to come up and see him. I did, and we sat down and talked about any options I had at this point as far as taking care of Mom and running the business. Al and I both felt it was the best decision to place Mom in a residential care facility. She was starting to fall more and needed more nursing-type care than I was soon going to be able to afford. I started going through Al's phone book looking for a residential care facility. There was one that specialized in Alzheimer's. I set up an appointment to go and see it.

The administrator was so nice and seemed to understand exactly what I was going through. She gave me a tour and told me they had daily activities and showed me the calendar with all the events scheduled each day. They had two sofas in the living room area where Mom would be able to watch her TV shows during the day.

She showed me a nice private room close to the living room and said my mom could have that room. Because it was close to the living area, I felt it was a great place and I was told I could bring my mother's entertainment center with her TV, along with her rocking chair, lots of family pictures and anything for her room that would make her feel at home. The administrator told me she would need to interview my mom to make sure she was the right candidate for the facility and that she would get along well with the other residents. We set up a meeting. I was at work that day and my mother's nurse was at home with her. The nurse told me the administrator didn't stay very long, and soon called me to say my mother was welcome. The costs were fifteen hundred for a semi-private room and two thousand for a private one. I explained my mother only had eighteen hundred a month income, but she would need a private room and I wanted the room that was available close to the living room. She said she would speak with the owners and they agreed to the eighteen hundred a month.

I felt this was the answer to my prayers. I had found the right place for my mother. The day Mom came to the facility I brought all her personal things along. Al had loaded his truck with her entertainment center, her rocking chair, and her possessions that meant something to her, including pictures. When we arrived I was told my mother wouldn't be able to have the room she was promised, that it was given to someone else. Now this was a very hard decision. The truck was fully loaded, Mom was with me, and I was mentally prepared to have her move in while I sat in the new living room with her while Al unloaded the truck with all her belongings. I felt I couldn't turn back now. I had no other options. The administrator showed me the new room Mom would be staying in. The room was double the size of the other room, and just a door down from the bathroom and two doors down from the administrator's office. The question I had was why was she being put in the men's wing and was told that right now that was the only room that was left. But they would move her to the first available single room on the women's side when it opened. I was assured since they were always close at hand she would receive good care. I made it clear Mom loses her balance easily and I felt she needed someone to help her to walk at all times. They said no problem.

While Al unloaded everything, Mom and I sat in the living room watching her favorite shows, and she was making friends she would never remember meeting a few minutes later. The only thing good about that day was Mom was very happy in her new surroundings. The administrator told me that for the first two weeks I needed to stay away, because my Mom would need to adjust to her new place and if I was to visit she would want to go home with me. I remember trying very hard to stay away the first week, but had to come see her during the second week. Mom was so happy to see me. She still remembered me and was smiling when she saw me and said, "Hi honey," and told her other roommates that I was her daughter. Mom seemed to have them catering to her every need. My mother's smile was all I needed to see. I was reassured I had made the best choice for Mom's new home. Or so I thought.

During the week I was away from Mom, I was able to get everything organized back at home and get back to the day spa. It wasn't but two days later at the spa when I received a call from Ricardo. He said he missed me very much and that Stella had told him not to give up hope and that I would return to him. I never told him what I had done about my mother. I didn't want him to think I was living alone. I told him that as much as I cared about him and all the wonderful memories I had with him, I loved my son and family much more. I asked him to respect my decision. We ended the conversation politely and he said if I changed my mind he was there for me.

A few days later, I received a call from the owner of the business next door to the spa saying the glass door of the spa was broken. I thought, oh no, here we go again. But this time I made sure the house was locked up tight since Mom was no longer there. I drove to the spa to find the same door broken. I called 911 to report it and waited for the police to come. I went inside and once again nothing was taken. I had the glass company come out put in the new glass door and went home to make sure everything was okay there. All was as perfect as I had left it. It was hard to sleep that night, being in the house all alone. I couldn't even sleep in my own bed, so I slept in the living room, with the phone right next to me, keeping one eye open and Mom's two dogs right next to me to alert me if they heard something. The more I thought about the glass breaking this time and nothing being taken, it was my gut feeling that Ricardo had hired someone to do it, just to try to scare me enough to call him and have him come to my rescue. But I never did. I never told Aaron or Al about the glass door being broken. Somethings were better off not being said. I was scared enough, just trying to handle all going on around me.

During that same week, I had many appointments with guests who had been trying over the last couple of weeks to get an appointment with me. Business was booming. It was a Friday night and I ended up working until eight o'clock and I had to keep reminding myself to be sure to get gas in the car on my way home. I closed up the spa and walked out to the parking lot that was completely filled with cars and lots of people walking around the area as any typical Friday night in downtown Palm Springs. I couldn't find my car anywhere. I searched the entire parking lot and it wasn't there. My car had been stolen. I knew Ricardo had it taken. I knew when I didn't call him to my rescue when the door glass was smashed that I would hear from him again. I just didn't know it was going to become so serious now. I was really starting to get scared. I called the police and it wasn't long before a policeman on a bike and another one in a patrol car pulled up. They got the description of my car and just as I was telling them the information, they heard of the same type vehicle that was found on the side of the road heading into the city where I lived completely on fire. I knew right away Ricardo was responsible. The car was stolen and I didn't have any gas. The thief ran out of gas, and the car they must have had following to make sure all went well, picked up the thief and decided to torch it so no fingerprints or evidence was left behind to trace. The police drove me down to the station so at least I felt safe. I couldn't tell them anything, because I was too afraid for my own life at that moment. I let the police officer know I had an idea of who had done it, but I couldn't say anything. I'm sure they sensed my fear. They told me there was a woman police officer that I could talk to anytime I wanted and it would remain strictly confidential. They suggested I call an organization called Shelter from the Storm, a 24-hour hotline for women in danger and needing protection. They would send someone to pick me up and give me a place to stay. I went to the police department lobby and used the pay phone to call the shelter. They were so kind. They said they could come for me, that their service could only be used once, and I could stay as long as needed. I told them I wasn't sure what I needed to do and I would call them back.

The police department was across the street from the airport. I thought I would walk across the street and try to rent a car. I started to walk towards the parking lot when a car pulled up quickly. I felt I was about to be killed. My heart was pounding as I quickly hid in the bushes outside the Palm Springs Police Station. I knew too much. I had to watch whatever I might say, or I would be the one being handed a shovel and told to dig my own grave. How could a sheriff from my own burglary be the one to have recommended him to me? Obviously she never did a background check. Ricardo had worked his way to the top of the drug cartel world from the time he was a boy hungry for a bite to eat. Nothing and no one was going to take him down this time. It isn't often I find myself terrified for my life. I believe when he had the door at the spa shattered, it was to make me have to reach out to him for help. That didn't work. This time he had the car stolen so it would scare me enough to call him for help. He would make sure I paid the price for going to the police department. He wouldn't believe me, if I told him, I didn't tell them anything. He already had two strikes against him from serving two terms in prison. I watched the shadow of a man slowly get out of his car and remove what looked like a riffle bag in the darkness of the night. As he slowly walked in my direction, I wanted to make sure I didn't make a move from behind the bushes. I quickly tried to call my daughter from my cell phone for what I thought to be my last call. How did I get to this place in my life, when all I ever tried to do was be the most loving daughter, mother and girlfriend? Now, not knowing if I would ever see my family again, it was so important to me to have this one last chance to say goodbye.

Everything I had worked so hard for was right at my finger tips and in a blink of an eye it would soon be gone. My adult life has never been easy for me, but as long as I was able to make sure my family was well taken care of, I was happy. Now my life and my family's lives were in danger.

I was able to reach Michelle. She didn't need any of this stress in her life. She has a beautiful newborn baby and loving husband. I was crying into the phone and could barely breathe telling her about the car being stolen, me at the police department, and now hiding in the bushes. I told her I was on my way to rent a car at the airport. But, wait, what is that I see? Is that only a man parking in the police department parking place holding a suitcase and now walking toward the airport, perhaps to save money on the parking? What a feeling of relief came over me. My heart was still pounding from fear. Thank goodness it was just a stranger and I still had a chance to make a mad dash across the street. I told Michelle I would call her the second I rented the car and hung up. I ran as fast as possible to get safely inside the airport, watching everything and everyone around me. I tried to rent a car but only had my debit card with me and they would not accept that as payment. Any credit cards I had, I had tapped out close to the limits. So I didn't use them any longer and was just busy making payments to pay them off. I called Michelle and explained what had happened and she said, "Mom, don t worry. I will come down and rent the car with my credit card. I'll leave right away." She continued, "I cannot be any part of this and take chances with danger to my family but I will be there right away and get the car for you." Michelle did exactly that. She came down, rented a car for me, then left as quickly as she arrived. I called her when I got home safely. Then I called Al and told him what happened. He made me pack whatever I needed and get up to his home to stay so I would be safe. That was one of the things I always loved about Al. He made me feel safe and that no harm could come to me. The insurance paid for my car being stolen and I used that money to buy a used BMW in great shape that Al had found for me.

Al and I talked for hours about the choices I had. I would sell Mom's house since it was in my name, pay off as many bills as I could, and close the day spa. I could always open another spa, but right now I needed to get away from everything. Move to Al's where I know I would be safe and be close to my mother so I could spend time with her every day. And that is exactly what I did. One of the hardest decisions I made was close my business and move closer to my mother and started living at Al's. I can always have another spa, but I only have one mother. I was so happy her mind had no idea of all that was going on around her.

Within the first three days on the market, Mom's house sold. Michelle came over and helped me have the biggest garage sale ever. I think that is when I decided I never wanted to own a bunch of stuff. What I did want, I put into storage, including all my spa decorations and appliances, just in case the day ever came for another grand opening.

CHAPTER 26
I Can Do This!

I knew I had to have a job, and living a half-hour away from Palm Springs, in Joshua Tree, wasn't exactly the place to make a huge amount of money. They didn't have a spa anywhere nearby. So, being a creative person I found the busiest beauty salon in the adjacent city of Yucca Valley where there were two rooms for rent. I rented one room for two hundred fifty dollars a month to do my facials. The other room was rented to a massage therapist. I then went to the only radio station in town and started doing heavy advertising for the next two months, describing my hour-long facial with hot stone back massage for twenty five dollars. The phone at the salon rang off the hook! Within my first week of advertising on the radio I was sold out for two months. You might think that is cheap since I always charged one hundred twenty five dollars a facial, but I needed to make money and I was a hard worker and I made a lot of money plus my tips were always five to ten dollars on each treatment. Soon, I was working with the massage therapist and I created a spa package of my facial followed by her massage, so it worked in my favor. Most people love a massage, but I knew once they had my facial/back massage with hot stones, they would spread the word. Getting both treatments back to back was even better. Within the next few months I found a local place, and I leased it for a year and brought the massage therapist with me and rented a room out to her and created the first day spa in that city. The business was doing very well, very quickly. I had regular standard appointments booking, same persons, and same time each week.

All the while I was still staying at Al's, working very labor-intensive work and watching over my mother the best I could. Al, for some reason started acting strange again and it created an uncomfortable environment for me to live in. My guess was he wanted to be able to see other women or something, especially since he would come up with the strangest reasons to start an argument.

I thought I had no place to run to this time. But oh yes, I did have a place to run to. I loaded everything I had at his home, my clothes, cosmetics, etc. and I moved into the room where I did facials at the day spa. Al and I remained friends; I just said I couldn't do this life any longer. It made me start looking at all the big mistakes I had made in my life regarding men I decided from that moment on I would never date or look at another man.

My life was filled with nothing but me making bad choices where men were concerned. I found it was easier to stay single. It was difficult because I am so filled with love and passion but if I was to ever allow a man in my life he would have to be exceptional very caring, warm, loving, passionate, kind, a generous man who is always thinking of what we could do to make the world a little bit better. He would have to be head over heels in love with me and adore me to pieces. There were never any bad words said to Al. I could only thank him for giving me shelter and being there for me at a time that was the hardest. To this day, I am grateful to him.

My new living quarters at the spa was one of my funniest challenges to date. I joined the local gym, so I had a place to go shower before and after work each day, plus get a little exercise at the same time. When I finished my day at work, I packed my gym bag with all my necessities, took my shower, came back to the spa, dropped off my gym bag, and went next door for a nice dinner. If I was really tired, I would rent a movie, pull out a cart that I had put a portable TV and DVD player attached, wheel it into the facial room, where I folded up my massage table and inflated my very comfortable queen-size bed., watched my movie and went to sleep. In the morning it was back to the gym to get ready for my day at work. I have to admit, it really wasn't as bad as it might sound. I lit some candles, often times had food to go, would put on music and escape into a beautiful place in my mind. Often that meant thoughts of Rock and how I dreamed of being held and touched by him. The spa had a nice office with internet, restroom, refrigerator, kitchen sink, and microwave, so I was quite comfortable.

I had the most wonderful client named Marsha who came to have her facial every Monday morning. I had confided in her that I had to move out from where I was living and I was staying at the spa. After a month of knowing I was there she told me she and her husband had purchased a duplex earlier in the year and had left it sitting just as an investment. She told me that if I was interested, they would fix it up and I could rent one of the units for two hundred dollars a month. I said yes, sight unseen. So Marsha and her husband (a general contractor) surrounded the entire property with cyclone fencing. It was a two-bedroom unit, connected by both garages to the second two-bedroom unit. My new two bed room home was completely gutted, everything new was installed and the fresh paint made it feel as if it had just been built. The property was huge. Marsha loved organic gardens and asked if she were to buy all the flowers, trees and plants, would I enjoy doing the gardening on the property? I said sure; I LOVE gardening! They also made a large fenced-in enclosed private patio across the entire front of my unit. Once inside the gate, it felt like I was in my own private world.

I moved in and turned that place into the most awesome private escape anyone could ever want. I turned the inside of the courtyard into a tropical paradise. I put in a big waterfall that had been in storage since The Guest House. I added special lighting, tons of tall, full tropical plants and looking out from the big glass front living room window one felt transported to paradise. Marsha couldn't believe what I did to the entire place, giving it a "Tommy Bahama" look. Thanks to thrift shops and a very creative mind, it was gorgeous. Once that was finished, over the next year I planted over 300 plants, trees, roses, and shrubs, along with filling four big garden beds with organic vegetables to harvest and was blessed with crops to share. Marsha would buy everything, and I would plant. My favorite place was inside at the end of a hard day, lighting candles, putting on music and taking a relaxing bubble bath to soothe my nerves. God was really looking over me, and I felt blessed being given so much abundance

Each week I would do my mother's hair, manicure and pedicure. I had spoiled her all these years and I wasn't about to stop now. I would tease her and say how I treat her like a princess and she would always respond by saying, "You know, I like that," and give me a big missing a few front teeth smile. Mom loved my visits and often I took one day a week to do other residents haircuts also. A place would be set up for me in the living room with a big sheet underneath the chair to catch the hair. We would gather in the living room to sing favorite songs together from CDs I bought of old-time favorites. I'd see these elderly Alzheimer's patients sitting around in the living room, usually never saying a word, but when the music would play, they remembered all the words. It was magical.

After a month I was called and told my mother had fallen while walking to her room, but she was fine. Then another week or so later I had another call that my mom had fallen out of bed but she was just fine. Since Mom couldn't recall the falls, I had to go by what I saw and what was told to me. My Mother didn't seem in any pain at that time. A short time later the administrator quit working at this home. The new person who was promoted to being the administrator was a caregiver/cleaning person. I was shocked that she was put in charge, but felt the owners knew what they were doing. Whenever I had any questions to ask regarding my mom and her care the administrator would say she didn't know, but would find out the answer. Soon the activities director became the new administrator. This third administrator was always telling me she was unhappy with the way the owners would never follow-up on giving her the assistance she needed. Soon they became understaffed. The turnover of staff was obvious, and I could barely remember the new ones I met when they would be gone.

In May I was called and told my Mother had fallen again and they were going to take her for some x-rays to make sure she was okay. I was later told the x-rays showed she didn't have any broken bones, but was bruised and would be sore a few days. I came to check on her and she did have some big bruises on her hip and arm, where she must have fallen. After seeing my mom, I asked if the doctor had ordered any pain medications but I was told no. She was put in bed to get some rest and they put a portable potty next to her bed. Someone now had to be responsible to lift her from the bed to the portable potty chair. My mom only knew how to use the toilet so unless she sat on one she was not able to relieve herself.

Keeping in mind her room was at the back of the men's wing every time my mom felt she had to go to the bathroom she had to holler for help to make sure they could hear her requests. I'm sure she drove them all a little crazy. But they knew she really didn't need to go and, I suppose, got used to tuning out her requests. With limited staffing, it was getting harder for the caregivers to stop what they were doing and give Mom the attention she required. It was at this point I should have been told the truth. The x-rays did show a hairline fracture on her pelvic bone, so I could make arrangements to move her to a skilled nursing facility.

The one I had previously checked out was more like a large hospital. But my mother's mind was still too alert and she would know I was putting her in a nursing home, as she would call it. Since this was a big money-making business I was told lie after lie so I wouldn't take her from there. I couldn't surprise anyone there with my visits since the place was in lockdown for the safety of the patients. They always knew when someone was coming because the door bell had to be rung and someone would actually have to come open the gate in order for anyone to enter. During the next two weeks my mom became very violent and could be heard screaming and hollering, "Won't somebody help me please!" When I called to check on her, because the phone was down the hall from her room, I could hear her hollering. I kept telling the person in charge that day that my mom was in great pain. They finally gave her pain medication and told me it was the Alzheimer's that was causing the change in moods. I also noticed other patients acting in the same manner. I had never been around this type of illness, and it was only recently President Ronald Reagan had been diagnosed. Alzheimer's was not a mainstream illness at that time and wasn't spoken about much. I knew there was a chance to expect that mood changes were possible.

One night after hours I decided to come by to check on Mom and found her needing help to be lifted onto the potty chair. By the state law only one person is required during the night shift depending on the number of patients. The problem was the girl they had just hired only weighed about 100 pounds. She was new and this was her first night on the job. She had not met the owners when she was hired. It was obvious she would not be able to lift my mother, so I assisted her. In the living room an older man had pulled down his pants and somehow tripped on them and fell on the floor. I also helped her with this man and spent the rest of the evening going room to room helping her. The girl said she would be telling the owners she would have to quit if more help wasn't given to her. I left in the middle of the night after Mom fell asleep. I had a fully-booked day at the spa and a few hours left to get some sleep.

The next morning I called Ombudsman. (They oversee any complaints given at any facility, and can shut down a place instantly if needed.) I told them I felt my mother was being neglected and they said they would come unannounced to check on her. When I got a call back from Ombudsman they said that one person was all that was required due to the number of residents. They assured me they would keep checking on her.

My mom's crying and pleading for someone to help her became unbearable for me. The sound was something I have never heard before. The administrator again told me that the doctor had come to the facility that day and checked on my mother along with others. He said she was becoming more combative due to her Alzheimer's, but I didn't feel that was the case and had my mother's doctor changed in order to get a second opinion. On another occasion I had called around 10:30 A.M. to check on my mom, and I could hear her in the background hollering for help. I asked if my mom had gotten up yet and had her shower, breakfast, and clean clothes put on her. I was told no, they didn't get to her yet but they would very shortly. I was upset and told them she needed help. I could hear her in the background. I called Ombudsman and told them I felt she was being neglected. By the time they arrived an hour later, Mom was sitting up and they were feeding her. So Ombudsman told me they would start making more unexpected calls.

One thing that I thought was a good thing backfired. When your loved one is placed in a gated home with padlocks and you have to ring a doorbell to get in, it gives them the chance to give a false presentation, as if everything is just perfect with fake smiles. They know ahead of time who is waiting at the gate.

As the second week continued with my mother saying she was in pain, I called my son, and asked him to come down and take a look at her. When he checked his grandmother, he requested the administrator make arrangements to have her taken to the emergency room right away to get some x-rays. This is when I found out she had a crack in her pelvis. When my mom returned, the administrator told me Mom would need to have regular therapy and that she would be fine. By now, Mom was on stronger pain medication, yet still in pain. The administrator finally moved my mother to the front bedroom she was originally promised. I insisted she be close to everything and everyone.

I did not like the changes I was seeing in Mom and I made a call to the social worker at the other hospital-type facility. I asked if my mom could be moved to that facility. I explained what I had seen and didn't believe this was the best place for my mother. The social worker set up an appointment to come meet my mother. The cook at the facility told me she was concerned because my mom was not eating like she used to. The cook and I were both concerned because my mother was losing so much weight. I began bringing her my homemade food each day, food that I knew she would like. When I was there I noticed she would eat everything. It made me start to suspect she wasn't being fed and given the personal care required while eating. This was another good reason to move her to a new facility. I also requested they start giving her more nutrition. I made sure her insurance sent nutritional supplements. I purchased some in the meantime. In July, the families were invited to come and celebrate the Fourth with a barbeque. This was the first time I got to meet the owners. I assisted in serving the food and brought in some extra food myself. It was the only "activity" that actually ever happened during my mother's four-month stay.

By now I started to notice other residents that had been doing nicely when we first came there, also had a change in their personalities. Many of the residents seemed drugged. These were the same ones who only a couple months earlier sat around the living room singing with me. By September my mother appeared to be half the size she was a few months earlier. One day I was called and told to come right away. My mother was hallucinating and was talking to people in her room who weren't there. I came right away and they were right. My mom was talking about her mom waiting in the car for her outside and she needed to go now. Also, she saw there was a man in the room with a hat on. I told her I would go get something for her to eat before she could leave. I got some of her favorite foods and fed her and she ate every bite as if starving. The hallucinations went away.

A staff member told me he had seen this happen many times before in other patients of his and that my mom was getting ready to die now. This was why she hadn't been eating, because her body was telling her to start shutting down. The administrator told me she was going to place a request for hospice to be called now because my mom didn't have very long to live. I believed them since they had much more knowledge than I did.

It was now October and my mother's birthday was nearing. I knew I needed my family to be able to spend as much time with her as they could before she passed away, so I planned a nice birthday party for her at my home, because I didn't want the family to see her in that type of setting, especially in the condition she was in. I hired a caregiver from the facility for the day. The caregiver told me not many family members come to see their loved ones as much as I did. It really made me feel good to know that I did everything I thought I could have done for my mom. It was a nice party. Aaron came, Michelle, her new baby and my son-in-law. Mom was smiling all day long. It made her so happy to see her family. It was so strange that Mom couldn't remember anything at all and yet she never forgot who we were.

Now, it was November and I received a call in the middle of the night. Mom had fallen out of bed and had hit her head on her nightstand. She was complaining of back pain, so the only caregiver on staff that night told me she had called an ambulance to have her taken to the ER at the local hospital. I explained that I was at home from work that day and had been throwing up all night due to the flu. I would not be able to get to the emergency room at that moment. She said she would call me the minute she heard anything. After no call back from the caregiver, I called the residential facility. The caregiver told me it would take a few hours more for my mom to have x-rays. I asked her what my mom was wearing when she fell and she told me nothing. My mom was naked when she fell. I asked if she could make sure my mom had some warm clothes and could she please take them to her. She told me she would take care of it. I went back to bed to try to recover from the flu.

The facility never called me but I heard from the hospital. They told me they were transferring my mom to a skilled nursing facility. Mom would be put on IVs for the next week because they found she was dehydrated and had a severe bladder infection. It was by luck that my mom had fallen that night, otherwise she would have died shortly afterwards. In the meantime, Mom started responding to the treatments. This was the very same facility where I had spoken to the social worker and set up the appointment to have Mom transferred. Mom started putting on weight again and even her memory was starting to improve. She amazed me with the things she wanted to talk about. Her body was now crippled in her lower region and no therapy would be able to help her. Her knees became locked in place and couldn't be straightened, but she didn't appear to be in pain any longer and was always happy to see me. I went to be with her every single night.

Mom lived another year. I still continued to do her hair and nails. Often I would just crawl up on the bed and lie by her side. I loved putting lotion on her arms. On my last visit, I was called into the social worker's office where it was explained to me my mother's body was showing signs of the probability of her dying soon. I should consider calling hospice, which I did that same day and hospice began seeing her at the facility over the next few days, while arrangements were being made for me to bring her home.

On the day Mom was to come home with me, I walked into her room and the staff was busy getting her ready to leave. She had just gotten out of the shower and had her hair washed. She lay on her bed getting fitted with adult diapers. I knew I would be the one to change them from now on.

My mother's things were placed in plastic trash bags. She was put in a wheel chair and the hospice team came to be with me during the move from the facility to my home, where they followed behind my car. The most amazing thing happened during that drive. I remember Mom being so excited she was going home to be with me. She laughed so hard when I told her I was springing her from that joint. It was then she seemed to be herself again and exuded so much happiness.

Earlier in the day at my home, Mom's hospital bed was placed in the living room, close to the large window overlooking the garden. The hummingbird feeders hung directly outside the window so Mom could enjoy the view. I didn't want her hospital bed to be covered in typical white cotton hospital bedding. Instead I purchased a bright tropical bedspread and matching sheets. I placed fresh-cut sunflowers throughout the room. Sunflowers had always been her favorite flower. She said they always made her smile. Now more than ever, I wanted to see her beautiful smile. She would soon arrive to hear her favorite big band sounds being played softly in the background.

The delivery men arrived and started bringing in Mom's hospice supplies and oxygen. I began to realize that I needed to make sure I did everything possible not to have this room look like a hospital setting. I wanted my family to spend time with their Grandmother and Great Grandmother in a warm, tropical, peaceful place. I thought the hospice team would pay frequent visits, so I also needed to make certain my home was different from the others they had been to. I wanted every person who entered these doors during my mother's dying process to have as pleasant an experience as possible. I thought about what the hospice team must see and hear in their daily line of work. I could never begin to imagine. So I wanted this place to be comforting for them also. That was my mission.

I had attended a seminar once that talked about death and dying. I learned something that I will never forget. When a new baby is delivered, a woman needs to have support to help bring the child into the world, from the nurses, to doctors, to family, right by her side helping her breathe and push. The end of life should be the same. Everyone is entitled to have a support system that helps you leave with dignity. Why is it we are so happy to join in on the birth process, but it's so hard for us to be the support system when someone has to leave us? They are both a natural part of life. Hospice and firefighters have one thing in common: both rush in while others are rushing out.

As I arrived at the Alzheimer's facility to pick up Mom, I was so excited about her leaving this dreary place that I had come to know much too well over the last year. My mother would always ask when she could come home. I had told Mom she was in a hospital, promising she could come home as soon as she was better. It would be a nice relief for me to not walk these halls any longer, reminding me of the pain my mom had suffered. I have always had a passion for the elderly. There was so much to be learned from their life stories. When my mom first entered the facility, I volunteered to work in the hair salon one day a week, cutting and styling the men's and women's hair. I could always count on some good stories. It was amazing how much of the past they could remember for short periods. I remember one woman telling me about working in a factory designing hats. She spoke of it as if it were yesterday. Through her story I could picture this woman in the prime of her life loving her passion of design and I'll never forget how happy she was to tell the story.

It isn't pleasant to watch the elderly wandering around the halls or sitting in wheelchairs making crazy comments as you pass by, let alone the smells. God bless the health care workers who have chosen to work in this field. You have to learn to understand their coldness as trying to self-preserve. It must be hard for them each and every day, knowing when they come to work someone might die and others are just existing. With no chance to help give back their patients minds, they just help them stay safe, bathe and feed them until nature's time runs out. God bless the family members and friends who are few, sad to say, that come for daily, weekly or bi-weekly visits to make sure their loved ones are treated with dignity, safety, cleanliness, and of course, fed properly. Most patients never remember them, and you feel so sad for that loss of connection.

CHAPTER 27

It's Time to Go Home

Today, as I walked into my mother's room I was able to tell her she was getting to go home with me. Her toothless smile was all I needed to let me remember life with this precious woman, how much of that life was shared with me. As the staff got her ready for her shower I sat in a chair staring out the window thinking, if only I could have done so much more for her. If only...

As the hospice team helped me lift my mom from the car to the wheelchair, they also noticed the dramatic change in her behavior. Mom was smiling and made a comment about how beautiful the garden was. She wanted to stop for a moment before going inside my two-bedroom paradise escape home. She wanted to see the waterfall and the beautiful garden, look at a hummingbird and try to remember all of it.

The hospice team helped her into bed. Sometimes she was in so much pain, even the morphine couldn't help. Over the next few days, my mother's complete hospice team would pay her a visit. I had heard of hospice but never understood what a blessing they would be in my life and the life of my mother. My family came to spend some peaceful time with her before she died. There were lots of precious moments I was able to share during that week. She loved her milkshakes. I had learned Mom was going through the dying process and I should not to try to force her to eat too much. It would cause her body more pain than necessary as it tried to shut down. It was better for her if her stomach wasn't full. It felt good not having to leave her side to go home, knowing she was home with me, safe and loved. God will take it from here.

The hospice nurse taught me how to change her Depends (I was never very good at that) and gave me directions for all the medications she would be taking. One afternoon when Michelle came to visit me, she brought baby Logan so Mom could see them one last time. While Michelle was there, the nurse had some private words for Michelle to also help her. When Michelle came back in the house she said that we needed to tell my mother goodbye and let her know it was okay for her to die and leave us and that we would be okay. I just started to cry my eyes out. Uncontrollable tears poured down my face. I wasn't ready to say goodbye. Michelle said she would talk to her grandmother and tell her it was okay to leave us now. After a short time, I walked close to Mom and sat by her side, and I told her that her body is tired now, and soon she needed to rest and go to sleep, and that it was okay for her to die, that she was at home safe with me and I would take good care of her. I told her I loved her and that I would miss her very much. Then she said, "You're Mine and I'm Yours Forever."

That night as I changed her I noticed she was no longer in pain. I put ice chips on her lips. I noticed her skin changing to become very dry. I couldn't sleep well that night and by 3 A.M. I got up and did some chores around the house while Mom slept. I sat and watched her lying there so peacefully and wondered what she was dreaming about.

In the darkness I lit some candles around the room and went in to take a bath. As I sank down in the hot water filled with bubbles I leaned my head back against the wall and as tears came down I said a special prayer to God and asked him to take my mom now. It was exactly after that moment when I heard her take her last breath. I got out of the tub with a towel wrapped around me and went by her side. I was told by the hospice team that the hearing was the last organ to die and that even though a person is dead, you could still talk to them for the next ten minutes and they might hear you. So as I held her hand, and touched her cheek softly, I closed her eyes and spoke kind loving words to her, giving her thanks for bringing me into the world and for loving me. I hoped she could still hear my final words as she went on her final journey to heaven.

I called the hospice nurse on duty and she came within a half-hour. I had already called the funeral home to have them come pick her up. The nurse had me fill out some paperwork in the kitchen, while the men from the mortuary placed my mom on a gurney. I walked into the living room and noticed for the first time my mother's legs were straight as she lay under the white sheet. I noticed her toes showing and went to cover them. The others smiled as I said I didn't want her to get cold. I was happy I always made sure her manicure/pedicure was done and her toes looked so pretty. I watched them outside as they lifted her up into the back of the white van and locked the gurney into place.

I felt numb as I walked back into the house. The hospice nurse stayed with me during the next hour. She had to have me count each pill and flush them down the toilet as she charted each different type. I told her it was okay to leave me, but I requested that she call the supply place and have them come to remove all the equipment as soon as possible. They arrived within the hour to remove the hospital bed I had placed in the living room next to the window so she could look out at the tropical jungle of plants and flowers I had created. I placed all the furniture back as if what had just happened didn't exist. I then drove to the drugstore to get some aspirin, and came across a decorative stone that read "Mother's Garden" and purchased it. I brought it home and placed it in the garden for her. I now knew the grieving process for me was beginning.

The night before my mother's funeral I sat alone in my room on the floor trying to think of what I was going to say to her the following day. As I wrote this final goodbye, I played her favorite Willie Nelson song, *Stardust*, and looked at a picture I had of my mom and dad dancing. The next day the family gathered around my mother's coffin outside at the cemetery: Michelle, Kevin, Aaron, his father Mike, Al and I. I gave each person a copy of the letter I had written to Mom. I started to read the letter out loud but had to stop for a brief moment as Michelle came to hold me and the tears poured down my face. It was hard to get the words out. Here is what my letter said:

Mom, we are with you now. You are released from pain and suffering. It is comforting to know you have many family members and friends who have gone before you who were waiting your arrival. Not once did you ever show any fear of dying. You knew you were safe from harm in a loving home where dignity and respect would be placed upon you, with lots of pampering which I know you enjoyed until the end. You knew my most peaceful place to be was taking my bubble bath. I smile knowing you let me clean, mop the floor, light the candles and then heard the water running for my bath. As I sank into the warm water and closed my eyes, I whispered out loud to God, my father, and my grandmothers, to please take you now. A minute later I heard you take your last breath of life. A few times you told me your mother was waiting in the car outside for you. You were right. She was. And I can only imagine what a wonderful journey you made with her. Please tell her thank you from me for letting you spend the extra time. Mom, you always said, you never missed a thing. You never wanted for anything and just last week you said, "I've sure had a good life. I got to do everything I wanted to do." This brings all of us so much comfort. So many times as I was taking care of you over the years, you said that I would get my reward in Heaven someday. I just want you to know you are getting your reward now. You have been a devoted daughter, wife, mother, grandmother and great grandmother, and a true friend. Through you, we have learned so much. Everyone has always said that I'm so loving, kind and giving. It was from you that I learned. You were always by my side, through my happy and sad times. You were able to raise me up when I was at my lowest. You always knew the right words to say. We have always said, "I'm yours and you're mine, Forever." Even in your dying days you were able to tell that to me. If I'm crying it is because I'm selfish. I will miss you, but in my heart you are always with me. It is those memories that will get me through the toughest times. You were the age of fifty three when my father died. The night I drove him to the hospital he asked me to make sure I helped take care of you. Later, from you, I heard he asked of you the same thing about me. Thank you Dad, I hope I made you proud while you watched me care for her. There isn't anything I would not have done. Thank you God for letting her stay long enough to see her grandchildren and great grandchildren. Mom it brings back memories of how much you used to love to dance. I remember your favorite song called Stardust. *I remember the day I took you to see Willie Nelson in concert, how you never got over getting to touch his hand and him kissing your cheek. I can only imagine the thoughts that must have passed through your mind as you listened to this song. You told me it was your song with my father. As I wrote this letter to you last night I played your song and held the picture of you and my dad dancing. I would like to share this picture with everyone here today. As I pass it around I want everyone here to picture you in heaven being reunited with your husband and being able to dance to your song once again.*

416

Mom, it is said that the light we see on the earth is the light of the sun. It is but a small candle in comparison to the light of God that you see now. I will forever think of you when I light my candles and know you are the brightest one. Mom, we are members of the church on Earth, you are now in the church of Heaven. While we are no longer able to kiss you or hold your hand, we will, through our thoughts and prayers, be able to kiss you and be kissed in return. With each memory, let our hearts be reminded that nothing can ever take away the beauty of you that we have known. For love remains a part of us forever.

I'm hoping that through this story and my mom's unnecessary suffering others can benefit from my mistakes and trustfulness. I would like to help you make informed choices when choosing a care facility. On behalf of my Mother, I filed a lawsuit against the first residential care facility I had placed her in. Shortly after my mother passed away, the case was settled out of court. There was no stipulation in the settlement that my mother's case could not be shared with others. Most cases like this are settled out of court and remain confidential. This is one reason why we don't learn more from others telling their stories. This case took two years and numerous hours of investigation to unclose the hidden truth of what went on behind closed doors. The investigative work tells the real story. It needs to be shared to make others aware of the lessons I had to learn the hard way.

The title of my case was "Big Money." This residential care facility, also known as a "board and care," is like so many, all about the money. It is a business and they can be huge money makers. Unfortunately you do not see much true old fashioned compassion for the elderly. Caregivers start out thinking this is a wonderful job, helping the elderly, but soon find out it is hard work and often are paid minimum wage and since there is a shortage of help, the turnover of staff is ongoing.

Some places don't get background checks completed in a timely manner, allowing for convicted felons to be hired before the truth is discovered. They are not governed by the same laws as a skilled nursing facility. Unless a complaint is made and Ombudsman is contacted, these places can remain unchecked for long periods of time. In my mother's case, even with Ombudsman being called twice, they could do nothing to help. Ombudsman's hands are tied in so many ways. If the residential care facility specializes in caring for patients with Alzheimer's disease, I've been told that it is even harder since the residents can't remember what goes on and are unable to tell anyone.

Within six months after my mother entered her residential care facility she suffered from untreated broken bones, hallucinations, malnutrition, dehydration, and a severe bladder infection. My mom, six months earlier, was normal by most standards for someone suffering from Alzheimer's. She walked, laughed, and was lots of fun to be around. She had a great personality. Mom was a little overweight and loved food. Now she was skin and bones, and I was told by the staff she was going to die soon. But by some miracle she fell out of bed and hit her head. The hospital staff saved her life. Hard to believe I was unaware of what was really going on behind the closed doors. For such a long time I felt it was my fault for what happened. But now I know it was the owners and caregivers that failed me and my mother. After the investigative reports came out, I was able to discover many unanswered questions.

The first administrator at my mom's facility quit a month after my mom's arrival to go manage another care facility. Shortly after, she was responsible for the death of an Alzheimer's resident who was found wandering on a major highway and later died from being hit by a car. Two days later another resident was found wandering. The state did step in and temporarily closed the facility. The person who took the administrator's place had been a caregiver/cleaning girl. She didn't have a high school diploma, any administrative training or nursing skills, and even had a prior arrest record. After a couple of months when she couldn't handle the job, she was demoted to a cleaning woman again. I thought at the time it was strange, but they convinced me she would be a great administrator and deserved the promotion. The next person to take her place was the activities director. I did not meet her for the first few months. I kept wondering when they were going to start having activities. I was told she was on vacation and returning shortly. I later found out through investigation she had been in jail on a drug charge and when she was released and came back to work they made her administrator. Later she also left to go work where the wandering patient had been hit by car. She is currently serving two years for selling drugs.

We all know that the elderly are on a lot of prescription drugs, many for pain. Caregivers are not required to take classes on how to administer drugs. Guess who was selling drugs out of the residential care facility? As a matter of fact, it became a big side business for the caregivers who are paid so little. Let's just say it was a bonus. In my case the owners only showed up once a week. What went on the rest of the time didn't matter to them as long as the big money kept rolling in. One of the first key witnesses who heard my mom's bones break was addicted to drugs. This was a common problem. This seemed more normal than not. My investigator went to check on her whereabouts because she didn't show up for her deposition. She was living with some local drug addicts, and they told the investigator she took a walk out in the desert. When the investigator walked out in the desert behind the house, he found her passed out in the hot sun due to the drugs. She happened to be pregnant. He was able to get her to shade. He got fluids in her. He told my attorney not to count on her because she wouldn't be alive in time for the trial. Other investigative work uncovered one resident at my mom's facility was left outside in the sun so long that he had burns and blisters. Another got out of the padlocked fence and walked down the street and fell into an open septic tank. Another man had gotten out and sat in a car and almost died due to heat exposure. There were deaths and many broken bones for other residents long before my mother arrived. I just had no way of knowing.

Sometimes, the food that was brought in by the owners was the kind given for free to low income people. By the time the owners got it to the facility it was past its expiration date. No wonder my mom stopped eating. I also found that many times food is placed in front of the person to eat, but no one comes to help feed. So the food is barely touched. The caregivers are so few and in this case had twenty residents to feed each day. On the subject of the owners, they falsified being there on paper. I never met them until three months into my mother's stay. Since there were twenty residents, most times there was only one person to take care of them all during the evening and bedtime. The ratio of caregivers required in a residential care facility per person is very low and seems impossible to give the best care needed.

As I said earlier, they would hire staff for minimum wage. There was no training, no background check, and some never met the owners before being hired and going to work. They were often left in charge of all the residents. Some would quit the next day. The morning person would arrive to find beds wet and Alzheimer's patients wandering around unattended. The staff would lose their jobs if the families were noticing and reporting that things were not in control. So lies were told to me. I was always trusting and looking for the best in everyone. I can tell you, I was taken in big time!

Looking back, I try to think of things I would have done differently. This type of business feeds off knowing you need them. Where do you place your loved ones when you have doubts? There are many families searching for a home, and most places have long waiting lists. Just to find placement for your loved one that will take their personal income without having to put them on state funds is very rare. So when you find what looks like a loving home that says they do not accept state funds and will accept your small private income, you feel that your prayers have been answered. The legislative regulations for residential home care or board and care facilities are not tough enough. Even though I called Ombudsman twice in my mom's case, it didn't help. Later, after the case settled, I did get a letter of apology stating that they wish they could have done more and were sorry they failed me. I must say that I very rarely saw family members come to visit, mostly because they were not recognized, or because they lived so far away. We assume our loved one is being cared for with dignity. My case settled for four hundred thousand dollars after two years. The attorneys took half and the investigator got twenty thousand dollars. I split the hundred and eighty thousand dollar balance with my half-sister, who never once offered to help me or bothered to even ask how I was doing. But she was her daughter, and it was the legal thing to do. My half-sister died not long afterwards with eye cancer.

CHAPTER 28

Don't Mess with My Mom

The year is 2001. The year of 9/11. Al-Qaeda terrorists attack the United States, bringing down the Twin Towers in New York City and crashing into the Pentagon in Virginia leaving 3,000 dead. An earthquake in India kills 20,000. A series of Anthrax attacks spreads fear of handling infected letters. Dale Earnhardt dies in the last lap crash of the Daytona 500. Apple computer releases the iPod.

After my mother died, I continued working at the day spa. My land lady Marsha respected my choice to bring my mother home to die. She asked if I would look after her husband's mother if they moved her from Florida and into the duplex next door. She would be completely independent and not need my help, just checked on daily, plus my rent would be free. So not only would I have a little company on the property, but now a little extra income. The emotional trauma and drama of all that had happened over the last couple of years made me want to work, come home and tune out the rest of the world. I was almost becoming a recluse, other than going to work.

One evening I was bored and feeling lonely. I went on the computer and decided to do a Google search of a name from my past, Chris Carpenter, the preacher man, the married editor from my local newspaper years past who had gone back into his original field of public relations helping to create a façade for a high ranking pastor in the Christian Community.

Looking up someone's name wasn't possible all that many years ago and I was surprised when I put in his name to find page after page of his work listed. He had become a top talk show host for a Christian Station. I looked up the radio station itself and found his name listed and how to send him a personal note, which I did. I told him how I had Goggled his name and was surprised to find him listed and hoped all was going well in his life. I didn't hear back for another two weeks; then, one day when I got home from work there was a long email message from him telling me that he was sorry for the delay in getting back to me, but that the very day I sent him the letter was the day he was burying his wife after a long bout with cancer.

He wanted to know if it was okay for him to call me. So I answered back and allowed for the call. He said all these years, finally he was in a position to offer me so much more in life than before. How it was a blessing that on this very day of his wife's death would I be sent to find him. And that it was God's way of picking me to find him on this day, of all days. He wanted to see me again. I needed to spend more time on the phone getting to know him again. Over the next few weeks we spoke for hours each night. He learned my dream vacation place was Bora Bora. He learned all about how I had helped my mother. I learned from him how he had been with the radio station for ten years and was just getting ready to retire, and how the Lord made this happen at this time in his life.

When the possibility of America going to war was looming, Chris flew to the White House with other ministers to help the President make the best decision for the American people. I learned how he was now in the spotlight and how recognizable his voice was. I told him how I hadn't been in a church since he told me how crooked and money hungry most of the big ones were. I told him he taught me not to trust someone at the altar, but to only trust the words in the Bible. I don't think he realized what an impact he made on me by confiding about what really happens in these big churches. Chris said it would be hard for many of his closest friends to accept his choice of being with me, and how they wouldn't understand our history. He told me if I didn't belong to a church that would have to change, since it was so important to him. I told him that because of him, I never gave up on God and always shared my greatest gift with others, and that was love. I just didn't believe in attending church on Sunday, paying my 10% and thinking I was good the rest of the week.

So, Chris was coming down to see me and take me to dinner. It was a very passionate and romantic evening, with him confessing all his love to me, although he was still grieving the loss of his wife. He wanted to plan a future with me. He said I was "The One." He brought me champagne and told me he was now a millionaire and I could take baths in champagne for the rest of my life if I wanted. He brought me perfume named Bora Bora and told me we would be traveling there soon. He ended up spending the night with me, and when I left for work the following morning, I left him sitting outside in the courtyard reading his dozens of sympathy letters his fans had written to him.

I didn't plan on putting trust into another man but this was different. Chris wasn't a stranger to me. When I returned home from work that day I was so excited to start this new chapter in my life. But all that was left was a long hand written love note saying how reading all the letters of condolence had affected him, and he couldn't stay any longer. He didn't feel it was right to bring his sadness into my life at this time. He was sorry, but he needed some time. I was disappointed when I didn't hear from him for a few months. Then, one day he called out of the blue and asked if he could meet me for lunch. I asked him what he wanted to talk to me about, and he said that his inner circle of friends would never understand him being with someone who didn't belong to a Christian Church, and that he had started dating. She was a friend of his wife and he had discussions about her being the one he should spend his life with, since she was a very active Christian in the church. So, I wished him well and never looked back. He was just one more man in my life who made me feel worthless.

How ironic I thought that this man chose another woman over me because I didn't belong to a church, and yet he was the one who had confided so many bad things about what really goes on that I lost all faith in the pastors since they were only human and this was a big money making business when you made it to the top. Chris had told me about one pastor who wanted to raise money for his trip to the Great Wall of China. Tons of money was mailed in from the tv viewers. But the pastor actually went to a Hollywood set and had the picture take of him standing in front of the Great Wall. The trip actually happened after the fact so the vacation was all paid for ahead of time. It was so deceitful. I am trying to always remember footprints and how when things go wrong not to fear because the Lord will always carry me through it. I knew the Lord knew my heart, and I didn't have to answer to Chris or any of his friends about my faith. My faith was living inside of me, and I would always do work to help others. By now my respect for most tv preachers was nil and thanks to Chris I understood that they are just human earthly men running a business. Not all are filled with greed needing to be worshiped and glorified. Let me seek the ones out on the streets helping the homeless, feeding the hungry and setting the example of what love should really mean. Show me those following in Mother Teresa's footsteps, and I will believe there is still good being shown silently that needs no boasting or bragging.

I knew inside of myself that I was lonely. I also knew I could never trust a man again. Nor could I believe words from their mouths since I will just be lied to again and again, and I had had enough. But I had so much compassion, so much kindness and love to give, so I went to the Hospice Office and registered to become a volunteer.

I was so impressed with the teamwork and how they helped me through my darkest days. They said they do not consider a volunteer immediately after the death of a loved one, but because of the way I was able to handle death and how I was able to focus on what needed to be done without falling to pieces, they would love to have me on their team. So, after two months of training I became an official hospice volunteer, going into people's homes to bring comfort to those still living and bring compassion and support to those dying. I declined to go into nursing homes as a volunteer at this point, and they completely understood why I needed to stay away. Going into private homes and taking on new cases continued. As each patient would die it was never easy to say goodbye and start anew. I was once sent to a lady's home that was in the middle of the desert and a few miles from anything, on a dirt road. The small house was filthy dirty and infested with mice. I cleaned and scrubbed the kitchen and made sure everything was sanitized as best I could, so she could have life a little easier. I felt in my heart that at least I made sure this sweet little lady would have a clean house when her time came. I learned a good lesson that day that has helped me ever since. When I told my hospice manager about the woman's living conditions, they told me never to put my personal lifestyle into someone else's life. Meet them where they are. Accept where they are, unless there is abuse suspected in the home. Just report it and never take anything into my own hands to correct. This advice really came in handy so many times later on. It taught me never to judge and to just show compassion and love, nothing more, nothing less.

By the following year, Michelle expressed concern for me doing nothing but working and visiting with the near dead. She said I was starting to get old. I was spending too much time alone hibernating, tending to the garden I suppose. She insisted I start looking for a job down in the desert, closer to her again, and get back to a healthier lifestyle rather than locking myself away behind a fence in my tropical paradise. I soon closed my day spa. This time is wasn't so hard. This business had served its purpose. It was fun to reflect and think how I was able to put the ad on the radio for twenty-five dollar hour-long facials and sold out immediately. At the end of the week I had made around a thousand dollars because the price was right and the treatments exceptional, plus the tips were amazing. The power of great advertising works, and proves that anyone can do well if they work hard and apply good marketing techniques.

The first job I found close to Michelle was working part-time three days a week for a local high-end beauty salon as a shampooer. I spent all day making ten dollars an hour from the stylists who pooled their money to pay for my helping them. The most money came in the way of tips, most often five-dollars per person for giving such a great shampoo and massage, due to my strong, well-trained hands. I loved the job, but Michelle soon found another one she wanted me to interview for. It was manager for a big cosmetics company retail store with a prominent name, located in the heart of Palm Desert in a high end outdoor shopping plaza. I interviewed and got the job.

Michelle let me move into her home with her family until I was ready to find a place to live on my own back in the low desert. Once I was with family and had the perfect job, I got back to being myself. I have to give Michelle all the credit for seeing I was slipping into a place not healthy for me and for encouraging me to leave the safety of my small, fenced-in world and start making a new life for myself. I lived with Michelle for close to a year when she helped me find (as she always does) the perfect place for me to live. I rented a large detached one bedroom casita that was built into the mountains in Big Horn sheep country off Highway 74 in Palm Desert in an area called Cahuilla Hills. Michelle helped by giving me a living room set, bed and so many other things to add to the things I still had left from my mother's house. The bathroom alone was worth the rental fee. It had a huge sunken tub with a skylight, a perfect place to rest my body, soaking at the end of the day, as I continued with my volunteer hospice work as well as managing an amazing cosmetics store.

Listening to nature became so natural to me. I learned of the one granite squirrel that would stand tall upon a rock and give loud warning sounds to all others around that a predator was nearby, and in this area, it meant coyotes. I would be in another room with my grandson when I would hear this unique squirrel sound and I would say, "Logan, come with me. There are coyotes outside." And sure enough, there they were, always two, never just one. I could always count on hearing them during the night as they would howl while they surrounded their prey and captured it. I would just lie in bed and pray for the poor creature that just lost its life to nature. Each and every day I would cut up fresh produce, and place a plate out for the baby chipmunks that would come down the hill the minute they would hear me open the back sliding glass door onto the patio. The owners of the casita lived in the main estate house down the hill from the casita, so I really was alone in the mountains with the wild things. My grandson loved my hummingbird feeder, as I would put a ladder next to it so he could stand up and look eye-to-eye with them. It was a beautiful sight to see, the wonderment in a child's eyes.

One time I walked out to the patio and next to an ice chest the wind must have blown a plastic bag and when I went to lift it up there was a rattlesnake coiled up, sleeping and resting peacefully. I slowly backup up into the house, closing the door. I called Animal Control and they came out right away. The man had no problem reaching in with his snake pole and catching it. I watched him as he walked down the hill while out-stretched in front of him was this dangling, twisting and turning rattlesnake. Instead of opening the door to the trucks container to drop it in, I watched in horror as he cut off its head. Later he came back up to the door and told me he usually takes them out into the desert wash area and releases them but he was a baby southwestern speckled rattlesnake and had he bitten me, since he was still considered a baby, I would not have made it to the phone to call for help. The babies have no control on how much venom to deliver and since his was so deadly I would have become paralyzed almost instantly. It certainly made me give more respect to the environment I had nestled myself in. Tarantulas come out at mating season and I only saw one of the big ones crawling across my front door way, and my landlord came and picked him up with a shovel and took him down the hill to the wash to let him go. Other than that, living up against a mountain was breathtakingly beautiful. I was so blessed that Michelle found this amazing place at a price I could afford.

CHAPTER 29

Eleventh Hour

I enjoyed working at the cosmetics store, and creating many fun special events. But I needed more. So, I continued my hospice volunteer work in the Palm Desert area for a special program. It was called the Eleventh Hour. The hospice program was created for a private hospice hospital that had eleven rooms and twenty two beds. It was for those that were in the later stages of dying, and the families would rather have them in a hospital, instead of dying at home. My volunteer job was to visit and sit beside someone dying who didn't have family so that no one ever had to die alone. It was one of the most rewarding volunteer positions I have ever had. To hold someone's hand, even when they can no longer speak, but letting them know they were not alone as they leave this world. I would gently apply some soothing lotion on their hands and arms. Other times, I would just pick up the Bible, knowing God would find just the right passage for me to read to them. I would tell them they were not going to die alone and letting them know I would not leave their side. I was always called in during the very last stages of the body starting to shut down. Death is easily predicted due to the body temperature and the feeling of the skin; the dryness, elasticity disappearing, and color of the skin. I would put ice chips on their lips and kept them free of food and liquids to help make the dying process much easier.

During this same time, Michelle and her family started attending a local Christian church. They never pushed me to go, but I was always invited and made to feel included as family. Because of Chris I had not wanted to attend a church for so many years. But for some reason, due to the loss of my mother and so many other losses, I felt the need to go into the House of Christ Our Lord and reach out, once again finding myself crying, asking for forgiveness, and to allow me to do more of God's work, as I felt I had been placed upon the earth to do. I could feel the presence of God through me and I asked to be lead to do his will.

During the following two weeks I kept reading about, hearing about, and even seeing billboards, about the local rescue mission. Someone mentioned to me that they had a relative who happened to be in charge of the women's division. I wrote her name down, and later that day placed a call to her, asking if she could use my volunteer help in any way. She was quick to say sure, yes, please, I really could use some help. I was so excited to meet Rachel. She had a great way with the women at the shelter. She could speak their kind of language that only street people seemed to understand. You couldn't put anything over on her; she was tough and street-smart. She knew how to walk the walk and talk the talk of these women who were homeless for various reasons drugs, alcohol, and prostitution, penniless, lost and without a place to go. Most have been sleeping on the streets or in many of these cases, somewhere out in the desert.

When I first arrived and met with Rachel in her office, it didn't take her long to get me started on the cabinets filled with paperwork that hadn't been categorized due to lack of help. They contained the clients' personal files, stating why they were staying, how the progress was going, and what their plans were for the future. It was all in my hands to file their stories away.

It made me think of how we all come into the world the same, but due to one reason or many, we are taught to survive and make some choices that are not always the best for us. And now these unfortunate women are left stranded at a facility for the homeless, asking for help, because the other option of living in the desert had taken its toll on them. Or they would have fallen victim to human trafficking and been sold for sexual services. This is the new form of modern slavery being controlled by the threat of violence and forced into prostitution or other forms of sweat house slavery. I could only relate and be reminded of my own life and the choices I could have made when I was asked to work for a very popular escort service for high end clients. We all have choices. These were women who had made bad ones. A few had lost their children to child protective services, and wanted to start a new life, to try to regain custody. Such a mixture of causes, and yet you could feel a special bond and a connection, especially since they were all homeless and in need of help.

The greatest part of this rescue mission success was due to it's being a Christian based ministry giving hope to those less fortunate with the reassurance that God loves, no matter what road they have walked. It is powerful to know you are loved when you can't even stand to look at yourself in the mirror. I learned that lesson from my weeks spent in the hospital so many years earlier.

After my filing was complete, Rachel asked me to go out into the living room and just get to know the women. Luckily for me there was an instant friendship. Thanks to my hospice training, I learned to meet them where they are, and listening was the key factor. They each have a story to tell. Just being there and listening, not judging, and giving them reassurance that there is value to their lives. It seemed to be what they really longed for. After the day was finished, I was going to join Michelle and family at their local Christian church and if a few of these women were allowed, I could take at least four with me. Rachel said yes to my suggestion and four women immediately wanted to go. I knew it was a good excuse for them to be able to feel the freedom of the outside world once again.

I went home quickly, changed and returned to the Mission. All four had showered and looked their best, which for some wasn't so easy as some had missing teeth due to drug abuse, and some were overweight due to eating whatever could be gotten out of a dumpster, and others were so skinny from not having proper nutrition up until now.

As I walked into the church I didn't sit with my family, but instead, the five of us sat in a row together. I could see how they loved being inside these four walls. When it came time for an altar call, all four of my riders walked up to the altar with me as they gave their life over to Jesus knowing they were forgiven for all their sins, tears pouring down their faces, a moment I will never forget. EVER!

The next time I came to do my volunteer work, others asked if I went again to church could I take them also. Soon the requests kept getting greater and greater. Pretty soon I had to ask others at the church if they would come and bring a group of the women. I had this one wonderful lady named Laura, and both she and her husband were staying at the mission. His name was Jeff and he was living on the men's side. After attending church with me, Laura told her husband Jeff, also a resident at the mission about the church service and how some of her friends were being saved at the altar. Jeff went to the man in charge of the men's wing and got permission for the men to also ride with me to church. But the only rule was no men from the men's side could ride in the same car as the women from the women's side. Nor could they sit next to each other at church. It was a strict rule that could cause termination of their living at the shelter. So everyone obeyed the rules. Soon, I was taking the men on one night a week and the women on another, plus I helped arranged rides for all of them. A caravan of cars came on Sundays and Wednesday nights to drive everyone. Each week, more and more became born again at the altar. And if only one had chosen that path, then the others would also walk up with that one person in support, arms wrapped around each other. For me, it was a sight to behold, knowing that one mention of "would anyone like to go to church with me tonight?" was the start of all this.

Whenever I drove the men or women back to the mission, I would stop at a fast food place and load them up on burgers, fries, and drinks to take back with them. It didn't cost much, but the special bond I built with each of them was priceless. I listened to their stories during the rides. Laura and Jeff once were able to go to church with me in the same car since they were a married couple. I had a very soft heart for the two of them, and I was proud of their progress. Soon they would be graduating from the mission's program and trying to find their own apartment. In the meantime, after church I took them grocery shopping instead of buying fast food. They requested more fruits and healthier things to eat.

Another time I took two seasoned street life women from the mission to the .99 Store during the daytime and gave them each ten dollars to buy whatever beauty supplies they needed. That small amount of money, to them, was like a thousand dollars. It felt so nice to give directly to the people, and feel the appreciation coming from their hearts. After the ten dollar shopping spree the two ladies and I had a nice lunch and talked about many things. One of them started to challenge me and said I do not have any idea what it is like to stand outside in the dark of the night waiting to come inside the mission for a meal, a shower and a place to sleep on the floor inside the chapel. They continued to say most volunteers help the best they can but not enough take the time to listen. Every one of them has a different unique story to share. Both of these ladies went through troubling times before being accepted to join the mission program. Living in the desert, or selling one's body in order to have drug or alcohol money was the worst. I was given credit for taking the time to listen and really caring, but if I could do what they did just one day in my life, then they would forever be a believer in me. So the challenge was set.

Well, I took them up on that challenge, and with them not knowing, or anyone else for that matter, I decided it take it upon myself to try for one day to walk the walk. I put on an old pair of jeans, a tee-shirt, wore no makeup, hair in an unkempt ponytail, and went to sit outside the mission in the cold that day without a jacket. I sat on the sidewalk with the others, just waiting until it was time to go inside. When you do go inside, you have to sign your name and go take a seat, women in the first few rows of stackable chairs, the men in the rest. Being in this church service was unlike anything I have known before. I experienced the pureness of gratitude, of wanting to be a step closer to God, and having the chance to receive a hot meal on this chilly night. After the half-hour service, we were allowed to start a line from the first row going first, working its way to the last row in the back. We entered the cafeteria in a long line, waiting our turn to get a plate, as piles of wonderful fresh-cooked servings of hot entrée and side dishes along with salad and dessert were served. The kitchen staff is run by a few paid workers, but mostly volunteers or people on the missions program, trying to find a way to fit back into society, once they graduated. There were a few of the people that night that I ate with that recognized me. The mission residents ate before the open to the line was opened to the needy outside the mission. Jeff was one of them who knew it was me but never said a word. He never mentioned knowing me and neither did I. After dinner we were sent back outside for another half-hour, forming a line to get back in to get a clean change of clothes, and allowed ten minutes in the hot shower. It felt awkward for me outside that door with only five women and fifty or more men. Most men smelled like alcohol and you could tell others were drug addicts. There were only 5 women and a group of at least fifty or more men. Being flirted with in this situation was not comfortable, so I had to work hard to be in

447

control and get respect. Around the corner of the building in a somewhat darkened alley from where I was standing was a drug dealer wanting to make some deals and wanting to keep all these people hooked on drugs, offering them the world. I noticed Jeff out of the corner of my eye watching over me like a protective angel. Just to make sure I was safe, he had my back. As we each entered the building again, we had to fill out our name and city we lived in. I was given a fresh set of clothes, shirt and pants to wear along with a surprising gift of Estee Lauder mini shampoo bottle, bar of soap, comb, toothbrush and tooth paste, (remembering how we gave these as gifts free to my cosmetic customers, but never appreciated as much as at this moment) and a towel, all with the warning of no longer than ten minutes in the shower. That part right there could have thrown me into a tailspin. Ten minutes to shower? Are you kidding me? I would prefer a half-hour bubble bath, but this was not the time or place to discuss that. Instead I was happy to enjoy the ten minutes allowed before bedtime. I kept my same clothes on again and left behind the free clean ones offered. When I came out of the shower, I was led down a hall back into the chapel, however this time all the chairs had been gathered and stacked in high piles. The row of chairs were set up as a wall that separate the five mats that were laid down for the five women on this evening. On the other side of the chair stacks were rows upon rows of mats laid out on the floor to accommodate the men. The mats, similar to yoga mats, each had a pillow, clean pillow case and folded blanket. It wasn't long before everyone had finished with the showers and was now ready for bed. The room was a steady loud stream of snoring. I would turn to my right and some lady was facing me sleeping and the same on my left. I tried to lie on my back, but for the next few hours all I could do was think of how blessed my life was. I also thought of the women lying next to me. What were their stories? They each seemed so nice, not strung out on drugs, but each had a hardened look to them where life had taken a toll. The program at the mission can only accommodate so many due to the amount of beds, and these women will just have to make due in the meantime until they can try to enter. The problem with some of the women is they get hooked on drugs and or alcohol, and make some money for their "John" in order to get the next fix. Once they are used up and get that trashed look they are still on drugs but so far into it they have lost all self-worth along with their looks. They have become just a means for a man to slap around and use for the sake of a dollar. In the middle of the night I slowly got up, went to check myself out and figured whether I slept three hours or five hours didn't matter. I came, and I saw enough, and now could hold my head up high when I met up with the two women who challenged me, and I could actually speak about their walk from a somewhat different perspective than before. Without question, it was a life-changing experience for me because now I knew, if I had to be homeless and seek help at a rescue shelter, I could actually do it and give back even more than what I might receive. Sometimes it's the fear that holds us back from trying things. But if we are brave and step outside of our safety zone it is a very powerful feeling to know you are capable of helping others that are in desperate need.

As timing would have it, a few interesting things happened that dovetailed together at the perfect moments. I had a group of men that I was very proud of who were graduating from the mission program. As a reward for them, I got permission to drive them to San Bernardino, an hour-and-a-half ride, and take them to the main church of the one I had been taking them to, the one that it had originated from. It had seventeen thousand members and I thought they would enjoy the drive, meeting new people, seeing the big church. They were so excited to attend, and as it happened on that early Sunday morning when we were to leave, there was a huge thunder storm in the desert. Streets were flooded and driving was not safe. I gave a lot of thought as to whether I should drive in this storm or not. If it was an ordinary circumstance, I would not have ventured out, but this was different. There were two men waiting with such eager hearts to attend this church. I knew they got up early, dressed and looked their best for the special occasion. To leave the rescue mission when you have no car and no money over a period of time makes you appreciate everything. So, I got in my car and picked them up and even though the ride was a little difficult at times, we made it in perfect time and got great seats. The service was amazing and after it was over we went to a special area for first-time attendees to come that was like a mini coffee shop with fresh pastries and refreshments being served. What was an especially nice touch was the pastor from the church came to meet and greet the potential new members. When we had our chance to shake hands I told him we were from the Palm Desert church and that both men belong to the rescue mission and were about to graduate. Bringing them here was my gift to them. I told the pastor that we had many people from the mission coming to the church now that we had many cars each week just to pick up the residents. The pastor then said to me, "Go back and tell your pastor that I am giving him a brand new van to use and now he will always be able to always pick up the people from the mission." Had I not gone in the storm that day, and brought blessings to these two men, there would not be a brand new van delivered to our church to always give a ride to those at the mission and others.

Another thing happened close to the same time. An opportunity arose to move into a home with a woman ninety years-old as a personal assistant, and at the same time Jeff and Laura graduated from the Mission with Jeff getting a permanent job at the Mission, giving them enough income to be able to move to their own affordable housing apartment. I gave them everything I ever owned and more, right down to the silverware, helping to make their new apartment turn-key furnished. I didn't need the things since I was moving as a live-in companion. If I put my belongings into storage, knowing that over time what I would have paid could have bought new. So it was a win-win. It helped them and I didn't need storage. They even came and helped me pack and transported it all. They were ecstatic in their new place.

Sadly, a few months later Laura was diagnosed with inoperable cancer and it was a very rough time for them. By an act of the Lord, I was just asked to see a hospice client that had just checked into the hospice care unit and needed our Eleventh Hour services. It turned out to be Laura! I was so honored to be her hospice person, to give her strength, and pray with her. At the same time her room was always filled with people from the mission coming to spend time with her. On the evening before her death, there must have been at least ten staff members, residents and Jeff in her room with the pastor who knew her from the mission. We made a big circle around her, holding her hands and praying and you could hear her sweet voice as she said "amen" when we were finished. She knew she was soon to leave us. She was brave and as prepared for her death as any of us could be. When I walked out into the waiting room, so many of the visitors were crying and emotional, but never did they let on while they were with her. Before the light of dawn she was gone, as if angels gently lifted her spirit away.

A few days later there was a big memorial service for her at the Mission. I will never forget when I walked out of the Mission after the service that day, how I knew my time and purpose had been served in that particular hospice program, my time spent at the Mission, and also my time at the church was complete. I know that must sound crazy but it is exactly how I felt. I was at complete peace knowing I did what I had been called to do. Because of that feeling I learned to listen to that voice much more often. I took a year away from anything that had to do with death and dying. I needed to recharge my own batteries since it might not show on the outside, but this work had taken a toll on my heart and spirit.

CHAPTER 30

Kevin, Could You Move Me?

Michelle always finds the best things for me. She guides me, teaches me, and is so very protective of me. She calls me her teenager since I step outside of the comfort zone often, especially when doing volunteer work. I like to choose work others would not do.

Michelle found a dream job for me with a top fashion house in Palm Desert. The average price for a piece of clothing was close to a thousand dollars. They paid a low hourly wage, but the commission structure was fantastic and if you could sell, you had the chance to make as much as most who had been there for some time, making close to one hundred thousand a year. Not bad money for a clothes selling job. I applied and got the job right away. The clothes sold in this store were very heavy knits and being in the desert, where summers can reach the 120s, you have to rely on the seasonal winter/spring business and make as much money as you can to get you through the entire year when your regular clients go home to their summer places.

The first and second years were amazing. I was making fifty thousand a year, and for a new person building a clientele, that was pretty good. Then the recession started to hit. People were not spending as much. Even the wealthy clients were tightening up their belts. I would often take clothes to my clients' homes for a private showing. They loved the special attention and once you know your customer well enough, you can spot collections that would fit her perfectly when they first arrived in the store, give her a call and set up an appointment with her.

One of my clients was this wonderful lady named Lea. She was able to walk and stand but mostly used a wheelchair or a cane to get around. Lea was a vibrant 89 year-old and she and her husband Tom lived in a secluded estate next door to the First Lady, Betty Ford, inside a private country in the city of Rancho Mirage. By coincidence was where I would do on call facials at the country club's private spa. Lea just happened to have been one of my facial clients for a few years before I reconnected with her at the clothing boutique. So, we already had a nice friendship established. Since I knew Lea very well, I would often pack up a garment bags full of chosen clothes, and take them to her home for her to try on. If I took ten thousand dollars in clothing, she would often buy six thousand or more. I got to know her family very well since Lea would bring her daughters into the store when they came to visit.

One day one of her daughters called me to tell me their father, Tom had died. They wanted to meet with me to see if I could help during the memorial service to dress Lea and be right by her side during the memorial celebration. It was an honor to be called in at a time when Lea needed me the most. It was held in the elegant banquet room at her club with wonderful catered food served and champagne flowing. It was a true Celebration of Life. The memorial service was packed with all the members of the country club along with personal friends and family, a few hundred attendees. After the service Lea asked me to wheel her here and there to meet and greet some of her longtime acquaintances at the country club. I never left her side.

I received a call a few days later from one of her daughters asking if I would meet them for lunch. There was something important they wanted to discuss with me. So, I met with them and they asked me to leave the store where I was working and come live in with their mom. I would have very little to do since they already had a housekeeper who cleans, but requested I be her companion, take her to doctor appointments, prepare her meals three times a day, and take the dog for walks. They would pay me a thousand dollars a week for five days, giving me two days off, when they would hire someone from an agency to cover for me.

I gave it a lot of thought. With the recession, it might be hard to make as much in commissions at the boutique. I would live rent-free; food included, and also could drive her car if I chose to. (Which was a Rolls Royce parked in her air-conditioned controlled temperature garage), and make fifty two thousand a year, practically a no-brainer for me not to consider. So, I talked it over with my family. I decided it was a good financial move, plus I really liked Lea.

"Kevin, could you move me?" This had become so common to say, since he already moved me five times or more in the last couple of years after Mom died. But this time I would give away everything I owned except my big screen TV, clothes, and cosmetics… to Laura and Jeff. I didn't see the need for anything more, and I'm sure this was one of Kevin's easiest moves for me.

My landlords always love me because I make the home much nicer when I leave than when I arrived. I used Q-tips on the window sills, deep-cleaned baseboards in every room, and scrubbed all the nooks and crannies. All they had to do was put an ad on Craig's List, post a photo and it was rented again!

My room at Lea's was huge a king-size bed, a sitting area for reading, and a nice private bathroom complete with tub. It took Kevin and me an hour to load and an hour to unload. We had already moved me so many times, we were really getting the process fine-tuned.

I helped Lea get ready for bed each night. In the morning, I would start my day getting up early, getting everything lined up for the day before she was awake, making my lists and checking them twice. I took her dog out for a long walk around the golf course each morning. Since she lived next to the Former First Lady Betty

Ford's estate, there were always Secret Service agents passing up and down the street and a guard at the gate to enter the driveway, but on the golf course side there was no obstruction to the view of the massive home that was in the shape of a single story large half circle that overlooked the golf course. One time Lea's little dog went onto the Fords' lawn instead of walkway. All of a sudden I heard a loud speaker go off saying, "Intruder on Property," over and over. I had to smile to think what the Secret Service agents must have viewed on their TV monitors, as they would see this little dog on the lawn looking for a place to pee, and me, holding the leash while staying on the walking path. What a beautiful, serene walk that was for me every day.

I would go grocery shopping, pick up her meds at the pharmacy, drop off clothes at the cleaners, and each day I would dress her to the nines. This is where my cosmetic/fashion stylist/hair stylist expertise came in handy. She was the most spoiled and pampered woman you could imagine. Lunch was usually at the club. The club staff knew her by name, as did all the members, but since they also knew of her husband, the entire staff, including chefs would come out to say a personal hello and ask how she was doing. Lea and her husband must have lived there for twenty-five years or more, the staff really seemed like family to her.

Every afternoon around four o'clock it was happy hour. That meant she had her cocktail while she sat at a gorgeous built-in bar in her living room. We put on her favorite FM radio station as she listened to music of her favorite singers, like Frank Sinatra. I never told her my story of knowing him. She had been there and done so much more in her lifetime than I could ever dream of. It was great fun for us each day to pull out a deck of cards and play poker. She taught me the game and she was very good. It was her favorite time of the day, enjoying playing poker during her happy hour. Prior to that, while she took her afternoon nap, I started preparing dinner; a salad, entrée, and dessert, so it didn't take long to serve her when Happy Hour was over. This is when I realized I loved being a personal assistant.

One weekend while I was away from her, Lea had taken her shower and fell, breaking her arm and injuring her hip. She would now need nursing care, more than I was prepared to give. The family decided to let me go and hire a nurse at this point. So as much as they didn't want to lose me, the job ended. They wrote me a wonderful letter of reference. I had now left two $50,000-a-year jobs in less than six months.

I also had another awesome client from the boutique, Jeannie. We socialized and were great friends. That is one of the great things that can happen when you build up a clientele in a high-end clothing boutique. They set up appointments with you so you are exclusively theirs when they arrive. Hours can be spent with just that one person in a large elegant dressing room, styling them from head to toe, pinning their alterations, as they sip champagne. You become a confidant and a therapist, knowing her every flaw to cover to make her look fabulous. I called Jeannie to let her know what had happened, how I had lost my job as a companion. She invited me over to have lunch and give support when I was taking deep breaths just knowing I had to start over once again, while trying to be strong and resilient. I had no place to live, but thank God, Michelle and her family took me back in, putting a roof over my head at least until I could find something else. Still in shock, and now June in the desert, the thought of not having my own place to live and no job was daunting.

Jeannie, I'm sure, from the moment she wakes up looks like perfection with an angel-given heart. I felt blessed to know her. She had always shown such kindness towards me. She knew I couldn't afford to run with a billionaire circle of friends. I was lucky I could go out for happy hour and special lunches on my budget. But Jeannie always invited me to be her guest at many special events, often including splashy high-end fashion shows with long runways and skinny models wearing thousands of dollars in clothes from each couture collection.

It seemed ironic that one of the fashion shows I attended was to benefit the Barbara Sinatra Children's Center. Barbara had been one of my private clients at the boutique. I dealt over the phone with her personal assistant, helping her select items from our catalogues that Barbara had picked out. Then I would personally deliver the order to her doorstep, only to be greeted by a housemaid and hand off the garment bags filled with clothes. Only once did I have the chance to have her actually set up an appointment with me and come into the store. As I walked all around the boutique with her looking at collections, I couldn't help but feel in awe of her beauty, elegance and grace, as she had aged well. I reflected on my younger days when I would sit across from her at age twenty-three, watching which fork she would pick up to eat her shrimp with, and I smiled from some sweet memories of moments of past. There wasn't a time that presented itself to mention knowing her as Barbara Marx. Who knows maybe one day she will read this book. It was just one of the many special moments resulting from Jeannie's taking me to special events.

During lunch at Jeannie's home we sat around sharing stories, with her showing me all her rare pieces of art, including collectables having to do with carnivals. Jeannie and her recently deceased husband were teenagers in love who married and started out their business having pony rides at the carnival where families would pay a few coins to let their children ride around in a circle. Later, the business grew and grew, and soon they were one of the biggest carnival companies in California, traveling from fair to fair all over the state. They changed the image of carnies taking your money, being low-life bums, to what now is a powerful money-making corporation with hundreds of workers and run more professionally due to all the state laws and regulations.

Jeannie's daughter happened to call while we were sitting at the table and I heard the mention of a carnival her daughter (who has now taken over the family business) was doing in Monterey. Just hearing the name "Monterey" and my ears popped up. After the call Jeannie was telling me about her daughter doing a carnival in Monterey and I said, "I'm without a job; see if she could use me." So Jeannie quickly called her daughter back (Thank goodness I had met her daughter while working at the boutique!), and asked if she could use me and her daughter said YES, but not just for Monterey, but if I could drive right up the following week to Sonoma she could use me there for three weeks with a weekend off, then Monterey for another week. I didn't hesitate ... YES! Just the idea of going home to Monterey was what I needed.

My lodging was all paid for and we got paid our hourly at the end of each carnival location. I was up for the adventure. It would be cool weather compared to the desert. I could save a little nest egg from the money at the end of each gig, and be gone for the next six weeks on a complete thrill ride! Well, not exactly.

I drove up to the Sonoma fairgrounds and quickly met Jeannie's daughter Dee. She took care of my gas mileage for the drive. When I was told I would be given a room I was thinking a motel or something but instead this was the start of knowing what it is like to live the life of the carnies. It looked like a wagon wheel circle where all these motor homes lined up for the traveling workers. Dee walked me over to mine. It was pretty small. It was a toy hauler. We knocked on the door and a nice girl answered and invited us in. She would be my roommate. She had a little puppy and it had just gone pooh in the room. That was going to be my room to live in over the next three weeks. The girl apologized for the mess and said she had just gotten the little puppy from the shelter and it wasn't quite house-broken yet, but she would make sure she cleaned up all the messes. She offered me the larger bed and she and the little puppy would take the bunk bed at the other end. So there I was, tired after the long drive, a lumpy bed in this little toy hauler that looked pretty good right at that moment, even though the bathroom had to be the very smallest I had ever tried to squeeze into. When sitting on the toilet the door just barely closed against my knees. Standing in the shower would have to be quick since the hot water lasted only a few a seconds.

I couldn't turn back now, so it was time to look for all the good. I drove to the closest store, loaded up on some food to get me through a few days, since space was at a premium, and stopped for Chinese to bring back for my roomie and me to have a little get-to-know-you party, since we were going to be together for the next three weeks.

Cindy, my new roommate was really nice. She had worked for this family doing carnivals since she was a teen. Now that she was older, she worked in Arizona for a telephone company and planned her vacations every year around this three-week event. She worked as a carnie at one of the games. She knew these games inside and out. Times were different from way back in the day. Now there is a commitment to safety, best quality equipment, modern appealing rides, games and food, and colorful, comfortable midway amenities, as well as beautifully landscaped rest areas. There was a special kid-friendly zone with rides just for the younger set. No scary monsters or fast rides, just good photo-op moments. The only thing to be on the lookout here for is perverts who just love to take pictures of little children. For the bigger kids and family times there was the merry-go-round and the tilt-a-whirl. For the thrill-seekers, there was spinning, turning, twisting, dropping and sometimes all at one time if you can handle it. And of course you have the spectacular rides, the giant wheel reaching 110 feet in the air, the whirling wave swinger, and the giant carousel.

The Heath Department is always checking on the individual booths filled with as much fattening things as you can imagine such as deep fried such as Twinkies and Oreo Cookies. There is cotton candy, candy apples and hundreds more things that are a must for all fair-goers. All the staff wear uniforms and are clean cut, and very engaging. My job, if you're wondering, was to work in the customer service booth, from morning until late at night, handling the complaints obviously, but mostly it was where military, fire, and law enforcement came to buy their discounted tickets. There were long lines all day long selling products like carnival beads, sun block, and disposable cameras. I never worked alone, always having another girl with me. We would take this little booth, open it up wide and set up displays and rock those sales. It was easy work, with super-long hours, but time went by quickly. We were relieved for an hour, just long enough to make it back to the toy hauler, eat a quick bite and relax. When the night's end came, all we wanted to do was just go back to our room, undress, have a quick shower and lie down, getting as much sleep as we possibly could before the new day started.

I met lots of great people, each of us trying to make some money while enjoying the atmosphere of lights, laughter, show time, kids smiling, pictures taken and prizes to be won. After spending three weeks in Sonoma, which I had always heard was a very beautiful place, I actually never got to see it. I made it as far as the grocery store and back. I loved getting bottles of splits of champagne to go with my baloney sandwiches, and every once in a while I would savor the meal of a corn dog and a candy apple. I will always find a way to make even the worst of times feel like the best. I had lots of experience with that.

When Sonoma was over, the cleanup finished, my roommate and her little puppy that I grew to just love to pieces had to leave to go back to Arizona. I then learned I would have the toy hauler all to myself in Monterey. I had adjusted to living in the toy hauler with its drop down dining table, benches and comfy sofa that made into additional beds if needed. I came to enjoy it very much. Being resilient and adapting to any and all circumstances I am faced with, I would remember times worse that made this entire trip look very nice.

I was so excited now about being on the road to Monterey and having this toy hauler all to myself that I couldn't wait to invite Michelle, Kevin and Logan to come spend the week with me. I was off for three days before I had to move back to the toy hauler, so I got us two small motel rooms and got to have my family come to spend some time in the place Michelle was actually born, a place that her husband and son knew nothing about and had never seen. We spent those days going everywhere tourists go. Spending time with my family, sharing places and times of Michelle's childhood, memories that I only knew, was priceless. We walked on the sand at Del Monte Beach and I pointed out where Michelle and I lived when she was a little girl.

I found my mind drifting back to the night that Rock came to visit. I never in all these years got over my love and lust for him. I often wondered what happened to him, was his life happy? Each time a certain song would come on the radio, it reminded me of him, of that one moment of love. Would my life have been better if he came to find me? But this was not the time to reflect so much about my lost love as it was about sharing the joys of Michelle and her life here before I moved to the desert when she was three. I could tell that even though she was just a little girl, this place remained in her soul.

After a couple of days enjoying the sights and waves of Monterey, Carmel, Pacific Grove and Pebble Beach, it was time to move into the toy hauler with my family. Michelle is opposite from me when it comes to adventures. She wasn't quite sure how she would adapt to living in a toy hauler. But I had talked to her every day for three weeks telling her how much fun it is to live on the grounds of a carnival and this would be the trip of a lifetime for Logan. Well, when I was in Sonoma, the toy hauler was parked away from the rides; however, not in Monterey. Nope, instead it was parked right within a hundred feet of the bumper car ride. Michelle was freaked out living in the little toy hauler (she is much more a hotel girl with room service), let alone having thousands of people, bright lights from the rides, music and more. Kevin is easy going and adapts to anything and never complains.

Then picture a little boy of nine years-old after dark in a carnival. All the lights, games, stuffed animals to win, let alone every child's dream of having cotton candy, and candy apples for sale right outside his door! This was like living at Disneyland in his mind. He thought he had the coolest grandmother known to man, I'm sure. Michelle toughened up and handled the next three days because her son was so happy. But on the third night after not sleeping very well the two nights before, Michelle was really counting on a good night's sleep, but just her luck, the carnival had a free ride night after the fair closed, so until 1 am, all the workers and their guests got to come and ride as many rides as they wanted for free. Right outside our living room!

The following day it was time for my family to leave to go back home. Michelle couldn't handle another day of living the carnie lifestyle. I spent a few days after I finished my gig at the carnival and enjoyed the beauty of the Monterey Bay including my favorite luxury of a bubble bath. Complete silence and rest. Again, before I left, I took a long walk on Del Monte Beach deep in thought of Rock. That one night, those beach front apartments standing right in front of me.

CHAPTER 31

Paying It Forward

When I returned to the desert, I had a little extra money to help me with a new start. As luck would have it, one of Michelle's long-time girlfriends had a clothing store in the desert and one in the mountains, Idyllwild, forty-five minutes above the desert floor. The village of Idyllwild is nestled in the San Jacinto Mountains, set among tall pines and legendary rocks. It has a small town atmosphere with many shops and restaurants along with a variety of small inns and cabins to rent. It's great for camping, shopping, rock climbing, and hiking. My new boss, Zoe, had gotten sick and needed someone dependable to run the business, at least until January. The timing couldn't have been better. I jumped at the chance for this job, where again, I didn't have to pay rent, and the village was so beautiful, just like you would see in a mountain resort brochure. Everyone in the village was very friendly. The town caters to tourists and it was so much fun to have this stress-free job, helping to grow this business for a friend of my family.

Zoe was a young, single mom doing the best she could to make ends meet and to provide the best for her daughter. Oh, how I could relate to that! Let alone a close friend of my daughter and many more I know.

Zoe was pleased with the job I was doing for her up in Idyllwild. Once the store closed in January for the winter months, she asked me to continue working for her desert boutique. I knew it would be very easy for me at the start of the season going back to work in the desert for another high end clothing boutique where I could make some good money, but for now, I just wanted to take the season off from working under any type of stressful job. I enjoyed being in the small mountain village with no cares, simple life, hardly any responsibilities.

I hadn't dated for years. I stopped considering being with another man. How could I trust anyone ever again? All I ever wanted was a Prince to fall in love with. Now, is that asking too much? The storybook romance of him falling madly in love with me and treating me like his Princess? He who would say, "You're My Everything," I will love and protect you, come share this amazing life with me? Having us spoil each other and making the remaining years of my life become the best ever.

But my hopes and dreams of that were few and far between. I had some major trust issues by this time and with good reason. Sometimes I would wear a wedding ring just so I wouldn't be approached. When asked if I was single, I would say no, doing everything possible in my power not to draw attention to myself. Even gaining some extra weight didn't seem to matter. Knowing what I do now, that would never have been a choice. I have had a very difficult time losing the weight ever since, which even further helped to lower my self-esteem.

Michelle would get frustrated with me and tell me I should get out more, have a social life, and start dating again, do things to make me feel desirable. But no one had caught my eye. I had given up on looking and if by chance the right man appeared and the chemistry was there I would be open, maybe. That is, if I even recognized him standing in front of me. In the meantime, all I wanted to do was focus on my work and get back into some type of volunteer work.

This time I was led to another area of hospice, but not helping end-of-life stage patients. I was drawn to help survivors with their grief. Not just any survivors, but children and teens who had lost a mother, father, sibling, grandparent or best friend. When children experience the death of a loved one, it can be confusing for them. They are often left feeling lost and alone while the adults around them are grieving.

Most children up until the age of seven or eight have no concept of death and grieving. They are afraid to talk about it because they do not want to cause more pain and crying around them. They try to cope with their own grief. In the desert, a program existed where every two weeks the child can go to a group class with kids in the same age range. Just meeting and playing with other children going through similar circumstances helps them to know they are normal and can express grief through arts and crafts projects when unable to verbalize emotions.

Children can't be kids at home because they feel it is wrong to be silly, to play and laugh when everyone around them is sad. But at this program, Mourning Star, they can be kids again and laugh, play games, even shed some tears. A very special bonding takes place and kids start to make friends again, now understanding how they feel is very normal when someone close to them dies. Snacks and craft time end the evening in a social setting, and they proudly take home their craft projects to keep in remembrance. The classes only last the length of the local desert school year of nine months, leaving the three summer months free

During the summer, they can attend Camp Erin, a grief camp that is held each year in the mountains of Big Bear in California. A hundred children come together from the surrounding counties of Riverside and San Bernardino. Children from all walks of life and age groups attend, all with one common bond, dealing with grief and coping with the loss of a loved one. Camp starts on a Friday afternoon, when the children are greeted by a friendly staff and the volunteers. They are divided into gender and age-specific groups.

They are given a Camp Erin T-shirt, lanyard, and backpack filled with fun things. A Camp Erin teddy bear and a homemade quilt are waiting for them on their bunks. Each child brings along a photo of their special person. After they meet their camp counselors, known as Big Buddies, the kids design a memory frame in honor of their loved one. They carefully place the photo in the memory frame and decorate it with words or stickers. On that first evening, in a special ceremony, each camper is given the opportunity to say something about their loved one as they place their memory frame on the Camp Erin memory board. This is followed by another special ceremony in a room filled with all one-hundred children, and the one-hundred Big Buddies and camp leaders. After the memorial ceremony, campers sing, dance and do fun exercises including running and playing. This helps them realize they are in a safe place.

They come to Camp Erin not knowing what to expect. A grief camp sounds so sad, but it doesn't turn out that way. On Saturday, right after breakfast, the children and teens start doing more craft activities like making wooden memory boxes that they can paint, place stickers on, and use photos in memory of the person who died. They might paint the box in their loved one's favorite color. Some kids write a message to their loved one. Soon it is lunch time. The meals are served in a big cafeteria and long lines are formed. They love the food and can go back for more as many times as they want.

After lunch the kids go back to their rooms, put on their swim suit or shorts, sandals, grab a beach towel and head down to the private lake. Their choices over the following four hours are swimming in the lake, fishing, canoeing, or playing in the water with the therapy dogs that are trained specifically to work with children. These dogs are amazing and as I played with my group of children, while helping to keep an eye on many, I always found myself drawn to the dogs at every opportunity. Each child held a special bond with the dogs and lots of petting was encouraged. It gave the dogs a deep feeling for each child they came to know. The dogs' intuition was almost magical.

Summertime fun always means ice cream, and the kids loved making sundaes themselves. We barely had a moment to rest up before it was time to walk back up the hill to the cabins, shower, dress, and get ready for dinner.

On Saturday night, all of the children walk in the moonlit sky and are guided by the volunteers back down a path to the lake's edge. Each child will light the candle inside the luminaria they made earlier. They have the chance to say that this is in memory of their loved one, naming them, and then tell a little bit about the person who died. For most of the children, this is a very hard thing to do. Most are unable to say very much at all. This is when I heard the weeping of these children who had reached down inside a hidden place and were able to feel the loss along with all the other children, not embarrassed in the dark, but rather comforted by the sounds of their new friends also crying. It was at this moment that even I had difficulty trying to fight back tears. You couldn't hear me cry, but tears flowed down my cheeks as the therapy dogs were released to go through the children, feeling their pain and coming to give unconditional love and comfort. These dogs were like angels walking among the children and once all the luminaria bags were lit they were placed on the large wooden raft and it was slowly pulled out into the middle of the lake. I couldn't help but be filled with emotion standing at the edge of the shore, watching these beautiful luminaries set adrift on the lake, while beautiful music was played.

Slowly the children walked quietly back up to the cafeteria. Once inside in the bright lights, dancing music was played, and dozens of boxes of pizzas were ready to eat. Desserts and soft drinks were served. Within a half-hour of the return to camp there was laughter, dancing, singing, neon necklaces swirling around, and fun to be had. They did what they needed to do.

Camp Erin is special for these children because the weekend is spent remembering the person who died and learning new coping skills to help with the healing process. Kids never, ever want to forget. Camp Erin helps them to remember. Camp Erin gives grieving children and teens a chance to be with other children and teens who have experienced the same thing. Just being together, the kids can look around the room and think, I fit in here. I'm not different here. These other people all get it.

After breakfast on Sunday the children gathered up all the craft items they made and their favorite part was signing everyone's T-shirt. I have my T-shirts safely stored in a cedar chest. Knowing I helped in even the smallest of ways made it all worth the effort, especially when the children gave me big hugs as they left to go home.

Doing anything to help in the community is just part of my existence. Even on vacation last year, I spent some more time in Monterey, and I was able to find a local food bank to help box hundreds of bags to be handed out. I also volunteered with Save Our Shores, where they gave out gloves and a big empty bucket to go out and collect trash along the ocean's edge. If we each do just one thing each week to pay it forward and make a difference, it all adds up.

When summer came I was asked to return to the store in Idyllwild. By this time, I had been a big help to the boutique's owner, and she asked me to live with her and her young daughter, rent free, in exchange for cleaning and helping to make meals. So, I spent four days a week in Idyllwild selling clothes, then drove back down to the desert to stay at the boss's house rent-free, and catch up on the cleaning, laundry, and meal planning, with two days to completely relax. Her large swimming pool also allowed, if not nude sunbathing, at least topless. I was able to save enough money to help give me a few weeks' vacation the following summer.

During this time, I was extremely busy going back and forth from one store to the other, and then the owner opened a third store, and soon a fourth. It was getting impossible to do my volunteer work, help at all the stores, do the business paperwork, sell the clothes, clean her house, and still try to have some private time. I was starting to get run down.

Meanwhile, Michelle had been busy over the last year studying everything she could get her hands on about health and nutrition. She had become a private Pilates instructor to the crème de la crème in the desert. She took on-line courses, and attended longevity conferences. She came to understand the importance of "you are what you eat."

When I was visiting her one day, I was enjoying reading the thick September issue of *Vogue*, when she tried to hand me a book called *Health Wars* that she wanted me to read. I looked at her and the size of the book on health (It wasn't a love story, for Heaven's sake!), and I held up my magazine and said; "Now really,

Daughter, which one do you think I will actually look at?" And I laughed away her attempt at trying to make me understand the importance of what she was trying to teach me. This type of thing went on all the time, Michelle always trying to teach by example, always encouraging me, letting me know how wonderful I already was. "But just think if you did this how much better you would be!" I honestly just tuned her out.

One day she called me to come over and watch a chick flick with her. An offer of wine I believe was in the mix of fun to be had as well. "Absolutely, Daughter," I said, "I would love to come spend some Mother/Daughter time with you." It is without a doubt that family time is my favorite time, seeing my grandson and enjoying the company of her amazing husband Kevin. He is more like a son to me than a son-in-law. I just love him and admire how he would do anything for his family. If I could have created the perfect person for my daughter, Kevin would be the design.

I got all settled down on my favorite reclining sofa in front of the big-screen TV waiting for our fun movie to begin. Michelle came into the room from her office and said, "Hey Mom, would you mind watching this quick video before our movie?" She said it was really fast but she needed to watch it in order to get certified in some online course she was taking, so I agreed immediately.

The video she put in was called *Food Matters*, and by the time it ended, I had tears in my eyes. I turned to her and said, "I Get It! Now I understand what and why you have been trying so hard to teach me." It took that one video, to be the life changer for me. From that moment on, I started studying every single thing I could get my hands on. There was a big event called "The Longevity Now Conference" held in Orange County that was three days long. She said, "Mom, I will pay your ticket for the weekend if you will please go with me." Of course I told her I would love to go. It would give me a chance to finally start learning more of what it is that excites her about these conferences. Plus, it would be another fun Mother/Daughter weekend. I don't even know where to begin to tell you all that I learned from that weekend. But again it was life-changing.

I learned what "superfoods" are, along with medicinal mushrooms, the importance of organic vs. GMO crops, the difference between smoothies and juicing, and why one is better than the other for detoxing, cleansing and healing your body. It was fun once we got back to the desert. You could find Michelle and me deep into the health food stores reading labels on all the products, completely cleaning out our kitchen cabinets and refrigerators. Once a month we drove two hours to Chinatown in downtown Los Angeles, bringing home products to make the healing medicinal teas.

Over the last four years, since starting this regimen to help stack the odds in my favor, I have had no need for medical doctors, no illnesses, not even a cold. I will continue to study all that I can about natural healing through plants and herbs, and using pure essential oils that have no fillers.

Michelle was so happy to see my life take such a dramatic turn. From then on the two of us went to the conference every year. We held parties at her lovely home to share the ideas and help educate friends. My life started to change as I became healthier. While living with my boss I started making her smoothies each day. I made us big wonderful salads, and healthy soups. Farmers markets became my grocery store.

Things started to become so clear and easy to understand. Our body is made up of cells. We need to give the right nutrients to feed these cells to give us a healthy life. When we eat the common American diet, we are eating because we like the taste, textures and the full comforting feeling food gives to us. We are required to eat in order to stay alive. But when we eat all the processed, chemically induced foods, they fill us up but they do not feed our cells. So, we are always craving more and more food until our cells are actually given something to help them survive.

If we eat organic, raw, gluten free, soy free, dairy free, vegan more often, that is ideal because we are feeding more nutrients straight into our cells. For me, I love to drink fresh cold pressed juices as often as possible. When you drink cold pressed, you get the most nutrients with the quickest delivery straight to your cells. The more you feed your cells what they need, the less you crave sugar and salty foods. I actually started craving the taste of the different blends of juice, and my cells were being nourished. When I juice, I try to juice as many greens as possible, such as kale, spinach, parsley, cucumbers, celery, broccoli and add some lemon and green apple for sweetness. I have so many recipes now that I have learned to be a juicing specialist.

I also love smoothies. They are not to be mistaken for juicing. Smoothies keep the pulp and you drink that as well. When juicing, the pulp is completely separated out of the juice. As the fresh juice travels through your digestive track it requires no energy or hard work for your body to process and the nutrients are quickly absorbed. Because the smoothies have pulp, the process is a little longer to work its way through you. Superfoods, such as raw organic cacao, maca, acai, hemp seeds, chia seeds, coconut water, organic kale, parsley, and berries can be added for a little sweetness. These are health building drinks.

Medicinal mushrooms that grow out of trees such as reishi, astragulas, porta and many others have a healing quality within them. You must continue drinking these Chinese herbal teas each and every day to help restore what has already been depleted.

I was at work one day thinking how nice it would be to live in my own place once again, not having to cook, clean or do anything for anyone but myself. I was just finishing selling clothes to a beautiful woman named Patti. I came to learn she lived close by and I said, "oh by the way, if you ever hear of a small place to rent close to here, I really could use one." Patti said, "I have a large room for rent, but I leave for Costa Rica on vacation tomorrow morning. How much can you afford to pay?" I told her a very small amount because I didn't make much money at this job. She said that sounds fine. "Can you come over right after work today? Then when I come back in two weeks you can live there." Patti had just gotten a divorce and hated to live alone so that would work out great for her. Just knowing someone lived on the property would reduce her feeling of loneliness. I took down the address and drove straight there right after work.

When I got to the address, it was inside a gated development. In my entire life, I had never been a part of something like this. The guard was at the huge electric gates waiting to check my name. Then these enormous gates opened to allow my entry. There was breathtaking desert scenery and a 360-degree view. The golf course was like green velvet with its rolling hills, lush landscapes and palm trees lining the way, as I drove up to her long brick driveway that seemed to go on forever. I was overcome by the thought that it just might be possible that I could live here. Getting out of the car, walking toward the large black wrought-iron gate, I could see a beautiful big dog running in my direction. "Rex!" I could hear Patti calling him. "It's okay, Rex," she commanded. Patti greeted me and opened the gate as I entered what was another world to me. Off to the right was a large casita a one bedroom detached guest house with full bath kitchen, large living room with fireplace, all completely designed and furnished in classic Spanish style. Patti said this is yours if you would like to live here. Can you even begin to imagine my expression and disbelief that I could live in my own home, not just a room, feel safe and secure at a price I could afford? This casita if advertised would have been five times what she was allowing me to give. Don't pinch me because I never want to wake up! I said YES, I would love to live here. Patti said great, she'd be back in two weeks and it was mine, a luxury golf estate, valued at close to four million.

A 5,117 square-foot home had 5 bedrooms, 4 baths, a library and an office. The master bath had a spa tub and huge shower, room enough for a party. From the great room/living room area, the 14-foot glass walls allowed the blend of the outside into the living room, as these glass walls opened up and disappeared. The panoramic view was spectacular. As we stepped outside to the salt-water pool with beach entry, there was an amazing outdoor cooking station with plenty of seating, some around the built-in fire-pit adjacent to the golf course.

I was in a daze as I thanked Patti for this wonderful opportunity. When I left, watching the huge gates closing behind me as I drove out of the property and back into reality, I was feeling numb. I thanked the Lord for His abundant blessings. The call was made, "Kevin, Can You Move Me?"

A few weeks later Kevin did move me in and he was very happy to see me actually have a roof over my head that was an actual house. I didn't have to clean for anyone, cook for anyone and could just BE. My grandson Logan started coming over to spend the night. I bought a pink beach cruiser and he would bring his bike and we would ride for miles around the development. Security passed by regularly to make sure we were safe and to check on all the other estates in the complex. In the morning before school, I would drive him up to the club house and we would have a big 5-star breakfast and be treated like royalty just because we lived there. Both Logan and I shared precious moments that I hope he will be able to remember all his life. Logan and I would wrap up with our blankets and snuggle on a big pull-out sofa bed in front of the big screen TV, with the fireplace blazing as we are ate popcorn and M&M s, a family tradition to live on forever with him, I hope.

We often watched animated movies we could sink our teeth into, and this quality time meant the world to both of us. It reminded me of the times I used to spend with my own son Aaron when he was little. Every once in a while I would catch myself calling Logan, Aaron.

Aaron my son had met and fallen in love with a woman who had three children. He married her and had a huge church wedding. Now they were expecting a child of their own. With him being a firefighter for a city two hours away and a new family, he had little or no time to drive down to spend time with his sister, her family or me. I would love to have shared this gorgeous home, clubhouse and all the amenities with him but now he had responsibilities and priorities.

Sometimes I would set up my massage table in the living room and invite my friends over for one of my intense 90-minute facial/massage treatments with candles glowing and the fireplace burning. Often times when friends were over I would teach them how to make superfood smoothies and give a class about what superfoods were all about. I met this one beautiful lady, Nancy, at the clothing boutique and we started talking about making smoothies. As we were so engrossed in the subject, I suggested she come over the next day. I was off and I wanted to give her a class on what she could do to help stack the odds in her favor for longevity.

Nancy lived in northern California and had a second home in the desert. She loved where I lived (who wouldn't, right?) and we laughed and spent a couple of hours sharing secrets about health as we knew it. An instant bond of friendship was made. Nancy's husband was in the medical profession and she had to rush off to meet him. Before long, we were doing things together when she came down to the desert.

Nancy invited me to northern California to visit her home, which was fabulous and located right on the Delta River. When I drove up to visit for my summer vacation, her husband took us for a long boat cruise. Nancy planted her garden, started her own composting, and really got into changing everything she and her husband were eating. It was helpful that they were already vegetarians. Nancy did a home exchange with a friend that had a condo in Monterey for a week and that person would get to stay in Nancy's home for a week in the desert. She invited me to spend the week in Monterey with her. I would arrive a day earlier in the week and stay at the hostel. I wanted to give her a tour of Monterey, Carmel, Pacific Grove, Pebble Beach, like she hadn't seen before.

I arrived earlier and thought I hadn't been to my father's and grandmother's resting place in the cemetery for years. The sun was out with clear skies. I bought some flowers and was going to clean off both of their grave markers and talk to them. Just as I was doing that, a funeral procession drove up with many cars to unload a grieving family and friends of the deceased. The site was directly across the driveway from where I was parked and in plain view of me. As I listened to the words being spoken, hearing the gun salute for a veteran, and at last, the bagpipe player playing, I have to admit, I got caught up in the moment. Hearing their sobs, feeling the suffering of loss, and understanding their grief, made tears come down my face, I spoke to my dad and grandmother in silence. I asked them to please bring someone special into my life, someone who I could fall in love with like Rock over forty years earlier. I didn't really want to be alone. It had been 9 years without dating.

As I left the cemetery, I knew I needed to plan some fun adventures for Nancy while she was here. I went to the store and picked up the Monterey Weekly newspaper that told of all special events and the entertainment for the week. I went back to the hostel, sat in the dining room and read page by page, making notes of things to do, when all of a sudden I saw Rock's name. He was still performing on the Monterey Peninsula. My heart skipped a beat, just knowing he was still here, still performing music on Cannery Row after all these years a different venue, but it was him. I knew I had to see him once again.

Nancy arrived and we went out for a wonderful dinner, and I told her of all the fun things I had planned to show her during her visit. Of course I told her we were going to hear a performer on the following night that I used to dance to forty years earlier. She loved all the suggestions. It was hard for me to sleep that night, wondering what I would wear, would he recognize me after all these years. Would he remember the night he came to visit me at the beach apartment? Would he remember the trilogy of *The Sea*, *The Sky* and *The Earth* he brought me as a gift? Would he remember I moved away for him so I could share the rest of my life with him?

CHAPTER 32

And There He Was

It was Wednesday night, August 24[th,] eight-thirty pm 2011. The place was crowded as Nancy and I entered the room and found our seats facing the stage. I started to sit down when I saw Rock from the back. He was busy fixing some wires before the show was to start. I excused myself from Nancy, and walked up behind him. I said, "Excuse me," as he slowly turned around and looked into my eyes. I said, "You probably don't remember me, but I used to dance to your music over forty years ago. My name is Sharon."

Have you ever seen the TV show, the Jefferson's when Mr. Jefferson would grab his heart as if he was having the big one? That is what Rock did. It was as if he had seen a ghost. He quickly gave me a huge hug and was completely speechless. The other band members climbed up on the stage, and he asked where I was sitting and if I was with anyone and asked that I please stay around until the first set was finished.

At that moment, it seemed as if there were no years to separate us. The look on his face said it all. I went back to my table and sat down, still numb from seeing him, being hugged by him, and now hearing his voice and the smooth sounds of his singing. After the first song played he asked the other band members to play *Hello*, The Lionel Richie hit. I couldn't wait till the band took a break. It was a beautiful choice and fitting song for the occasion.

As the music stopped playing, and Rock came over to our table, I could feel my heart wanting to jump outside my chest. I introduced him to Nancy and let him know how much I was enjoying hearing him sing after all these years. His voice was pure perfection. I told him I still lived in the desert and that I had been living there the last forty years. I had no idea he was still performing here. I told him my daughter (who he had met when she was three) was married and had a child of her own now, and that I also had a son who married a woman with three children and now had a child of their own. He said he was married (at those words the happy that was inside me left briefly as I faked a continued smile) had three daughters who were grown now, some with children of their own, beaming as he spoke of his five grandchildren with pride.

Earlier in the day Nancy and I met a wonderful couple while we were having lunch at the lovely Casanova restaurant in Carmel. Scarlett and Randy happened to be on their honeymoon, and as we were talking and sharing stories, I suggested they come out that evening and join us for the entertainment and dancing on Cannery Row. Thank goodness just then this great couple arrived and joined our table. It turned out Randy was a singer and it just happened to be a Jazz Jam night, and all local entertainers came up on the stage to do their thing. So Rock pulled Randy up on the stage to sing *Proud Mary* and the crowd was dancing and the room became instantly filled with high energy. Towards the end of the evening, Nancy left to go visit with Randy and Mandy. It gave Rock and me a chance to talk.

I asked him if he remembered my living across the bay in the apartments on the water at Del Monte Beach. He said yes. I asked him if he remembered the record album, the Trilogy of The Sea, that he had given me as a gift. I could see it in his eyes, the memories starting to come back to him as he smiled and said he was still reeling from seeing me again after all these years and how beautiful I still looked.

Rock said his life was a bit complicated now since his wife was very ill. I changed the subject quickly as I didn't want to be reminded. But I did remind him how he had given me a brown portable cassette player with a special cassette he had created just for my drive to the desert to help keep me company while we were apart, helping me to know he would be coming to join me soon. Then I looked up at him and said, "But you never came there to find me."

I told him it was the music and the memories that helped me to survive the hard times over the years, and it was such a surprise to see his name in the paper and that he was still performing on Cannery Row all these years later. He didn't speak much, but his eyes never left me, as if still in a daze from seeing me as well. It was as though he was tuning out what I was saying and was in a trance with his recollection of those times so many years ago.

It was time for me to leave. As I got up to leave, Rock came around the table and gave me a big hug. He asked if he could walk me to my car. I said sure, and he escorted Nancy and me. His eyes said it all. He opened the car door, gave me one more hug, and said he hoped he would see me again. I told him I would be leaving soon to go back to the desert, but would be returning the following month. He lightly kissed my forehead and looked into my eyes, then turned and walked away. No words needed to be said.

After returning to the desert, Patti told me she was going to be selling her estate to downsize, since the economy was in a recession and other places in the desert could be purchased for a great price. It didn't take but two weeks to have a cash sale and another two weeks for us to move out. I loved every minute of the past year and living in such luxury every day. But I also know it takes some waves to appreciate when the ocean is smooth, just like in life.

Luckily I keep my belongings to a minimum and as I leave wherever the Lord has put me I always leave it better than how it was found and always give away anything extra that I accumulated so it helps benefit someone else. That's the secret of not ever getting attached to material things. In the big picture, they really have no meaning. I laugh to myself, to know that when I'm dead and gone it will take only a couple of car loads to the Goodwill, and there won't be much work for my children! Kevin, can you move me?

My boss was happy when I told her I needed to find a room and she invited me to come back to help her and her daughter once again. This time it was really nice to get back to my boss's home and help her once again with organization, cleaning and light meal preparation in exchange for room, a win/win situation. I really appreciated living there much more the second time around.

The following month I returned to Monterey again. And between 2011 and 2013, I made 7 one week trips. I started coming alone from then on. I had mentioned to Michelle and Kevin when they came to stay at the carnival, how I wish I could find a way where I could afford to visit here more often. They found the Hi-Hostel listed in the phone book, drove there and went for a tour and told me how great a place it was for me. It has a super large living room, extra-large kitchen and many different rooms with bunk beds dorm style and for under thirty five dollars a day. It was always filled with tons of travelers from all over the world. I started staying so many times and knew the manager well enough to walk in the door and tell him, "Honey I'm Home"

I did go back to see Rock once again and when the music was over and it was time to leave, the he asked if he could walk me to my car. We left the building and headed out into the street, I felt like I was in a movie scene from the movie *Cannery Row* with Nick Nolte and Debra Winger … the way "the Row" was completely empty of cars, the pavement wet from the low fog drifting in. As I pointed to my car parked down the block and across the street, Rock offered me his hand and the two of us walked hand in hand in the middle of the road to get to my car, a picture that will live forever in my mind, just the two of us, as if no one else existed. Those forty years of separation were as if it never happened. During that short walk, for those few moments, I knew when the time came and I died that I could actually say, "I loved once." When we arrived at my car, Rock was the perfect gentleman, and no words were left to be said.

I started working hard and always trying to save saving enough money to return to Monterey for summer visits. The more I visited Monterey the more I felt a huge difference in my spirit, the total essence of me. I never really wanted to leave my hometown all those years ago, especially to go to a place I had never even been before in the middle of summer with a little girl, no car, and limited cash. Looking back on just that first part of the journey, it is amazing how the Lord always had my back, then, and continuing ever after. I always believed I had a guardian angel as time went on, and I soon had no doubt. It continues to this day, a special intuition. I have learned to listen to and trust as I got older.

Life was good; a job and boss I liked, a nice roof over my head, a swimming pool to splash around in, and food on the table. I was feeling blessed. This next trip I took to Monterey was really a personal journey, enjoying the sights, sounds and sun on my body, long beach walks and bike rides. This time as I drove back home to the desert I had a crazy intuition that told me I needed to move from my boss's home. I couldn't shake the urge. I loved it there, but it was a different feeling than normal. It was more of an intuitive feeling that I should move.

I looked online and found an ad for a room to rent. I called right away to speak with the owner, and she said she didn't live in the home, but she rents it out to some business professionals who were hardly there and great tenants. A woman and two men, lived there now, but one of the men was moving out. The home had four bedrooms, three baths, pool, sauna and it would be available in two weeks. The room I would rent also had a bathroom inside. I got the address to go take a look and as she was telling me where it was located, I realized it was in the same development where Michelle and her family were living. Then I started to understand there must be a reason the Lord was bringing me to be close to her. So I called Michelle right away and asked her to come with me to check it out. I already had my checks made out for my deposit and first month's rent, just in case.

As Michelle and I pulled up in front of the home, it looked really nice on the outside and was within walking distance of Michelle and her family. We looked at each other and couldn't believe the odds of this happening. Michelle and I walked up to the door, rang the bell, and a tall nice-looking guy with wavy graying blond hair down to his shoulders greeted us and invited us in. The artwork and some of the pieces in glass showcases were worth thousands of dollars. The home was immaculate, the property with pool was large and well maintained. One of the male roommates who lived there now had been there for three years and used to rent a room from the owners when they lived there. So they had left the home in the care of this gentleman to make sure everything was well cared for. One of the men had moved out so that meant if I moved in there would be two men and two women. That worked for me. I loved the home, the pool, my private room with bath. If I can sleep in the hostel co-ed with men and women, then I surely can move in with three strangers and be close to my daughter and family. I handed over the checks and Michelle and I left. Michelle just always looks at me like she never knows what to expect and this time was no exception. She's the practical one, always skeptical and always protective of me. Kevin, Can You Move Me?

Two weeks went by quickly, and on the day Kevin and I arrived at the home to unload my belongings, I was able to meet the man in charge. He was the nicest man. Soon another man appeared, and then the original man I had met came home from work. I asked where the woman was that was living there and they said she had moved out a week prior, and it was rented to a man and he had moved in the day before me. Kevin never said a word, but I could tell he was thinking about how I was going to be living in this house with three men. Sort of a three's company turned around. Now I was the "Jack Tripper" of the household. I think from all the experiences I have had, and the fact I felt this was the Lord's doing that all would work out just fine. I had my big screen TV, a comfortable reclining chair, my seashell decorations, bathroom and walk-in closet. I also had a small portable refrigerator, so if I wanted to hibernate in my room at any time I could.

What more could I possibly want? I nicknamed the three guys, "The Rock Star" was the one with his long hair, in his forties and always trying to pick up the chicks. We lived close to a casino and during the week he would make a few trips over there to go dancing, pick up some girl and bring her home. With my room being the closest to his, I would have to use ear plugs since the screams from making love into the middle of the night often times would get really loud. The following morning I would tease him and say, "Couldn't you get her to scream a little louder?" Then there was "The Case Worker," a Mexican guy in his forties who was a hard laborer, doing maintenance and landscaping for a large country club nearby. I named him that because he always brought home a case of beer after work and enjoyed relaxing with his brews, especially while watching the games on TV. The third and most wonderful of them all I named "The Therapist." Everyone needs their own therapist, don't you think? Often times he would knock on my door and start a conversation about something and would end up standing there talking to me for an hour. I had a slight problem once with the Case Worker, but let's just say he never bothered me again and leave it at that. It was interesting living with three men. I learned a lot. Perhaps this was another reason I chose not to let men near me any longer (laughing).

Living so close to Michelle was the best part. I could ride my pink beach cruiser over to her house all the time. She asked me to promise her that during this year that I would concentrate on myself instead of worrying so much about everyone else, and to continue on the path to health that I had started on already. She always felt badly that I hadn't dated in what now would be twelve years, but she understood I had some self-worth issues, along with trust issues. Even if the Prince was standing right in front of me, I might not recognize him. Now that Rock was out of my fantasies, I had to learn not to live in a dream world any longer. Instead, I just chose to keep to myself, always working hard and when I wasn't working, I was still doing my volunteer work to help the grieving children and still going to Camp Erin in the summer with the kids. Michelle wanted me to get some counseling since she knew I had suppressed many emotionally traumatic situations all my life. She felt it was what was stopping me from allowing anyone to get close to me. I had lots of social friends but no one except her and my family did I allow in my inner circle surrounding me.

Michelle would have fun in her kitchen, always trying new things. Her kitchen became known as "The Nutri-Cafe." Her husband Kevin and my grandson along with all his buddies would come over just to taste all the wonderful things she would make.

On her never-ending quest for the best superfoods on the planet, Michelle was always creating new concoctions in her kitchen. Then it happened; "TRUElicious Raw Superfood Bar" was created. Michelle, now being a Pilate's instructor, in between clients, would take a corner of her bar and eat it. Soon her clients wanted to try a piece of the bar and fell instantly in love with it. She had created a bar now in demand. There was nothing, not even close to the high level of nutrition on the market then or now. TRUElicious is Organic, Raw, Gluten Free, Soy Free, Dairy Free and Vegan. It worked out great that just by chance she made her dose of daily nutrition into a bar forms. The fact that it tastes delicious on top of being healthy was a big plus.

About the time Michelle started making these bars, a new law in California passed called the Cottage Food Law. It allowed Michelle to make food in her home and sell it. Lucky her! It was quite a process to go through since she was the first one in her city to actually get this permit. The health department came to her home for an inspection and she passed with flying colors. Michelle started doing trade shows and local events which created more demand for the bars. She started to get many local stores that wanted to carry the TRUElicious Bars.

To keep up with the demand they decided to go for broke and created a more professional packaging. They opened a family-owned and operated TRUElicious factory in Indio, California. The Director of Production is Kevin, her husband who oversees the daily operations. They have their son Logan starting learning how to work in the business from the ground up after school. Their kitchen is, certified Vegan, Gluten Free and USDA Organic. Michelle and her creation of TRUElicious are in Whole Foods. Her bars are sold in the refrigeration section and not sitting on the isle with the multitude of bars that are just glorified candy bars with fillers, chemicals, and ingredients you can't pronounce. Since Michelle's bars are raw and all organic, they selling very well because customers prefer the bar to be fresh. I'm so proud of all she and her family have done in such a short time, and the continued success of this business, as the mainstream public becomes more aware. The sky is the limit.

My son Aaron works full-time in law enforcement and I have always respected his need for privacy due to his work. His marriage didn't work out as planned and, I keep what he does to myself and don't talk about it much. But I can tell you one thing; I have such an abundance of unconditional love for him. The older he gets, the closer I am in his life and I cherish every moment. As a Mom, I just want them to be happy, healthy, do good things to help others in the world and always remember Love and Peace is the answer. I have been blessed with two grandchildren I love more than life itself. Michelle and I are extremely close, and since I make many mistakes from poor judgement, she is very protective of me. Michelle has lived every day of this crazy life with me.

Since Aaron was raised with his father, I was able to build a very special relationship between the two of us. If I need help in an emergency, Aaron would come to my rescue. But ninety nine percent of the time, he has not known the whole story of my life the way Michelle has. I was ashamed to have him know some of the choices I made, and Michelle carried the burden. As mentioned previously, I haven't dated for so many years now. No drama and no trauma in my life. Plus I gave up watching news on TV. If it is something important, I will read about it in social media, but I cannot sit in front of a TV that is filled with bad news and propaganda. It is even hard for me to get used to four letter words being uttered in today's music. But I guess it is a way of expressing anger for a world that is out of control.

I try to keep my life very simple and filled with love, laughter, happiness and music. My dreams for my future are maybe, just maybe, one day my Prince will actually come for me. It would be nice to have an actual home to live in where I didn't have to move. I am so tired of moving. (I'm sure Kevin is tired from all the moves he helped me make, for which I would be forever grateful). I dream of a place to live where I could bring friends and spoil them. Maybe one day at some point even being secure enough to own a pet. If it's a male cat or dog, I will name him Prince. (Laughing) As for now I am into healing, serenity, and giving unconditional love to all I meet, while always looking for the good in everything. I keep active with my volunteer work and paying it forward as often as possible.

I also will give the readers of my journey the opportunity to have contact with me, the author via Facebook. I thought how often can you read a book and feel free to make comments or ask questions of the author directly? So, please when you're finished reading, "like" and "get notifications" on my Facebook.com/AuthorSharonRow page. Plus you might have friends that can benefit from reading one of my chapters, for example my mother's story of Alzheimer's and let them know they are not alone in their journey.

The summer of 2013, I decided to take some time off from working at the boutique and was offered a job to house-sit for five weeks. The estate was located in a private country club, high above the Desert floor, a view overlooking the Coachella Valley, with a huge infinity pool where the flow of water looked as if it was filling the miles of the green velvet golf course down below.

I was able to earn enough money to help pay some bills and still had enough left over to be able to take my summer vacation in Monterey. I stayed at a hotel on my arrival day, just so I could enjoy the peace and quiet of being alone and have the luxury of a candle-lit bubble bath with some of my favorite music playing in the background. I always burn my current favorite songs just for my trips. I enjoyed a glass of champagne, toasting to the times I survived and to the new adventures in store as I go forward. Then I spent the following few days at the wonderful Hi-Monterey Hostel, my home away from home.

As I was sitting in the dining room of the hostel, I saw a post on Facebook, where my daughter's close girlfriend, Chloe, was at a restaurant within walking distance of where I just happened to be. I quickly left to go find this sidewalk café along the walking path of Cannery Row. But I was too late. I must have just missed her. I texted her to tell her where I was and she texted back saying she was with her best friend named Natasha. Could I join them for happy hour at Schooner's at 5 o'clock? I said sure, I would love to.

CHAPTER 33

Full Circle

I looked forward to going to Schooner's Coastal Kitchen and Bar, sitting on top of Monterey Bay on Cannery Row. It offered us dining with an ocean view. When I arrived, Chloe and Natasha were enjoying a glass of wine and I ordered my wine and we all shared delicious appetizers. The view was spectacular and the girlfriend stories started to flow. Natasha, I learned, also was a long-time friend of Michelle's. All three of these girls worked at a popular gym together as spin instructors over fifteen years earlier. Chloe now was a certified raw food chef and had a growing clientele that she caters to, delivering fresh-pressed juices, organic soups, and fresh raw salads daily. Natasha is the general manager for a large spa corporation, creating the ultimate in spa luxury and pampering. It was expanding into Monterey, Florida, Times Square, Maui, San Diego, Arizona, and across the country.

Natasha was also getting ready to publish her first children's book benefiting rescue animals, featuring the real life story of her own dog "Jack Brown." Natasha told me when I first sat down that I was the perfect person to help her the rest of the summer. She needed someone to stay at her home in August and part of September to pet-sit for Jack and her cat Puss, while she traveled to help open up the new Maui spa. She also needed me to help with social media when her book first got published. She titled me, "Director of Chaos," helping to manage her schedules, making her healthy smoothies, juicing and salads while giving her peace of mind, knowing her pets were getting TLC while she was away.

For me it was Home Sweet Home. Natasha lived a block from Cannery Row. And hearing the seagulls and seals were going to be music to my ears. I thought, wouldn't it be wonderful to find a job here full-time and be able to come back full-circle to where I was born and raised. There is something to be said about where you took your first breath of air that will remain in the soul of you. Of course, living in perfect weather conditions year-round between 60 and 70 degrees isn't hard to take either, especially since I have lived in the desert for so many years in extreme summer heat. Now, to spend my retiring years in paradise sounded great.

I went online looking for jobs locally but found nothing that would pay me enough money to make the move. I did get one call from a large clothing chain that had a store in Monterey and also in Palm Desert. I applied and was able to take that new job when I returned home for the interview. I left the boutique where I had worked the last three years. I like change and move with the flow knowing that when one door closes another opens and it is usually better. When I interviewed for the new store in the desert, I asked if when the summer came and they started slowing down, would it be possible for me to transfer to the Monterey store, then come back again the following season, and the manager said that shouldn't be a problem as long as they are hiring in Monterey and I keep my sales figures up high here.

So, in December, I started to work in the #1 store in the company out of over 700 stores. I learned from the best and the amount of business was incredible. Each day, women were waiting in lines just to get rung up. The sales were fast-paced, going from one customer to the next, non-stop for five hours a day, five days a week. Part time worked well for me and I was able to write

UNSUPERVISED and loving it. The months just flew by.

When summer time approached, I called the Monterey store and the manager said yes, they were hiring, and I told her what my sales were and she said she really needed me. I asked how soon could she use me, and she said, "A month ago!" So as soon as I could get up there that would be great. Thank goodness my sales were extremely high and I proved to be worthy of a job transfer. The Palm Desert store expected me to return in November to start the new season, so basically, I was on loan. But I decided I would take whatever I could get, just to get back on my birth soil and walk the beach, smell the air and enjoy life to the fullest. I found the job easy enough, but now the tricky part started. Where would I live? I again went online to check out rooms for rent. I was coming from really beautiful homes in the desert with pools, where I could afford, to now room searching the Monterey Peninsula, where even the smallest run-down hole-in-the-wall room, started at nine hundred to a thousand dollars a month. I was getting a little discouraged in my quest, but not giving up hope.

It was Michelle's 45th birthday and all she really wanted from me was a 90-minute foot massage, which would be really fun for me also. I'd get to have complete Mother/Daughter time, share stories, a bottle of wine, and laugh. During the massage, I told her, "Michelle, I was able to get approved for my job transfer, but I am really having a hard time finding a room to rent." She said, "Hand me my phone." I said, "I already looked, and there is nothing." She said, "Let me try anyway." So I handed her the phone. Michelle asked me how much I could afford to pay for a room, and I said, "Six hundred dollars." The first ad she read to me said, "Master bedroom with private bath, sliding glass doors overlooking a large back yard with garden. Six Hundred Dollars." I said, "What?" I asked her the city and she said, "Marina." I said, "That's great, not too far from Del Monte Shopping Center where I will be working and it is where I used to live when I was a teenager, where I lived when I was married to your father, and where I brought you home from the hospital when you were born. Let's call and see if it's still available.

The lady on the other end of the phone sounded very nice and said it was still available and I told her a little about myself and I would like to have it. She agreed to rent to me sight unseen. I said thank you and what is the address to mail out a check first thing in the morning. I got a pencil and paper and started writing down the address, just at the moment Michelle's husband and son were coming in the room from the garage. As I wrote the numbers and the first word to the address, I said, "I know this home, and you are not going to believe this, but I used to own that home when I was nineteen years-old. It was the home I brought my daughter to from the hospital the day she was born. And today is my daughter's birthday and she just found your ad for me. I know when you open the front door your living room is straight ahead, and when you look off to the left, you see the dining room and kitchen and off of that is a step-down living room with a fireplace that has sliding glass doors that overlook the huge back yard." She said, "Yes!" and added, "I am looking out my window right now and you won't believe this, but I see a beautiful rainbow like I have never seen before. I know this is the Lord's work." All of us were in disbelief that such a miracle just happened. That was the confirmation I needed to know this was the right move at the right time and it was all in God's plans for me. Even Michelle, who wasn't so happy about my move, knew it was meant to be. What were the odds of this happening, a million to one?

A month later I gave away everything that wouldn't fit into my SUV, and down the road I went, back to the place I left forty-one years earlier, failing to meet Rock and living happily ever after. It took me all these years to have the chance to return home. This was my chance to start a new life, to make new memories, seeing the past as the past, embracing all the struggles and tribulations and look towards the new light of day, the miracles to be found and the goodness everywhere.

I had a new job, and I was available for volunteer work if needed. Just a great life ahead filled with possibilities. I loved my landlady, Joan, who lived in the home that I used to own. It was the weirdest feeling walking into this home forty-five years later, seeing it as it is but at the same time, remembering how it was. I walked out into the backyard and soon learned Joan was a gardener and worked in the yard every day. She had a little dog, and two cats. I knew in the deepest part of my soul that the Lord had placed me here in a warm loving home where I could feel safe, loved and be able to give help back to this kind woman when needed.

Joan had worked in the deli of the top nutrition grocery store on the Monterey Peninsula for twelve years. She knows what superfoods are and lives her life eating as much organic and healthy food as possible. I started doing daily juicing and smoothies and made sure I kept Joan as healthy as possible. I knew there must be a reason I was needed here for her, too. Joan had a large load of compost delivered to fill some big garden boxes and help the surrounding plants and flowers with fresh nutrition. I bought tomato plants, zucchinis, watermelons, bell peppers, beets, parsley, and so much more, and four months later all the plants and flowers were full-grown, and I walked out to the organic garden each morning to pick my daily food, always feeling blessed for all given to me.

Often, I invited my desert friends to drive up and spend some time in Monterey. My friend Patti, who had rented me her beautiful casita, came to spend nine days with me. I gave her the grand tour of the Peninsula, taking her to all the fun places, like Loulou's Griddle In The Middle for breakfast, Schooner's for

Happy Hour, The Monterey Plaza Hotel on Friday nights for music on Cannery Row, and Spanish Bay in Pebble Beach to see and hear the bagpipe player at sunset. I had perfect weather to take her to my favorite Del Monte Beach where I had lived and fell in love with Rock.

The apartments directly on the sand still look the same and Patti fell in love with the view. Since she has a little dog she loved the idea of one day bringing her dog here to take daily walks in the summer when it was too hot in the desert. Patti asked, if she leased a home in the same apartments where I used to live, could I stay there and look after the place and she would come up on occasions for mini vacations and spend the summer months there. I said I would love to live here again, right on the water, bringing me full-circle from where I lived with Michelle before I moved away. What was the chance of that? This would be a dream come true. Since I had already lived with Patti on her fabulous estate and rented her casita, I knew she was really considering adding this Monterey location to her lists of favorite places to go and stay.

When I got back home I couldn't help but lie on the sofa and close my eyes just dreaming of the possibilities. Could this really be true? Don't pinch me. I never want to wake up from this dream. Would I be able to return to the apartment that meant so much to me? Both have such meaning. One where I felt I was at home where Joan, always made me feel safe and secure. I thought I would house-sit, and still keep my room in Marina also. It will be like having your cake and eating it too. A place to go for the warmth of feeling like family, home cooking, lots of love and kindness, and I was especially looking forward to being there during the holidays, helping to decorate Joan's Christmas tree and smelling the turkey in the oven at Thanksgiving, but right now in my dreams it was still summer and I couldn't believe I was moving into the same building where I used to live in. It was not the exact same apartment, but only a few doors away and looking out my bedroom window at the same view, able to see the ocean waves and the buildings across the bay that would light up when night fell.

As I slipped deeper into my dream, I took my beach towel and walked on the sand down close to the water's edge. As I lay on my big pink towel, wearing my black bikini, I could feel the heat of the sun and hearing the sound of the surf and occasionally the sounds of children laughing. I love the way my body is snuggled down in the sand, warmly surrounding my body. No oil for me. I want the pure rays of the sun, even looking forward to a slight burn on my cheeks. My body was used to the desert sun and I already had a nice tan, so this afternoon would just refresh and make me feel healthy. I remembered as a teenager lying on this same beach, spraying my body with a mixture of baby oil and iodine to enhance my tan, and spraying my hair with peroxide to give me that California Girl look. Now here I was again, with not a care in the world. I had a job I loved, a family at home that loves me, a place close by where I felt like I belonged, and now I'm lying in my favorite spot of my entire life, feeling the sun on me.

The only thing missing was my Prince-one who would adore me, make me laugh, kiss my forehead and look me in the eyes. I went sound asleep, deep in those thoughts, and feeling the warm sun on my face, when all of a sudden, I was a little bit startled with my senses telling me someone was standing above me looking down. I looked up and I could see the figure of a man, but couldn't make him out. I put my hand up to block the sun from my eyes to get a clearer look. I asked, "Who are you?" and he said, "I'm your Prince and you are my everything. I want you to be my princess. I know all about you, all the hard times your life's journey has taken and I want to spend the rest of my life with you." As I saw his hands reach down for my hands to lift me up towards him ...

The Alarm Went Off.
I Woke Up and He Was Gone.

Made in the USA
San Bernardino, CA
20 June 2017